REACTING TO THE PAST

GREENWICH VILLAGE, 1913

Suffrage, Labor, and the New Woman

Mary Jane Treacy, Simmons College

W. W. NORTON & COMPANY
NEW YORK · LONDON

BARNARD
REACTING TO THE PAST

OTHER TITLES IN THIS SERIES

Patriots, Loyalists, and Revolution in New York City, 1775–1776, Second Edition
      Bill Offutt
The Threshold of Democracy: Athens in 403 B.C., Second Edition
      Josiah Ober, Naomi J. Norman, and Mark C. Carnes
Rousseau, Burke, and Revolution in France, 1791, Second Edition
      Jennifer Popiel, Mark C. Carnes, and Gary Kates

Also available

Charles Darwin, the Copley Medal and the Rise of Naturalism, 1862–64
      Marsha Driscoll, Elizabeth E. Dunn, Dann P. Siems, and B. Kamran Swanson
Confucianism and the Succession Crisis of the Wanli Emperor, 1587
      Daniel K. Gardner and Mark C. Carnes
Defining a Nation: India on the Eve of Independence, 1945
      Ainslie T. Embree and Mark C. Carnes
Henry VIII and the Reformation Parliament
      John Patrick Coby
The Trial of Anne Hutchinson: Liberty, Law, and Intolerance in Puritan New England
      Michael P. Winship and Mark C. Carnes
The Trial of Galileo: Aristotelianism, the "New Cosmology," and the Catholic Church, 1616–33
      Frederick Purnell Jr., Michael S. Pettersen, and Mark C. Carnes

W. W. Norton & Company has been independent since its founding in 1923, when William Warder Norton and Mary D. Herter Norton first published lectures delivered at the People's Institute, the adult education division of New York City's Cooper Union. The firm soon expanded its program beyond the Institute, publishing books by celebrated academics from America and abroad. By midcentury, the two major pillars of Norton's publishing program—trade books and college texts—were firmly established. In the 1950s, the Norton family transferred control of the company to its employees, and today—with a staff of four hundred and a comparable number of trade, college, and professional titles published each year—W. W. Norton & Company stands as the largest and oldest publishing house owned wholly by its employees.

Copyright © 2015 by W. W. Norton & Company, Inc.

Associate Editor: Justin Cahill
Project Editor: Jennifer Barnhardt
Editorial Assistants: Travis Carr and Penelope Lin
Managing Editor, College: Marian Johnson
Managing Editor, College Digital Media: Kim Yi
Production Manager: Ashley Horna
Marketing Manager, History: Sarah England
Design Director: Rubina Yeh
Book Design: Alexandra Charitan
Permissions Manager: Megan Jackson
Composition: Jouve International
Illustrations: Mapping Specialists, Ltd.
Manufacturing: Sheridan Books, Inc.

Permission to use copyrighted material is included on page 259.

Library of Congress Cataloging-in-Publication Data

Treacy, Mary Jane.
  Greenwich Village, 1913 : suffrage, labor, and the new woman / Mary Jane Treacy.
    pages cm.— (Barnard. reacting to the past)
  Includes bibliographical references and index.
  ISBN 978-0-393-93890-6 (pbk. : alk, paper)
1. Women—Suffrage—New York (State)—New York.   2. Women—Employment—New York (State)—New York.
3. Women—New York (State)—New York—Economic conditions.   4. Women—New York (State)—New York—Social conditions.   I. Title.
  JK1911.N7T74 2015
  324.6'23097471—dc23
                                                                                                    2014047936

W. W. Norton & Company, Inc., 500 Fifth Avenue, New York, NY 10110-0017
wwnorton.com
W. W. Norton & Company Ltd., 15 Carlisle Street, London W1D 3BS

1 4 5 6 7 8 9 0

ABOUT THE AUTHOR

MARY JANE TREACY is Professor of Modern Languages and Literatures and Director of the Honors Program at Simmons College, where she teaches first-year Honors seminars as well as Spanish and Latin American Studies. She has been involved with the Reacting to the Past pedagogy since 2005, when she played a minor spy in the court of Henry VIII and then set out to write *Greenwich Village, 1913* for her course in Roots of Feminism. She has taught *Greenwich Village* in both Women's and Gender Studies courses and first-year seminars. She has just completed a prequel, *Paterson 1913: The Silk Strike*, and a new game on the aftermath of political violence in Argentina, *Argentina 1985: Contested Memories*. A member of the RTTP Editorial Board, she has the privilege of reading and play-testing new games that take her to all eras and parts of the world.

CONTENTS

3. THE GAME

Labor and Labor Movements

Bohemia: The Spirit of the New

GREENWICH VILLAGE, 1913

Suffrage, Labor, and the New Woman

1

PART 1: INTRODUCTION

BRIEF OVERVIEW OF THE GAME

It is 1913 and the four square miles of lower Manhattan called Greenwich Village are humming with rebellious free spirits, who have gathered here to lead a "renaissance"—a new beginning—in American life. Their goal for the new century is to break down conventions in order to open up radical new possibilities for living in the modern age. Individuals will develop their full human potential through "vital contact" with marginalized social groups, social interactions between men and women, sexual freedom, and artistic and literary experimentation. Bohemians living in the Village are seeking a revolution centered in the body and the spirit. These Villagers and their friends gather at Polly's, a tiny basement restaurant near Washington Square, to talk about the new world they hope to create.

Others have their eyes on Polly's as well. Suffragists, inspired by the brash tactics of newcomer Alice Paul, have come to win the bohemians' support for a huge suffrage parade down Pennsylvania Avenue in Washington, D.C., on the eve of Woodrow Wilson's presidential inauguration. This is to be a bold show of force by the young suffragists, who plan to demand an amendment to the U.S. Constitution to give women the vote and to demonstrate that suffrage and women's political equality must be our top priorities today.

Over in Paterson, New Jersey, the Industrial Workers of the World (IWW) have been spurred on by a recent victory in Lawrence, Massachusetts, to organize a strike by silk workers protesting poor wages and the changes that new technologies have wrought on their artisan traditions. Facing police brutality and press censorship, the IWW and the Socialist Party have sent leaders to Greenwich Village to seek the bohemians' support in prioritizing the needs of the working class. Soapbox speeches, open-air rallies, parades, and pageants turn Polly's into a site of riotous debate.

The game that you will play over the next few weeks brings into contact and conflict major issues facing a modern and rapidly industrializing nation: women are demanding more legal rights and a political voice; the labor force is organizing to improve work conditions and to limit the power of an ever-expanding industrial capitalism; and bohemians are challenging prevailing views on marriage, sexuality, and the family. All seek social change, but each group has a radically different vision of the New America and its citizens. *Greenwich Village, 1913* asks players to consider these views and understand the kind of society these groups hope to establish.

In *Greenwich Village, 1913*, you will be asked to assume the role of a person who actually lived during this time or of a fictional character whose story has been based on the lives of several real individuals. Using the Historical Background and Core Texts sections found in this game book as well as the role sheet given to you by your instructor, you will try to persuade others that your character's views merit their consideration. Some players, in character, will share your opinions, while others will oppose them or hope to take your ideas in different directions. It is up to you to find your allies and work out a historically accurate "worldview" to present at Polly's restaurant.

Factions

Some players will be members of the Suffrage faction; others have joined the Labor faction. The Suffrage faction hopes to persuade Villagers to join them in Washington, D.C., to affirm that gender equality is the most pressing issue of the day. The Labor faction, on the other hand, asks that Villagers join them in convening a Paterson pageant to demonstrate that class solidarity is the more pressing issue.

Wild Cards

There are "Wild Card" characters in Greenwich Village, not affiliated with either faction, who have specific secret tasks as well special powers to endow others with influence and winning points. Players should pay attention to Village celebrity Mabel Dodge; Max Eastman, the new editor of *The Masses*; and notorious anarchist Emma Goldman.

Indeterminates

Most players are Indeterminates; that is, they are bohemian Villagers and their friends who have come to Polly's just to eat and socialize. Villagers, while generally supportive of both suffrage and labor reforms, will have to listen to the factions in order to choose how they would like to direct their energies and talents. Regardless of their political and intellectual commitments during this game, most Villagers remain individualists: writers who hope to publish their work and public intellectuals who strive to influence national culture. They will assert themselves, vie for attention, and seek out ways to make their ideas known.

Greenwich Village, 1913 is a game about setting priorities and finding solutions in the face of the new century's many challenges.

PROLOGUE

The following vignette asks you to imagine that you are a talented young woman living in a small town at the beginning of the twentieth century. Although your society allows you some new freedoms, it still demands that you marry and raise a family as your primary social role. And yet you have heard that there are some neighborhoods in American cities that have attracted women and men who are experimenting with new social arrangements and overturning prescribed gender roles in order to foster self-fulfillment, professional opportunities, and deep social change.

Life at its Fullest

ike many of your generation born in the last decade of the nineteenth century, you are enthralled by the possibilities of the twentieth. A whole new world has opened up: telegraphs have yielded to telephones; travel by rail has found a rival in the automobile; the phonograph and radio have brought Tin Pan Alley right into your home. Dance crazes have swept up the entire nation. You have recently learned the turkey trot and once even tried to do the daring shimmy. Yes, 1913 is just the year to be young and ready for adventure.

Alas. Most of your new ideas have come from avid readings of the *Ladies' Home Journal* and *Collier's Magazine*. While other women are attending lectures on Dr. Freud and his interpretations of dreams or viewing the oft-mocked painting *Nude Descending a Staircase*, you are still living at home in this small Midwestern town, waiting for something to happen. As a member of the middle class and of "old American stock," you have been trained in the Victorian values of respectability and decorum, rules of propriety that have especially crippled the spirits of many of your girlfriends. To be sure, some are going off to colleges in the East, but these schools are far away and cater to social elites. You cannot afford to go.

Worse still, your parents are intent on your finding a husband and settling down. It's not that you don't want to do this; it's just that you have never left home. You don't know who you are or what you want. How could you even begin to choose a mate without ever having experienced life?

Right now the issue of women's suffrage is once again in the spotlight. After decades of quiet maneuvering to persuade the states to ratify suffrage one by one (or, some would say, stagnation), the National American Woman Suffrage

Association (NAWSA) seems to be undergoing a sea change. Reports say that young women who have recently been involved in suffrage agitation with those Pankhurst women in England are bringing similarly noisy stunts to Washington, D.C. Those old NAWSA dowagers, still wrapped tight in their corsets, are going to have a battle on their hands when they confront Alice Paul and Lucy Burns. These two gals claim that a suffragist needs to throw off ladylike behaviors and take to the streets. Paul, they say, is even planning a huge suffrage parade to coincide with Woodrow Wilson's presidential inauguration. Won't he be surprised to see thousands of women on Pennsylvania Avenue stealing his thunder!

Suffragists have come to your town, decked out in their yellow sashes and "VOTES FOR WOMEN" buttons. You have been thrilled to sneak out to hear them. They seem different from other women, daring and perhaps a bit disreputable. Instead of going to the homes of the town's "best families" and talking about suffrage over tea in the parlor, they climb up on a box to speak their minds right there in the street, even talking back to the men who heckle and insult them. Once you saw suffragists walking confidently down Main Street, smoking in public. You thought that they must not have lives like yours with its measured paces, its missionary associations and ladies' literary societies, its predictable Sunday roast beef dinners. You long to join these women, to gain confidence in yourself, to talk so freely, even with men.

Ah, men. The boys of your town are a wholesome lot, future grain dealers and furniture salesmen. There is plenty of money to be made, as your father tells you, in this quickly developing region, but really, what will wealth do if you are stuck with a plodding bore? No, you want to experience something more than this. You want—dare you say it—passion! You want to know what it is like to be swept up, to love, and to forget about marriage, mortgages, and babies. You know that there are men who are different, dashing, and ready to change the world. You have read about Max Eastman, the new editor of *The Masses*, a revolutionary magazine that your library wouldn't order but that you found at a suffrage rally. They say he is really handsome. Then there is Jack Reed, an up-and-coming journalist, who has gone to Paterson, New Jersey, to report on a real up-in-arms silk workers' strike that is drawing national attention. These are men who wouldn't spend all night talking to you about the price of wheat or their job in the new department store. These men are exciting.

Maybe they are bit too exciting. Maybe they'd be better to dream about than to know in person. They say that Eastman, Reed, and the rest of that set are part of a larger group of men who want to overturn the government and bring chaos into the streets. They are socialists, anarchists, like that Alexander Berkman who attempted to murder the industrialist Mr. Frick in cold blood a couple of years ago. Or maybe they are

Wobblies—you can't really tell the difference—who want all the workers to join together and overthrow capitalism. Your father tells you that there are good union men in the American Federation of Labor, like those he has hired in the factory, but these International Workers of the World are hotheads, rabble-rousers, vagrants, bums. Can their IWW really stand for "I Won't Work?" You are afraid of them and avoid the outskirts of town where they congregate by the railroad tracks. Once when you were by the park, you saw one standing on a soapbox, haranguing passersby. You didn't stop to listen, but you heard a large roar of support when the man yelled "solidarity" and "class war." This was excitement of an entirely different stripe.

Still, you are twenty years old now and bored to tears. You've done all you can do in town. Yes, you have joined the Tuesday Club and read your poems to the ladies, thereby gaining a reputation as "artistic." You have even published some jaunty descriptions of local events in the society pages of the local newspaper. But this is not enough. You want to do things. To write serious pieces. To feel free for the first time in your life! You are determined to get away to one of the few places in America where you have a chance to taste life at its fullest: Greenwich Village in New York City.

HOW TO REACT

Reacting to the Past is a series of historical role-playing games. After a few preparatory lectures, the game begins and the students are in charge. Set in moments of heightened historical tension, the games place students in the roles of historical figures. By reading the game book and their individual role sheets, students discover their objectives, potential allies, and the forces that stand between them and victory. They must then attempt to achieve victory through formal speeches, informal debate, negotiations, and (sometimes) conspiracy. Outcomes sometimes part from actual history; a postmortem session sets the record straight.

The following is an outline of what you will encounter in Reacting and what you will be expected to do.

Game Setup

Your instructor will spend some time before the beginning of the game helping you to understand the historical context for the game. During the setup period, you will use several different kinds of material:

- You have received the game book (from which you are reading now), which includes historical information, rules and elements of the game, and essential documents.

- Your instructor will provide you with a role sheet, which provides a short biography of the historical figure you will model in the game as well as that person's ideology, objectives, responsibilities, and resources. Your role may be an actual historical figure or a composite.

In addition to the game book, you may also be required to read historical documents or books written by historians. These provide additional information and arguments for use during the game.

Read all of this contextual material and all of these documents and sources before the game begins. And just as important, go back and reread these materials throughout the game. A second and third reading while *in role* will deepen your understanding and alter your perspective, for ideas take on a different aspect when seen through the eyes of a partisan actor.

Students who have carefully read the materials and who know the rules of the game will invariably do better than those who rely on general impressions and uncertain memories.

Game Play

Once the game begins, class sessions are presided over by students. In most cases, a single student serves as a kind of presiding officer. The instructor then becomes the Gamemaster (GM) and takes a seat in the back of the room. Though they do not lead the class sessions, GMs may do any of the following:

- Pass notes

- Announce important events (e.g. Sparta is invading!). Some of these events are the result of student actions; others are instigated by the GM

- Redirect proceedings that have gone off track

The presiding officer is expected to observe basic standards of fairness, but as a fail-safe device, most Reacting to the Past games employ the "Podium Rule," which allows a student who has not been recognized to approach the podium and wait for a chance to speak. Once at the podium, the student has the floor and must be heard.

Role sheets contain private, secret information which students are expected to guard. You are advised, therefore, to exercise caution when discussing your role with others. Your role sheet probably identifies likely allies, but even they may not always be trustworthy. However, keeping your own counsel, or saying nothing to anyone, is not an option. In order to achieve your objectives, you *must* speak with others. You will never muster the voting strength to prevail without allies. Collaboration and coalition building are at the heart of every game.

These discussions must lead to action, which often means proposing, debating, and passing legislation. Someone therefore must be responsible for introducing the measure and explaining its particulars. And always remember that a Reacting game is only a game—resistance, attack, and betrayal are not to be taken personally, since game opponents are merely acting as their roles direct.

Some games feature strong alliances called *factions*: these are tight-knit groups with fixed objectives. Games with factions all include roles called Indeterminates, who operate outside of the established factions. Not all Indeterminates are entirely neutral; some are biased on certain issues. If you are in a faction, cultivating Indeterminates is in your interest, since they can be convinced to support your position. If you are lucky enough to have drawn the role of an Indeterminate you should be pleased; you will likely play a pivotal role in the outcome of the game.

Game Requirements

Students in Reacting practice persuasive writing, public speaking, critical thinking, teamwork, negotiation, problem solving, collaboration, adapting to changing circumstances, and working under pressure to meet deadlines. Your instructor will explain the specific requirements for your class. In general, though, a Reacting game asks you to perform three distinct activities:

Reading and Writing. This standard academic work is carried on purposefully in a Reacting course, since what you read is put to immediate use, and what you write is meant to persuade others to act the way you want them to. The reading load may have slight variations from role to role; the writing requirement depends on your particular course. Papers are often policy statements, but they can also be autobiographies, battle plans, spy reports, newspapers, poems, or after-game reflections. Papers provide the foundation for the speeches delivered in class.

Public Speaking and Debate. In the course of a game, almost everyone is expected to deliver at least one formal speech from the podium (the length of the game and the size of the class will determine the number of speeches). Debate follows. It can be impromptu, raucous, and fast-paced, and results in decisions voted on by the body. Gamemasters may stipulate that students must deliver their papers from memory when at the podium, or may insist that students wean themselves from dependency on written notes as the game progresses.

Wherever the game imaginatively puts you, it will surely not put you in the classroom of a twenty-first-century American college. Accordingly, the colloquialisms and familiarities of today's college life are out of place. Never open your speech with a salutation like "Hi guys" when something like "Fellow citizens!" would be more appropriate.

Never be friendless when standing at the podium. Do your best to have at least one supporter second your proposal, come to your defense, or admonish inattentive members of the body. Note-passing and side conversations, while common occurrences, will likely spoil the effect of your speech; so you and your supporters should insist upon order before such behavior becomes too disruptive. Ask the presiding officer to assist you, if necessary, and the Gamemaster as a last resort.

Strategizing. Communication among students is an essential feature of Reacting games. You will find yourself writing emails, texting, attending out-of-class meetings, or gathering for meals on a fairly regular basis. The purpose of frequent communication is to lay out a strategy for advancing your agenda and thwarting the agenda of your opponents, and to hatch plots to ensnare individuals troubling to your cause. When communicating with a fellow student in or out of class, always assume that he or she is speaking to you in role. If you want to talk about the "real world," make that clear.

PART 2: HISTORICAL BACKGROUND

GREENWICH VILLAGE, 1913

You have arrived. According to writer Floyd Dell, himself a new Villager, Greenwich Village is built of historical layers that can be examined archaeologically: an Indian hunting ground in the wilderness, green farmlands of Dutch and English settlers, pastoral suburbs beloved by nineteenth-century artisans, a patrician enclave around Washington Square, and finally today, in 1913, when its winding streets lead to what another recent arrival, Hippolyte Havel, has called a "spiritual zone of mind"—a small republic of radical thought.[1] "The Village" is New York's **bohemia**: an urban gathering place for rebels, free thinkers, the avant-garde, and seekers of personal and artistic transformation.

Because its narrow streets remain inhospitable to heavy traffic, the Village has been able to maintain its comfortable neighborhood "feel" in the midst of bustling, industrial New York City. This is what has attracted young intellectuals from New England and the Midwest to the cheap apartments and bistros that have come to characterize the neighborhood as a space apart and refuge from both the crass reality of urban commerce and the dullness of Small Town, U.S.A.

Yet it would be wrong to assume that Greenwich Village has lived in isolation from the profound changes that have transformed the nation since the end of the Civil War. To be sure, the Protestant elite, whose families accrued their fortunes in the early years of the last century, still inhabit the Greek Revival homes on the north side of Washington Square. It was they who only a few years ago commissioned the construction of the Memorial Arch in the nine-acre park, in an effort to cultivate refined taste through public art. Described by philanthropist Henry Marquand as "the arch of peace and good will to men" that will bring "rich and poor together in one common bond of patriotic feeling," the landmark coincides with demographic shifts that have seen the decline of patrician "Old New Yorkers." In their place have come waves of immigrants occupying the streets to the west and south of the Square, filling the park with their running children and boisterous street vendors.

The Village has recently seen the arrival of another social type, the college graduate who is determined to bring about social change by "settling" among the poor in run-down buildings that are now called tenements. Like the English at Toynbee Hall and their American counterparts—Jane Addams in Chicago, Lillian Wald in the Lower East Side, and Mary Kingsbury Simkhovitch in Greenwich House over on Jones Street—these young people have set up large communal households and offer services to their less fortunate neighbors: English classes,

Bohemia can refer to two distinct places. The medieval Kingdom of Bohemia was located in what became the Czech Republic, so Czech people and products were commonly referred to as Bohemian. In the nineteenth century, European artists began to imagine a connection between the freewheeling lives of Gypsies, who they believed had come from Bohemia, and the rebellious spirit of impoverished artists and writers living in urban slums. By the late nineteenth century, plays, novels, and operas had made the bohemian an easily recognized type: poor, artistic, free-spirited, and in conflict with the mainstream values of society.

arts and crafts workshops, kindergartens for children, clubs and activities for the youth. It is through this "social housekeeping" that they hope to challenge the corruption of a political system that predestines the majority of newly arriving immigrants to destitution. It is through cross-class alliances, they believe, that social reform can be achieved.

Villagers saw the effect of upper-class concern for the working poor just four years ago in 1909, when the shirtwaist workers went on a walkout to protest their fifty-six–hour workweek and terrible wages. All these new loft buildings, like the Asch Building over there on the corner of Washington Place and Greene Street, have factories on their top floors; the spacious rooms allow for rows upon rows of garment workers to cut, stitch, and finish their pieces using the natural light that pours in the windows. When Jewish girls, whose families flocked to the Lower East Side to escape the pogroms in their native Russia, and Italian girls from the Village finally demanded better hours and wages, the bosses set hired thugs on them as the police watched or hauled the girls off to the Jefferson Market Courthouse, treating them as if they were common prostitutes. That is when the society ladies of the Women's Trade Union League joined forces on the picket line and put the authorities on notice that they could not hurt working girls without facing serious consequences. Tragically, only two years later some of these same brave garment workers succumbed to the worse industrial fire in the nation's history when the Triangle Shirtwaist Factory on the upper floors of the Asch Building went up in flames. Since there were few ways to escape and, even worse, the owners had locked the doors to keep the girls from pilfering the merchandise, over 146 people lost their lives in just over thirty minutes. A crowd of Villagers could only stare in horror when workers threw themselves out of windows as they were burning alive.

Today Greenwich Village may be known for its brains, its dash, and its rebels, but look a little closer: it can tell you how an old society is giving way to the new, how social classes and ethnic communities stand apart but also come together, how greed and corruption coexist with idealism and utopian dreams.

You'll now want to set off for Polly's, a famous little restaurant over at 137 MacDougal Street that caters to the bohemian set. This basement room has been arranged to ensure conviviality rather than elegance (for that you'd go to the posh Brevoort Hotel close by on Fifth Avenue). Polly's current cook—that same Hippolyte Havel with the notorious bad temper—has made up three long trestle-style tables just for you. He may set down some cheap food on each table to signal the beginning of the game. After all, a home-cooked meal at Polly's costs only 20 cents.

FEDERAL CENSUS 1910

The population of Greenwich Village is 124,603. Of these, 55,000 are foreign born and 48,000 are native-born children of immigrants.

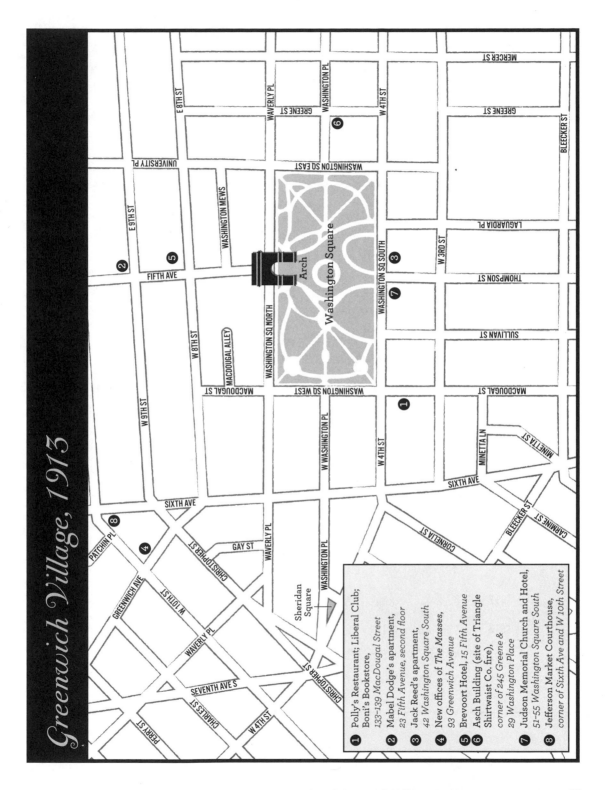

Greenwich Village, 1913

1. Polly's Restaurant; Liberal Club; Boni's Bookstore, *133–139 MacDougal Street*
2. Mabel Dodge's apartment, *23 Fifth Avenue, second floor*
3. Jack Reed's apartment, *42 Washington Square South*
4. New offices of *The Masses*, *93 Greenwich Avenue*
5. Brevoort Hotel, *15 Fifth Avenue*
6. Asch Building (site of Triangle Shirtwaist Co. fire), *corner of 245 Greene & 29 Washington Place*
7. Judson Memorial Church and Hotel, *51–55 Washington Square South*
8. Jefferson Market Courthouse, *corner of Sixth Ave and W 10th Street*

WOMEN'S RIGHTS AND SUFFRAGE

Chronology

1848   Elizabeth Cady Stanton's "Declaration of Sentiments."

1869   Stanton and Susan B. Anthony establish National Woman Suffrage Association (NWSA).

1869   Lucy Stone and Henry Blackwell counter with the American Woman Suffrage Association (AWSA).

1869   Wyoming allows women to vote in local and state matters.

1870   Utah gives women the vote.

1870   Fifteenth Amendment to the Constitution gives the vote to male former slaves but denies the franchise to women of all races.

1890   Alice Stone Blackwell, daughter of Stone and Blackwell, unites the NWSA and AWSA into the National American Woman Suffrage Association (NAWSA).

1893   Colorado gives women the vote.

1896   Idaho gives women the vote.

1910   Washington State gives women the vote.

1911   California gives women the vote.

1911   "Antis" establish the National Association Opposed to Woman Suffrage (NAOWS).

1912   Kansas, Oregon, and Arizona give women the vote.

1913   Alice Paul and Lucy Burns take over NAWSA's Congressional Committee to push for a constitutional amendment for woman suffrage.

1915   New York State referendum on woman suffrage.

Women's Rights and Suffrage, 1776–1840

Who should participate in a democratic society? All of its members or a select few? If only some deserve full membership, what kinds of qualifications should they meet? Should they own property? Fight for the nation in times of war? Read and write? Understand the official language? Who should decide on these qualifications? In the United States, the struggle for voting rights by disenfranchised groups cuts to the heart of debates on the nature of citizenship, political power, and the place of gender and race in the fabric of national identity.

Although the Declaration of Independence (1776) declared all men to be equal, the Founding Fathers extended full citizenship in the new nation only to those whom they believed to be autonomous rational beings; that is, only those adults of European background who owned property could vote. Almost all of the young states interpreted this to exclude men who did not own land, as well as all women and all children who were assumed to exist in a natural state of dependence. Black and native peoples were denied citizenship altogether. By the 1830s, however, the political climate had begun to move slowly toward more inclusion. Not only did the ideal of universal suffrage extend participation in electoral politics to white men of all social classes and conditions, a movement of religious renewal and spiritual fervor ushered women into the public domain, mobilizing to bring reform to the nation.

By mid-century, change was in the air. Prisons, hospitals, and the mental health care system were foremost on the list of institutions in need of improvement. Nevertheless, the primary catalyst for social reformers proved to be the South's "peculiar institution" of slavery. Encouraged by the evangelical spirit of the Second Great Awakening to spread the ideals of their religious faith, many Protestant women like Angelina Grimké (1805–1879) were inspired to speak out against slavery as an intolerable "crime against God and man." And yet this view was not universal. Reformers watched as political leaders fought over the extension of slavery into the Western territories, the interstate traffic in slaves, and a fugitive slave law that would open Northern communities to bounty hunters seeking runaway slaves. Northern white and free black people flocked to abolition movements: William Lloyd Garrison's American Anti-Slavery Society (1833) that demanded immediate abolition as well as moderate groups that advocated a gradual process in order to prepare the enslaved person for a life of liberty. Many white women saw a special connection between their own condition and that of the slave, seeing both as oppressive. Women created local Ladies' Anti-Slavery Societies and even ventured out from their domestic circles to gather names for petitions against slavery that they would send on to state legislatures, as some had done earlier to protest the Indian Removal Act (1830) that banished native peoples from their lands. A few emboldened women even took to church pulpits to speak publicly on the horrors of slavery before mixed audiences of men and women, acts that challenged the public's tolerance of slavery just as they transgressed the customary confinement of women to the home and private spirituality.

Northern women's burgeoning political activism was not only scandalous to their male contemporaries, but almost unthinkable. It was also dangerous. Both men and women abolitionists faced hostile crowds that regularly pelted them with rotten food, dung, and even rocks. One abolitionist meeting place was burned to the ground. Maria Stewart, a freewoman speaking in Boston in 1831, was run out of town by angry mobs. The outspoken South Carolinian Angelina Grimké, who came from a prominent slaveholding family, was warned not to return to her native state under threat of death. Yet in spite of intimidation, rejection, and public ridicule, activist women gained confidence in their rhetorical skills and learned how to organize public opinion for their causes.

Women's Rights, 1840–1870

For all their contributions to the antislavery movement, women did not find that many male leaders of their churches and abolitionist societies welcomed their participation as equals. Indeed, when a newly married Elizabeth Cady Stanton (1815–1902) attended an international antislavery convention while on her honeymoon in London, she found to her dismay that the women in attendance were seated behind an opaque curtain, far out of sight. Behind that curtain she met the elder Lucretia Mott (1793–1880), a Quaker with a strong abolitionist background, and together they took on the cause of women's rights. It was not a new topic. The English political theorist Mary Wollstonecraft's major work *A Vindication of the Rights of Women* had been published in the United States in 1792 and an educated elite had discussed how the concept of **natural rights** might coincide with women's seemingly biologically ordained roles as wives and mothers. Nevertheless, this discussion of rights had little influence on the laws and customs of the new nation. To the contrary, most states adopted British common law and its concept of "coverture" in which a married woman became legally "covered" by her husband, who enjoyed ownership not only of her property, wealth, and wages, but also of her body and her children. In addition, no woman, single or married, could sign a contract, serve on a jury, gain a formal higher education, enter the professions, work for wages equal to those of men, or hope to effect a change in her condition except by petitioning men to act on her behalf.

Many years before she found herself marginalized in abolitionist circles, Stanton had chafed at her subordinate role as a judge's daughter who longed for the education given to her brothers. Once married and living in Seneca Falls, New York, Stanton acted on her desire for reform by working in support of New York's Married Woman's Property Act (introduced in 1836 and passed in 1848), which was to allow married women

Eighteenth-century European thinkers of the Enlightenment period asserted that human beings had certain "**natural rights**" that no worthy government could violate. These included life, liberty, and property (ownership of one's person as well as of things). Sound familiar? You'll see that the belief in man's natural rights is the foundation of the U.S. Declaration of Independence.

control over their real estate, personal property, and income. This first step to overturn legal restrictions on women, however, did not accord women control over their own wages, leaving working married women completely vulnerable to their husbands' wishes and debts. There remained so many indignities and constraints placed on women even after passage of the Act that Stanton and her friends decided to hold a Woman's Rights Convention in Seneca Falls: two days of speeches, conversations, and setting the stage for what was to become the first women's rights movement (1848). It was

In the 19th century, American women most often referred to their movement as "woman's rights" and "woman suffrage." By the early 20th century, the name tends to shift from the singular to the plural, as in "Votes for Women."

here that Stanton presented her Declaration of Sentiments, a formal call to rebellion that included the revolutionary idea that women should attain the franchise. Based loosely on the Declaration of Independence, Stanton's manifesto ignited a nationwide demand for social, legal, and political equality for women.

Stanton's ideas were shocking to many who felt that woman's sacred place was in the home, supporting her husband and raising the next generation of citizens. The assertion that women were first and foremost individuals with natural rights to equality and therefore should participate in the life of the nation not only threatened to undermine women's domestic social role but also troubled believers in the power of female virtue to reform society. To throw women into the rough-and-tumble of political life would be to insist on their participation in the corruption and sinful greed that woman, from her pedestal of purity, could help to change.

Stanton would have none of this "**cult of true womanhood**"[2] assigning elite woman to a social role of idealized domesticity. As a mother living in a small town with few urban conveniences, however, Stanton was often called to stay at home to care for her household and seven children. Her enthusiasm seldom daunted by the limitations of her daily life, Stanton crafted the ideological framework for women's rights and sent an unmarried activist friend off to bring the message to a waiting public.

Susan B. Anthony (1820–1906), a liberal Quaker active in both antislavery and temperance movements, met Stanton in 1851. President of the Rochester Daughters of Temperance, Anthony viewed the consumption of alcohol by both native-born men and new immigrants as particularly injurious to the well-being of women and children: alcoholism, misspent wages, and domestic violence had led many families to misery and economic ruin. Yet Anthony soon became convinced that the goal of protecting women was not sufficient; women would have to assert themselves as equal members of society. Thus she was drawn to the women's rights movement that had been flourishing in upstate New York. Her political work with Stanton lasted for over fifty years as the two brought the women's rights message to the entire country, creating the first wave of activism to gain political power and thereby to make real changes in women's lives.

Cult of True Womanhood or **Cult of Domesticity:** an ideal of women confined to the separate, private sphere of the home where they would cultivate the virtues of piety, purity, and domesticity.

While the women's rights movement began to simmer, regional tensions between the North and South came to a boil. With the Southern secession from the Union in 1860, Northern abolitionists turned their attention to debates over what to do next: give concessions to the Confederacy? Permit slavery in some parts of the nation? Demand complete emancipation as the condition for rejoining the union? Coalition groups in the North, called Loyal Leagues, fanned popular support for what was quickly becoming a devastating war (1861–1865). Stanton and Anthony joined the effort, forming the National Woman's Loyal League (1863) that further honed women's political skills: their petitions, backroom lobbying, public speaking, and cultivation of influential male allies were strategies to secure legal rights for people of African descent as well as for white women. At the end of the war, women's rights activists, especially the New York faction, expected that their efforts would pay off: white women and black men and women together would gain the franchise and rebuild the nation. Members of the Republican Party, however, chose to concentrate on rights for enslaved men to the exclusion of women's enfranchisement. The Thirteenth Amendment to the Constitution overturned slavery (1865), the Fourteenth Amendment granted citizenship to "all persons" born or naturalized in the United States (1868), and a Fifteenth Amendment was proposed to grant voting rights to all men regardless of their race or previous condition of servitude (1870). Women, it was argued, should wait.

Debates over the Fifteenth Amendment split the women's rights movement as well as the friendships and political alliances that had forged a unified political front between activists of many different points of view. The women and men of the Equal Rights Association, formed to work toward a true universal suffrage for all, were now asked to choose allegiances. Lucy Stone (1818–1893), dubbed the "morning star of the women's rights movement," argued that the movement should be happy that at least one disenfranchised group had obtained the franchise. Mincing no words, the former slave and abolitionist Frederick Douglass (1817?–1895), a strong supporter of women's rights since 1848, proclaimed that the black man's vote was critical to overcoming the violent injustice perpetrated upon his race. Yet others, like Stanton and Anthony, asserted that white, educated women deserved the vote more, both for their decades of activism and for the wisdom and personal qualities they could bring to an awaiting nation in need of women's participation. The debates were contentious; the words, immoderate. Stanton's injurious attacks on immigrants and black men who had gained the vote appalled many former supporters. This ideological struggle partially, but not entirely, divided reformers along racial lines. Sojourner Truth (1797–1883), a former slave, abolitionist, and pro-suffrage speaker, also believed that the enfranchisement of black men alone would further disempower the newly freed black woman. Caught between the political needs of her race and her sex, Truth maintained her affiliations with both groups during an increasingly fractious time.[3]

Discord Over the Fifteenth Amendment, 1869–1890

Ultimately what was called the "Negro's hour" prevailed and the Stanton/Anthony opposition turned away to form an all-women's National Woman Suffrage Association (NWSA) in 1869. While Stanton hoped that the organization would take on a larger reform agenda addressing marriage, contraception, divorce law, and the biblical argument for the subordination of women, Anthony concentrated her activism on suffrage, asserting that this was the only way that women could attain the power to improve their condition. Both leaders publicly contested the meaning of the Fourteenth Amendment, which had described the citizen as a "person" who was born or naturalized in the U.S. but had included the descriptor "male" when referring to the citizen who could vote. Following their "New Departure" strategy, Stanton and Anthony went to the polls in New York state to demonstrate that women were included under the definition of "person." In 1872 Anthony was arrested after she tried to cast her ballot and refused to pay a small fine that she saw as unlawful. She explained her actions in a whirlwind speaking tour through fifty towns in neighboring counties, asserting in her speech that "it was we, the people, not we, the white male citizens, nor yet we, the male citizens; but we, the whole people, who formed this Union. And we formed it, not to give the blessings or liberty, but to secure them; not to the half of ourselves and the half of our posterity, but to the whole people—women as well as men." Nevertheless, three years later in *Minor v. Happersett,* the Supreme Court of the United States determined that the Fourteenth Amendment had affirmed female citizenship but not women's right to vote.

Yet other women's rights advocates, such as Lucy Stone and her husband Henry Blackwell (1825–1909), supported the Fifteenth Amendment and felt that Stanton and Anthony had betrayed their abolitionist values, made even worse by their accepting financial support from an antiblack Democrat for their newspaper *The Revolution.* Stone and Blackwell countered in 1869 by forming a Boston-based American Woman Suffrage Association (AWSA) that would limit its activities to suffrage, attracting those men and women who did not approve of the NWSA's intrusion into issues of faith and family as well as many African Americans who supported the organization's greater sensitivity to the difficulties they faced during the post-Reconstruction era.

After years of acrimony, the two organizations, encouraged by the efforts of Lucy's daughter Alice Stone Blackwell (1857–1950), joined forces in 1890 to become the National American Woman Suffrage Association (NAWSA), first under the leadership of an aging Stanton, then of beloved "Aunt Susan" (Anthony), and finally the latter's protégée, Iowan Carrie Chapman Catt (1859–1947). The two suffrage camps, once divided in their efforts, now joined together under NAWSA to win the vote for women in the twentieth century.

Struggles for Suffrage, 1870–1913

By the end of the nineteenth century, women across the country were organizing in large groups on behalf of their communities. A revival of **temperance** campaigns in Ohio and the Midwest turned into a national "crusade" against the liquor industry as well as local saloons. Marching, praying, and singing women invaded these all-male enclaves, wielding female morality as their primary weapon. By 1874, the Woman's Christian Temperance Union (WCTU) was building an organization of some two hundred thousand members, while its energetic leader Frances Willard (1839–1898) used her "Do Everything" campaign to move this powerful group to support suffrage.

African American women in the North as well as in the South developed an extensive network of women's clubs to benefit the needy and uneducated, most of whom did not enjoy the support of whites-only women's clubs and benevolence organizations. Secular clubs of elite black women—some 400 strong by 1900—joined to form the National Association of Colored Women (NACW) in 1896 under the leadership of Mary Church Terrell (1863–1954), with the motto "Lifting as we climb." Meanwhile, religiously affiliated women formed the Women's Convention (WC) of the National Baptist Convention, seeking to bring into its ranks the "everyday common women" who labored almost exclusively in domestic service or agriculture. Both club and church women's movements, no matter how distinct in their membership and focus, saw that they could meet their goals only if women had more political influence; indeed, WC leaders by 1912 were insisting on the franchise as part of their demands for equality.

Although the first wave of women's rights leaders were exceptionally long-lived, most did not see the success of their dream to have an amendment to the Constitution affirm woman's right to suffrage. In spite of a flurry of organizing at the state level, by 1910 NAWSA appeared to some supporters to have become stagnant, with some expressing that they were "in the doldrums." This perception was not entirely accurate. Due to the success of NAWSA's plan to recruit wealthy women of high social rank, suffrage had become respectable, having fought off the stigma of anti-male fanaticism that plagued the women's rights movement in its early years. While this new "gilt-chair movement" abandoned the challenge to domestic relationships and social mores, it did encourage moderates to join suffrage efforts, thereby building a mass base of support. Indeed, some Western territories and states had already enfranchised women: Wyoming in 1869, Utah in 1870, Colorado in 1893, and Idaho in 1896. In 1909 NAWSA moved its headquarters from Warren, Ohio, to New York City, a center of suffrage activity, in a sign of renewed energy and momentum.

Nevertheless, national suffrage had been stalled for years by legislative maneuverings and congressional apathy. NAWSA had just about given up its hope for a "Susan B. Anthony" amendment. Although it kept

The **temperance movement** sought to limit the use of alcohol in order to protect women and children from family violence, poverty, and abandonment. To that end, its members targeted saloons—men's social spaces—to picket, protest, and even attack. The Temperance Movement would lead to legal prohibition of alcohol in 1919 (later repealed in 1933).

a nominal Congressional Committee office in Washington D.C. this body could not have been expected to accomplish much with its budget of only ten dollars a year. Fighting for suffrage in state legislatures seemed more strategic, particularly in the West where a pioneer spirit promised to open the way for women's rights. This tactical shift resulted in success: suffragists fought and won in Washington State in 1910; California in 1911; and then Kansas, Oregon, and Arizona in 1912. Slowly but surely, thought NAWSA leaders, the suffrage states would reassure the national public that women would vote sensibly, family life would remain intact, and feminine decorum would continue to mark a difference between the sexes.

This plan did not endure for long. Alice Paul (1885–1977) and Lucy Burns (1879–1966), newly returned to the U.S. from graduate study in England, had become enthusiasts of the British militant suffragist movement and had come home ready to ignite the "Votes for Women" struggle with a new spirit. Taking over NAWSA's Congressional Committee, they adopted spectacle and civil disobedience as political tools. Paul and Burns represented a new generation of suffragists who were attuned to a "new woman" ready to leave demure "**parlor politics**" in order to make use of working men's traditional shows of force: open-air speeches and parades through city streets. Attuned to a newly developing consumer culture, they understood the need to "sell" suffrage in order to attract new followers, with events that combined a celebration of femininity, political activism, and popular entertainment.[4] By 1913, the suffrage movement had its official colors: the yellow of sunflowers, which spring up in the wake of the plow and therefore symbolize civilization, and white, suggesting the purity that women would bring to politics. These colors adorned sashes, blouses, hats, buttons, and banners; those who sported them harangued onlookers from soapboxes and street corners, marched in parades of thousands down city streets, and captivated audiences with allegorical pageants celebrating women's heroism. Suffrage had become fun.

However, African American women found themselves rebuffed by the "National," the name given to the predominantly white and middle-class NAWSA. At issue was a growing intolerance among white Americans toward the enfranchisement of citizens deemed "unfit," such as black men and newly arrived immigrants. Not immune to racist and **nativist** sentiments that permeated mainstream culture, some white women who had been working toward suffrage for decades deeply resented their continued marginalization while uneducated men had the vote that they could use, sell, or squander. NAWSA itself did not fully welcome African Americans, especially as it now faced its own "Southern question." Although support for suffrage had come slowly in the South, by the turn of century white Southern women were working toward enfranchisement through state organizations affiliated with NAWSA. Many supported NAWSA's state-by-state ratification policy rather than a national

Although elite women in the nineteenth century were expected to focus on the domestic sphere, they often engaged in political life through discussions, lectures, and entertainments within the home. This kind of "**parlor politics**"—debating ideas in the room of the house most accessible to visitors—allowed women to maintain an acceptable femininity while also involving themselves in the pressing issues of the day. Many suffragists of the early twentieth century maintained this practice, while the young suffrage set preferred to venture into men's public space to proclaim their views directly, loudly, and boldly. Nevertheless, you can observe some activists' anxiety about this challenge to woman's idealized role in their emphasis on woman's beauty, purity, and nurturing maternal instinct.

Nativism is a political movement or perspective that seeks to safeguard dominant U.S. groups and their cultures in opposition to immigrants and traditionally marginalized groups.

amendment because the South's "states' rights" policies would allow the states to exclude African American women from the polls. Suffragists could then argue that enfranchisement of white women would add to the number of white votes in the state, thereby rendering the black vote insignificant. At the same time, NAWSA leaders hoped to move the national "Susan B. Anthony" amendment forward. To do this, they needed the support of the South. Thus the "Southern question" was a sticky one for NAWSA members whose activism was rooted in the antislavery movement or who found the racist rhetoric repugnant. Their choices seemed to be either to tolerate the use of suffrage for white supremacist ends or to abandon hope of a national amendment. It was a conflict over social justice and "expediency," a debate that was never adequately resolved between a cherished principle and the success of the movement.

While Paul and Burns were shaking up the staid members of the NAWSA leadership, pro-suffrage forces in the Eastern states also revved up their activity. Harriot Stanton Blatch (1856–1940), daughter of Elizabeth Cady Stanton, returned to New York after living some twenty years in her husband's native England. The United States that Blatch encountered was vastly different from the one she had left. The old Anglo-American ways were disappearing. Immigrants from southern and eastern Europe had brought not only their languages and foods to the country, but their socialist and anarchist politics as well, demonstrating a working-class identity that challenged the "American" skilled laborers who had found unity in their trade unions. In New York City, immigrant women were a particularly active presence on city streets: shopping, going to and from work, stepping out at night to attend dance halls and to enjoy movies at the storefront nickelodeon theaters. Even elite and middle-class women were more visible: many now went to college and, though still excluded from a number of professions, were making their mark as civil servants, academics, teachers, and even ministers. In places like Greenwich Village, a magnet for those seeking professional as well as personal freedom, women were displaying their talents as public speakers, artists, poets, journalists, and actresses.

Blatch soon saw an opportunity to bring professional and working women together to improve conditions for both, but especially for those factory girls whose unrelenting labor was fueling the nation's wealth and the workers' discontent. Her Equality League for Self-Supporting Women (1907) attempted to bridge an economic and cultural abyss. When the shirtwaist workers—those sewing the popular blouses or "waists" that freed women from the cumbersome dresses of a generation earlier—voted to strike in 1909, they were backed by progressive society women who joined their pickets, accompanied them to court, and paid their bail. It was a short-lived solidarity. Even after elite women joined with workers to protest the factory conditions that would lead to the terrifying Triangle Shirtwaist Factory fire in 1911, the alliance did not last. Society and middle-class women concentrated on suffrage, arguing that the vote would bring political influence. Working women, while supporting suffrage, sought more often to improve their immediate conditions.

A tactician who enjoyed the game of politics, Blatch welcomed Alice Paul as a kindred spirit but focused her own attention on Albany, the seat of New York's state legislature. From 1911 to 1913, she concentrated on forcing state legislators to bring a referendum on suffrage to voters, using backroom lobbying, cajoling, and forceful dealing as well as public displays of women's demands for suffrage. From the outset, Blatch saw the utility of suffrage "stunts and gimmicks"—such as open-air rallies, parades down Fifth Avenue, and trolley tours upstate—to build a mass emotional connection to suffrage, even as she used them in a battle of wits with her politician opponents in the state's capital. These gimmicks were costly, however, and Blatch inevitably turned uptown to the wealthy for the funding and publicity to reach her goal.

In January 1913, Blatch won the legislators' approval for a referendum. As this game begins, she faces the even more challenging task of moving male voters to accept a "true democracy." She has until 1915 to convince the electorate and is mobilizing her new organization, the Women's Political Union (WPU), to build emotional support through "shows" of suffrage. Meanwhile, Blatch's considerable war chest has attracted others. Alice Paul shows interest in coming to New York, an idea that Blatch firmly opposes. And Carrie Chapman Catt, Blatch's opposite in temperament and political strategy who prefers a moderate and gradual approach, returns from abroad to revive her New York Woman's Suffrage Party (WSP) and to gain some control over the WPU. New York is populous and has great symbolic value: it is a prize that suffrage leaders are eager to win.

The Antis

In the nineteenth century, mainstream public opinion was unanimous in its astonishment at the temerity of elite women to demand the vote. Even a generally supportive Henry Stanton refused to attend the Woman's Rights Convention when his wife insisted on advocating for suffrage. Lucretia Mott feared that the women would be laughing-stocks if they pushed forward such a motion, and several of the Convention founders initially refused to sign the Declaration of Sentiments because they considered it too extreme.

SUFFRAGIST:

A U.S. term to describe all those who favor woman suffrage.

SUFFRAGETTE:

Originally a pejorative British term used to describe militant suffragists who took to the streets and defied the law. Later both U.K. and U.S. suffragists took the name as their own.

SUFF:

An informal name for a suffragist.

ANTI:

An informal name for an anti-suffragist.

REMONSTRANT:

An old-fashioned name for an anti.

At the time religious teaching and social custom, with the support of rudimentary evolutionary scientific theory, determined that there were innate physical, emotional, and spiritual differences between men and women that needed to be fostered for the well-being of the individual as well as for the health of society as a whole. An *anti*, someone who opposed suffrage, might have argued his or her case in the following ways:

- Did not God give woman a different path in life and make her subservient to men (Genesis; St. Paul's Epistles to the Corinthians and Galatians)? Moreover, has not science found that sex differentiation and specialization of function are marks of higher life forms? So too, the specialization of men and women into distinct sex roles marks an evolution of civilization. Just compare primitive societies to our own. By relegating the sexes to separate spheres of activity and influence, men taking charge of public affairs and women finding their crowning glory in the home as wives and mothers, a society assures the strength and well-being of the human race.

- Although woman is too frail to take part in the rough-and-tumble of politics, her emotions and intuitive knowledge prepare her perfectly for a domestic role. She brings the next generation into being; therefore no activity that would diminish her reproductive capacity should be encouraged. Learned physicians such as Harvard Medical School's Dr. Edward Clark have fulminated against college education for women; the rush of blood to the brain during study would, he argues, surely draw it from the reproductive and nervous systems. To allow women to weaken their bodies as well as their spirits would be suicide for the species.

- The primary unit of society is not the individual, as suffragists claim, but rather the family. The family is one unit with one public voice. Man has been assigned the role of leader and protector of the family; indeed, it is his physical strength that serves to keep hostile outside forces at bay. But it is woman who, through example, tames the aggressive nature of man, channeling it toward productive ends. Woman is no drudge; she reigns supreme in the home. She too participates in public debates of the day, but her power lies in her influence on her husband and male children. She can do more good and be more effective in this way than by voting. The men, in turn, provide for her, seek her counsel, keep her safe, and cherish her womanly nature.

- There is no inalienable right to the vote. Our republican government grants a voice to some of its members—ideally the most fit—to make good judgments. These leaders have the duty to respond wisely to public opinion and to convince others to follow their lead by moral, or even physical, force. This is what political life entails and it is no place for a woman. Her citizenship does not require that she vote. Indeed, she should enjoy the luxury of relief from the burden of political life to tend to the higher calling of the family. The nation needs citizens who fulfill their social roles so that the entire society can thrive.

- If women take on the prerogatives and duties of men, men will eventually take on feminine roles. Neither sex is suited for the work of the other and so this reversal will bring personal unhappiness, familial disintegration, poorly managed economy, weakened government, and even the dissolution of society into anarchy!

The belief in separate **spheres** assumed that men were meant to act in the rough-and-tumble public sphere of work, politics, and social life, whereas women should find their place as well as power in the home and similar domestic spaces, such as schools, women's clubs, and church activities.

To the nineteenth-century belief in separate, **gendered spheres**, antis in the early twentieth century added a concern about the state of democracy, a reaction to the enfranchisement of former male slaves and immigrants, the latter assumed to lack any tradition of democracy or understanding of "American values." The beliefs of these antis might be summarized as follows:

- A healthy nation must draw on the leadership of the most fit: those who are educated, thoughtful, and aware. The higher social classes have the skills to run this nation and should not be deterred or held back by the ideas of the unfit. If we give the vote to all women, we will double the influence of these unfit.

- We have already given the vote to thousands of illiterates, some barely arrived on our shores, who have no understanding of the importance of the franchise. They sell their votes for a few cents or a few drinks.

- The building blocks of society are the social classes—not the individual or the family. It is to the upper classes that we must turn for the well-being of all. Whereas the male elite protect our welfare in their governing of the nation, the female elite inspire with their benevolence. Because elite women engage in charity work with no interest in personal gain, they bring virtue to the public sphere.

Just as the meaning and goals of suffrage changed over the decades following Elizabeth Cady Stanton's proclamation of woman's right to the franchise, shifting social norms and political exigencies also influenced opponents of a public voice for women. While most antis continued to base their objections primarily on the different nature and duties given to women, they joined with others who had more self-serving objections to the vote. The brewing and liquor industries, for example, were convinced that women would vote as a bloc for prohibition, and therefore galvanized to finance anti-suffrage campaigns. Similarly, railroad, oil, farming, and manufacturing interests, particularly the textile industry that depended upon female and child labor, lobbied strenuously to defeat suffrage efforts. Finally, the men and women who worried that a universal suffrage would bring in far too many "unfit" remained opposed. By 1911, the various groups would join forces through the formation of the National Association Opposed to Woman Suffrage.

Votes for Women

The suffragists were in some ways as diverse as their opponents. In addition to their many differences in age, region, race, social class, and political views, the women who campaigned for suffrage in the early years of the twentieth century were as much the heirs of nineteenth-century intellectual traditions as they were examples of "restless women" who sought to have an impact on a society that was rapidly industrializing and urbanizing. As they organized, paraded, and lobbied for political participation, the suffragists were forced to address among themselves the ideology of separate spheres, the entry of women into the wage labor market, and their voting goals for after suffrage was attained. There was no single suffragist position.

Most suffragists did not completely reject the notion of sexual difference. Indeed, they argued simultaneously for woman's natural right to political equality with men and that women were domestic, nurturing, and maternal by nature. The vote, they claimed, neither would nor could diminish a woman's inherent womanliness. Some suffragists countered the antis' claims that they "unsexed" themselves as a "screaming sisterhood" by publicly displaying their conformity to feminine roles: pushing their babies in carriages during the suffrage parades, holding baking demonstrations, and publishing cookbooks of their best recipes. Few women joined anthropologist Elsie Clews Parsons in noting that attacks on suffragists' gender identity were "very painful to most persons and so the charge of unwomanliness has ever been a kind of whip against the would-be woman rebel."

Many pro-suffrage women not only included the concept of womanliness in their political arguments but also presented woman's allegedly domestic nature as the very reason for woman's right to the franchise. Female voters, they argued, would address the social wrongs ignored by their male counterparts—child labor; impure food for sale; filthy, unhealthy streets in urban areas; dangerous work conditions—and throw out the corrupt politicians and their political machines. By focusing on woman's "duty" to bring "home values" to public life, rather than her "right" to enter the political sphere, temperance organizations as well as the woman's club movement brought hundreds of thousands of women to suffrage work.

African American women turned to the concept of womanly respectability in their attempts to counter both racial humiliation and sexual assault. Nannie Burroughs (1879–1961) of the Baptist Woman's Convention, for example, argued that domestic life instilled a sense of self-worth in black children that helped them survive in a racist public sphere. In spite of rebuffs from NAWSA and the

Congressional Committee, black suffragists persisted in their efforts to join and to persuade the predominately white national groups to speak out against segregation and **Jim Crow laws**, and to organize among themselves. The vote, for these women, was key to building black political power that would lead to a "new day" for black citizens, providing protection against discrimination and unsafe practices in employment and supporting women in the face of physical and sexual abuse by men.

Like African American women, many immigrant and working women hoped that suffrage would allow them to secure long-lasting reforms for industrial labor: the eight-hour day, minimum wage, elimination of night work, and job safety.

As investigative reporter Rheta Childe Dorr (1868–1948) proclaimed in 1910, there were nine million women in the paid labor force throughout the country and therefore nine million outside the domestic control of fathers and husbands. The rising middle classes had sent their girls to college and into the semi-professions of teaching, nursing, social work, and librarianship. High school graduates were filling the increasing numbers of office and clerical staff positions spurred by the growth of businesses and governmental bureaucracies. Work, these women asserted, was desirable both as a vehicle for self-development and as a way of achieving financial independence. Professional and "business girls" alike wanted to put their education to use and take part in enterprises that "mattered." Even though they still encountered restrictions in law and medicine, limitations on advancement even in those spheres open to women, and vastly unequal salaries everywhere, they saw in the vote an opportunity to address these remaining inequalities. As M. Carey Thomas, president of Bryn Mawr College, suggested, the twentieth-century suffragist was seeking to change American society to reflect a social revolution that was already underway: "the old-fashioned arguments for woman suffrage are being pushed into the background by the urgent practical need of the ballot felt by women today."[5]

Although many suffragists saw the vote as their final goal, hoping that the franchise would bring about the public voice that they deserved, others saw it as a starting point to address the many limitations on women's lives. Following Elizabeth Cady Stanton, whose memory was now marginalized as too radical in the mainstream suffrage movement, they wanted to address issues related to the family and domestic life. These feminists—a term that began to be used around 1913—were all suffragists, but not all suffragists were feminists. Elsie Clews Parsons was one of the first to chip away at the belief in the essential nature of the nuclear family, while other members of

BY 1910:

77 percent of schoolteachers were women.
79 percent of librarians were women.
100 percent of nurses were women.

IN 1910:

80 percent of African American working women not engaged in agriculture had jobs as domestic servants or laundresses.

BY 1920:

92 percent of the nation's office workers were women.

New York's woman's conversation group Heterodoxy challenged the notion of woman as homemaker, designed new living quarters that removed women from the kitchen and nursery, questioned women's loss of their last names upon marriage and loss of citizenship when they married foreign men, and struggled to create companionate relationships with men both in and outside of marriage. When the "Susan B. Anthony" amendment to the U.S. Constitution was finally ratified in 1920, giving American women the vote, Crystal Eastman hopefully prophesied, "Now we can begin."

LABOR AND LABOR MOVEMENTS

Chronology

The 1880s through the 1910s saw an almost constant flow of industrial actions, strikes, and violent conflicts between workers and owners of industry throughout the United States. Only a few are listed below.

1869 Knights of Labor established, a cross-class and cross-trade labor organization.

1886 American Federation of Labor (AFL) established, consolidating many small trade unions.

1886 Settlement movement begins in the United States, including Hull House (Chicago, 1889), Henry Street (NYC, 1893), Lenox Hill (NYC, 1894), and Greenwich House (Greenwich Village, NYC, 1902), among many others.

1892 Anarchists Emma Goldman and Alexander Berkman plan the assassination of Henry C. Frick, business partner of Andrew Carnegie; the attempt fails, but brings national attention to the anarchist movement.

1893 Western Federation of Miners established to protest the changing conditions of the mining industry.

1894 Strike against the Pullman Palace Car Company (railroad cars), the first national strike, threatens the country's transportation system.

1901 Socialist Party of America (SPA) established.

1901 Anarchist Leon Czolgosz assassinates President William McKinley.

1903 Women's Trade Union League (WTUL) established, hoping to organize women within the AFL.

1903 Congress passes Anti-Anarchist Immigration Act, allowing the state to deport anyone suspected of anarchist acts or "philosophical anarchism."

1905 Industrial Workers of the World (IWW) established to organize all trades as well as unskilled workers.

1909 General strike of women garment workers in New York City, called the "Uprising of the 20,000."

1911 Triangle Shirtwaist Factory fire takes 146 lives and stuns the nation.

1912	"Bread & Roses" strike against American Woolens Company in Lawrence, Massachusetts.
1912	Socialist Party candidate for president of the United States, Eugene Debs, garners 12 percent of the vote.
1913	Paterson Silk Strike in Paterson, New Jersey, begins to protest poor working conditions as well the transformation of the silk industry.

Labor and Labor Movements, 1800–1900

If Jeffersonian America had created an ideal of the yeoman farmer who tilled his land and lived in mutually supportive interdependence with his fellow citizens, this democratic dream did not take into account either the rise of the planter class in the South or the mining and ranching interests that were to transform the Western Territories. Moreover, the rapid industrialization that took place in Northern cities after the Civil War strained the American self-image as a small town or family farm to its very core.

Once railroads crisscrossed the nation, goods could be manufactured in one place and shipped to the increasing numbers of urban centers with relative ease. Those with a large amount of capital to invest could control the manufacturing process from beginning to end. American business tycoon Andrew Carnegie, for instance, owned coal and iron mines, the blast furnaces and finishing mills to make steel, and the railroads and ships needed to bring these products to points of distribution. And mining was not the only industry to be consolidated into large corporations; the meatpacking, grain processing, and even tobacco industries also became national enterprises, as did investment banking, which was needed to provide funds for continual growth and expansion. Soon the Rockefeller, Swift, Pillsbury, Duke, and J.P. Morgan families became household names. Their huge conglomerates manufactured goods more cheaply, gained unprecedented power, and were interconnected through mergers, **trusts**, and common boards of directors. This corporate capitalism concentrated wealth in the hands of a few—by 1890 one percent of the population owned approximately 50 percent of the nation's wealth—while making the United States an economic power.

A **"trust"** refers to a monopoly, or ownership of an entire industry in order to eliminate competition. A corporation that wants to grow by taking over other corporations across the country—in violation of state and local laws prohibiting such practices—places all of its companies into a trust (a holding company) which serves as the supervisory body.

By the first decade of the twentieth century, Americans of every political view were wondering where corporate capitalism was taking them. Did it represent the natural evolution of technological progress? Was it building an economic prosperity that would ultimately be enjoyed by all? Seizing the power of the government? Creating a heartless society?

Leading the United States into imperialist wars, like the Spanish-American War of 1898, to gain new markets? This anxiety about the new corporate capitalist society generated a widespread desire for reform that gave the Progressive Era its name. Republicans, Democrats, followers of Theodore Roosevelt's Progressive Party, populists, and suffragists joined with workers and revolutionaries in calling for change. Of course, each group had its own understanding of the "good" society and plans for how to create it.

Labor in the East

By the late nineteenth century, the majority of wage earners were no longer farmers and artisans, but industrial workers concentrated near large factories and often living in shabby barracks-like dwellings. These workers were not the native-born youth who had first left the farms to seek independence outside the family enterprise; rather, the new worker tended to be foreign-born, part of the waves of immigration from southern and eastern Europe that characterized the transformation of eastern cities. With different languages, religions, and cultures, they shared little other than surprise that America did not offer them the prosperity that had been the stuff of their dreams. A few groups hoped to make their fortunes and return home; most were slowly adjusting to a life of toil; a few were determined to join the bosses, using their national origins to more efficiently exploit the labor of their countrymen. A small number were determined to rebel.

These immigrants found that American factories and the smaller "shops" were unlike anything that they had experienced in their home countries; even those who had suffered great poverty were not prepared for the disruption of everyday life and values wrought by industrialization. Artisans formerly respected for their skills remained unemployed. The dignity of scholars or community elders went unrecognized. Religious holidays and the Sabbath passed unobserved. Patriarchs sent their daughters into the factories as unskilled "learners" to support the family. Production was rationalized; that is, subdivided into parts with each worker engaged in repetitive tasks that gave little satisfaction or sense of accomplishment. Workers found that speedups demanded their constant attention, while advances in technology enabled factories to add more machinery at a time when safety precautions were mostly absent. Accidents were common and severe. Workweeks averaging 55 hours included mandatory unpaid overtime in many trades. Wages were kept as low as possible, often below survival levels; entire families often had to work "inside" or at home, pooling their income to gain the barest of necessities.

As the United States was expanding its economic strength, there was little consideration for the "hands" that produced its wealth. To the contrary, big businesses were becoming anonymous moneymaking machines; owners had little contact with those whose lives they controlled. Boards of directors demanded profits, middlemen disciplined the labor force, and workers enjoyed few regulations to guarantee their health and safety, reasonable wages, or decent work environments. Divided by ethnic differences and the competition fueled by the daily arrival of thousands of new immigrants looking for work, the labor force seemed increasingly powerless.

Yet American workers were seldom complacent or retiring in the face of poor wages and bad working conditions. From the mid-nineteenth century, skilled craftsmen, mostly native born of English and German stock, joined together into trade unions to negotiate for specific goals. Since skilled workers were highly valued and courted with the highest wages, these **craft unions** served their members well. Soon the carpenters, cutters, drapers, and other skilled workers had become an "aristocracy" of labor. Although the Knights of Labor, one of the first labor organizations (1869), reached out to both skilled workers and the middle class in hopes of building a working-class identity, its efforts could not overcome the well-established craft identity of workers, nor withstand the increasing repression of organized workers after the Haymarket Massacre of 1886 in Chicago.

The Haymarket Square Massacre (1886) began as a clash between police and workers and led to the conviction of seven anarchists and execution of four, who were later proved to be innocent of instigating the riot. It marked the start of an official crackdown on radical labor organizers.

In 1886, the American Federation of Labor consolidated these small trade unions into a national organization for working men only. The AFL claimed that its "pure and simple" trade unionism protected it from "electioneering" in order to focus entirely on the economic interests of its members, the elite of the working class. By 1900, under the leadership of Samuel Gompers, the AFL would represent itself as the conservative alternative to the growing radicalism of American labor movements.

Focusing on skilled, male, native-born workers, the AFL and its many Locals (individual craft unions) did not attend to the changing nature of industrialized work: industries were demanding a constant supply of unskilled workers rather than the craftsmen who had flourished before mass industrialization. Although skilled workers had gained in negotiating strength through unionization, the vast majority of the new industrial workers were left adrift, obliged to accept the lowest wages. Thus they became highly desirable to potential employers who no longer needed a large pool of skilled labor.

Many of these unskilled workers were young women between the ages of fourteen and twenty-four who were generally not considered worthy of anyone's organizing effort. As the AFL saw it, these teenagers were temporary laborers, working until they married or merely to supplement their family's income. Moreover, many Locals asserted that women should not be working at all and attempted to bar them from the union, just as they had done with blacks and immigrants. Although these union members hoped to maintain patriarchal authority in the home through ensuring wives' continued economic dependence, they also recognized that women were employed

A **craft union**, as its name suggests, is an autonomous organization that includes only those workers with a specific skill or trade.

precisely because they were paid a much smaller wage than men in the same industry. Labor leaders feared that the widespread entry of women would not only undercut the male wage, but also support the new technological advances that both de-skilled the labor and drove out the male workforce. It was better for all, they believed, to demand a "family wage" that would allow men to support their families and allow their wives to remain at home.

Yet proponents of this view did not consider the many women permanently in the labor force nor the majority they held in certain industries, particularly the textile and garment industries. In asserting that women were not amenable to organization, they did not pay attention to the specific conditions of women's lives: the inability of many women to meet at night due to family responsibilities and social decorum, as well as their discomfort debating in the backrooms of local saloons, a men's social space that was often used for union organizing. Most labor organizations not only ignored but also actively rejected women's participation; this opened the way for groups organizing on the basis of gender to lead working women into the fray.

Settlement workers, suffragists, and other reformers were instrumental in developing and financing organizations to benefit the growing numbers of "working girls" in American cities. Hoping to protect those whom they perceived to be vulnerable, these "allies" even created a Consumers' League (1890) to raise awareness among middle-class housewives of how their demand for cheap goods affected workers' lives. No matter how sympathetic, these allies generally discouraged organizing in favor of legal and political reforms. Believing as they did in cross-class alliances, these elites undermined the growth of a working-class identity and challenged the belief that there must be a class struggle between labor and capital.

Woman's Work

From 1890 through the early years of the twentieth century, both native-born and immigrant women entered the labor force in unprecedented numbers. Although almost 90 percent of the women over 35 years of age were married, the decline in the birthrate across all racial groups and classes meant that far fewer years of their lives had to be dedicated to child rearing. As commercial industries took on many aspects of household production, women no longer faced the labor-intensive tasks of sewing and laundering clothing, baking, canning and preserving food, and making their own soaps and candles. Similarly, the arrival of clean-burning gas fuel and running water made it easier to clean for the smaller family. The material conditions were in place to allow women to leave the domestic sphere at least for specific periods of their lives: before marriage, in the event of a husband's disability or death, or in times of financial need.

Women entered a workforce that was highly gendered as well as stratified by social class, race, and ethnicity. Historian Alice Kessler-Harris has found that jobs available to women in the beginning years of the century were based on a hierarchy of perceived proximity to gentility, respectability, and traditional work in the home. These include, from most to least desirable:

- **Teacher, nurse**. These professions reinforced the feminine virtues of nurturing and caretaking.

- **Department store buyer, professional in business and medicine**. These were assumed to be occupied by women who did not marry.

- **Office worker, department store clerk**. These jobs were lower on the hierarchy because they served others. Although they paid less than a factory wage, they were still more desirable.

- **Factory worker, waitress**. Women who worked these jobs had too much access to strangers and unknown customers to be entirely respectable.

- **Domestic service**. The lowest rung of the hierarchy.[6]

Among the jobs open to working-class women, factory work provided better wages and an emerging economic and social independence while remaining more or less respectable. Nevertheless, this work was subject to a gendered hierarchy as well: men's work was often determined to be skilled labor and therefore commanded higher wages, while women's adaptation of domestic skills such as sewing or food production was categorized as unskilled.

"Americans" were preferred for the higher ranking jobs; indeed the professions and semi-professions often restricted their workforce to native-born whites. Even factories sought to improve their reputation for hiring a "better sort" of worker by restricting their jobs by ethnicity and especially by race. Factory work in New York City, which relied so heavily on immigrant labor, was further subdivided by national origins. In 1910, for instance, 52 percent of all Italian working women were employed by the garment industry, mostly fabricating men's clothing. Italians also dominated the making of candy and artificial flowers. Jewish women also worked in the garment industry, but 60 percent of them worked on women's clothing. Black women, excluded from the trades by discrimination, tended to work in domestic service, which, although least valued of women's labor opportunities, could be seen as an improvement over agricultural work.

All women who entered the labor force at the beginning of the century would encounter restrictions on the kind of work available to them and the wages they could command. Their hope was to claim some agency within an economic system that used them as a pool of cheap, "unskilled" labor. Or, as the *Report on Condition of Woman and Child Wage-Earners* (1911) explained about the working woman: "The moment she organizes a union and seeks by organization to secure better wages she diminishes or destroys what is to the employer her chief value."

The Women's Trade Union League, 1903

Although the AFL refused to organize female workers, wealthy settlement worker William English Walling and former union organizer Mary Kenney O'Sullivan established the Women's Trade Union League (WTUL) at the 1903 AFL convention. Under the jurisdiction of the AFL, it was to be a national united front to bring women workers into existing unions, such as the International Ladies' Garment Workers' Union, the International Cigar Makers' Union, and the Neckwear Makers. The founders turned to "women of social importance," such as Margaret Dreier Robins and her sister Mary in New York and Jane Addams in Chicago, as well as to well-known working-class labor organizers, such as Leonora O'Reilly, to establish WTUL branches in industrial cities throughout the country: New York, Chicago, and Boston as well as St. Louis, Kansas City, and Los Angeles. Assuming that young women workers ignored or feared unionism, WTUL members pioneered the street rally and soapbox speech to challenge worker apathy. Yet they also veered away from official AFL policy by supporting walkouts and spontaneous strikes, walking picket lines, appealing to strikebreakers, organizing consumer boycotts, generating publicity, and building strike funds. The WTUL helped workers organize strikes and negotiate with bosses; once a shop was considered strong enough to work within the male-dominated unions, the WTUL tried to broker its affiliation with an AFL Local.

The WTUL often questioned how its parent organization's policies served women. When the AFL opposed a minimum wage, fearing that it would become a ceiling rather than a starting point for negotiations, and rejected the restriction of working hours as contrary to the freedom of contract, WTUL officials countered that a girl of fourteen could gain no real benefit from such theoretical freedoms. In later years, WTUL favored protective legislation such as a general minimum wage and a particular one for sweatshop labor, an eight-hour workday, limitations on night work for women, and prohibition of work for women two months before and after the birth of a child. It lambasted the Asian Exclusion Act (1882) that the AFL supported as protecting the native-born American worker from foreign competition. Although the WTUL was criticized as leaning toward radicalism due to its principles as well as organizing practices, the organization gradually shifted its focus toward developing women's political power through suffrage.

THE AMERICAN FEDERATION OF LABOR:

1897: 265,000 members
1920: 4 million members

WOMEN WORKERS IN ORGANIZED TRADE UNIONS:

1900: 3.3 percent of all women workers
1910: 1.5 percent of all women workers

From the outset, the WTUL attempted to place working-class women in its leadership. It was not to be the traditional charity organization or ladies' reform society. Indeed, many of its elite allies were eager to leave the protected world of high society and to engage in meaningful work, to "do things," and to "change the world." The majority of allies—independently wealthy, college-educated, and usually single women—formed close, even lifelong, friendships with their working-class counterparts, often financing their studies, vacations, salaries, and medical needs and sometimes living with them for long periods of time.

Nevertheless, elite women brought values and social norms to their relationships and to the organization that could rankle, hurt, and offend other members. Primary among these attitudes was a refusal to consider social class as a significant factor in women's lives. Elites believed in "sisterhood," a unity of women who shared a physical and emotional femininity that would overcome social difference. They saw work as a liberating experience of self-fulfillment that would launch the independence of the century's New Woman. Yet the women they organized valued their working-class identity and did not want to rise "above" it. Ideologically committed to class solidarity, they considered their sex as a less determining factor than the exploitation of their labor. As to work, they saw no glory in repetitive, unskilled tasks with no opportunity for either advancement or relaxation. Marriage could be a welcome relief from the squalor of factory work. Since the majority of working girls handed their paychecks directly to their families, envelope still sealed, there was little expectation that work could provide a means of individuation and self-reliance.

The vast differences in experience put cross-class alliances to the test, undermining them through misunderstandings and personal attacks. Deep friendships sometimes could mend breaches of trust. Yet working-class members of the WTUL who chafed at the patronizing attitudes of their allies often resigned from the organization in protest. Many returned after facing continued exclusion from the unions to juggle their commitments to labor and sexual equality and seek fellowship among their own class.

The Uprising of the Twenty Thousand, 1909

There was one moment when the "fragile bridge" between labor and elites seemed to triumph. On November 24, 1909, the shirtwaist makers of New York City, 85 percent of whom were young women, went out on an industry-wide strike. Supported and financed by the WTUL and its wealthy friends, working women proved that they were a political force to contend with in American labor.

Unlike many industries that had consolidated to form large corporations, the garment industry of New York City was fragmented into small factories, smaller shops, and even the workers' homes, where piecework could be done by an entire family. Manufacturers of women's clothing, particularly the popular shirtwaists—blouses whose simpler iterations were worn by working girls and whose elaborately embroidered and pleated variations often occupied a lady's wardrobe—had to employ a fast and flexible workforce to produce their goods on time while undercutting their competition. New York "waist" companies thrived due to the huge number of immigrants streaming into the largest port of entry in the United States. Rejecting highly skilled tailors and seamstresses, the New York factories sought out the unskilled young, teaching them to perform only one of many tasks, such as sewing buttonholes or setting collars. If they were very young—and the factories routinely employed and hid child laborers between ten and fourteen years of age—they pulled off stray threads.

Yet even this was not enough for small manufacturers, many of whom were immigrants themselves, to maintain their businesses. Seeking ways to cut expenses still further, the bosses set into place working conditions that pushed the girls to their limits. Factory owners allowed overseers to subcontract labor within the factory; that is, the higher-ranking employees could hire their own workers, whose labor would now have to support two levels of bosses. Sometimes workers were paid by the piece, forcing the girls to work as fast as possible; others received a weekly wage but endured constant speedups. Apprentice workers received particularly low pay and even had part of their wages withheld until they had completed a trial period satisfactorily. It surprised no one that many of these apprentices were found lacking and dismissed without receiving back wages. Workers could be required to pay for electricity, rent their chairs, bring their own thread and needles, even cart their own sewing machines to the shop. They were fined for talking and singing as well as for sewing errors. Garment workers bitterly complained about other conditions of their ten-hour days: factories were filthy; cloth dust permeated the air, giving them respiratory diseases; shop leaders addressed them in foul language; sexual assault, both verbal and physical, was commonplace.

Discontent finally came to a head after the Leierson and Triangle Shirtwaist Factories locked out workers who were organizing for the International Ladies Garment Workers (AFL Local 25) over the summer of 1909. On November 24, workers convened at Cooper Union's auditorium to hear the AFL and WTUL leaders repeat their customary statements when Clara Lemlich (1886–1982), a draper and organizer, took to the podium and called for a general strike. Unexpectedly, the girls rose as one, vowing to strike until a settlement was negotiated. Enthusiasm spread, giving rise to what was to be known as the Uprising of Twenty (or Thirty) Thousand. Although this strike was carried primarily by Jewish workers—the "Americans" were more reluctant to strike than the Yiddish-speaking organizers—it claimed a place for all working women in the public eye as strikers took to the streets to walk on picket lines, harass the "**scabs**" that might take their place, and sell the newspapers that would build their strike funds.

Striking workers often hurled the insulting term "**scab**" at workers who refused to strike or who were hired to take the strikers' places. Verbal harassment of strikebreakers was a common strategy to shame and discourage fellow workers who did not or could not condone a strike.

The participation of elite women in the WTUL was important to the short-term success of the strike effort. Not only did society women stand on picket lines to keep the police in order and go to the courthouse to provide bail for those arrested, they also brought press fanfare to lower Manhattan to keep the strike in the public's eye. When Mrs. Alva Belmont or Miss Ann Morgan invited workers to their exclusive Colony Club to talk about workers' lives, the event received newspaper coverage. When beautiful suffragist Inez Milholland did her turn on the picket line while dressed in an extravagant evening gown, it was noticed. When chauffeured limousines brought some working girls to the picket lines, uptowners paid attention. Although there were disagreements within the WTUL about the importance and the notoriety given to the "mink brigade," the multi-class alliance of women held until strikers refused an offer that increased wages without permitting unionization. Some allies were appalled. They had supported strikers as victims of exploitation, but could not accept an assertive working girl negotiating the conditions of her labor.

Anatomy of a Strike

The first decade of the twentieth century was awash in strikes: the Uprising of the Twenty Thousand in 1909 and 1910; the 1912 "Bread and Roses" strike in the woolen mills of Lawrence, Massachusetts; the Paterson silk workers' strike in 1913. These had all become legends in the East. But for all their frequency and apparent simplicity—workers withdrawing their labor to protest or to negotiate with employers—formal strikes were complex events to ignite and maintain. Unlike walkouts, strikes did not happen spontaneously. Even the workers whose suffering was most acute seldom rebelled openly against their condition until they could imagine the possibility of success. In the 1910s, labor organizations and political groups flocked to areas of unrest to build up enthusiasm for "industrial action." The agitators they employed, orators who could stir the emotions of a crowd, built a solid base of support as they channeled popular discontent toward the specific goals of their organization. Sometimes groups worked together harmoniously, as when the International Ladies Garment Workers Union (ILGWU), the Women's Trade Union League (WTUL), and the Socialist Party of America joined to support the shirtwaist strike. In other cases, groups vied with one another for workers' allegiance and political clout. In Lawrence, for instance, the radical Industrial Workers of the World (IWW) dominated the process of organizing the strikers, building the ranks of its membership by thousands after only a few days of intervention, much to the dismay of socialist organizers and town leaders alike.

Once a strike began, leaders from the parties and unions would move in to organize the workers and to maintain their courage until negotiations could bring about a work agreement. These outsiders brought considerable strike-management experience and coordinated the efforts of the different factories and shops to ensure that the various trades within the factories worked toward the same goals. They encouraged the recalcitrant, established legal counsel for those who would be arrested, set up strike funds, and provided soup kitchens for workers and their families. Often well-known and easily identifiable, organizers were targeted for arrest and frequently barred from entering a town by local police. Since organizers such as Bill Haywood and Elizabeth Gurley Flynn often had a national reputation, their arrival signaled the serious nature of the effort, as well as providing the publicity needed to garner public support.

Strikes, particularly those of long duration, were difficult for their participants. Strikers who had made less than a subsistence wage now had no income and few reserves. Factory owners would try to bring in strikebreakers, often people from ethnic and racial groups who were in even greater economic need than the workers. Picketing strikers often became ill from the heat or the cold. They could easily feel demoralized when fellow workers returned to the factories after settling with the bosses in their specific craft or after simply giving up the fight. Elizabeth Gurley Flynn often said that an organizer had to keep the strikers busy at all times, even all weekend, lest they shift their focus from the struggle of the working class to the needs of their individual families. Thus the skilled organizer would not only motivate strikers, but would also plan entertainments such as workingman's balls, children's meetings, and family picnics, which included encouraging speeches and the welcome experience of a joyous outing.

In the first decades of the twentieth century, strikes were provocations; picketing, unprotected; and free speech not yet considered a right. Workers therefore faced serious and often violent response to their actions: factory owners hired detectives and known "sluggers" to beat up strikers; police routinely roughhoused those on picket lines, arresting many for "unlawful assemblage," "incitement to riot," "obstructing sidewalks," and other offenses; judges condemned the arrested to days in filthy jail cells or even the dreaded workhouses. Factory owners hired prostitutes to harass and intimidate women strikers, sometimes beating them, but most often comparing the strikers' activities to their own streetwalking. Agent provocateurs posing as workers encouraged violence in hopes of providing a rationale for increased repression. Hotheaded strikers, too, retaliated with force as well as with sabotage against factory machinery. With firearms and other weapons as unregulated as workplace conditions, labor disputes could and often did become deadly. In the dizzying atmosphere of a strike, workers turned to their strike committees for information, took turns walking the picket line, sought out news, and tried to figure out who was friend and who was foe. Sooner or later, they would get word on negotiations with the bosses and answer with their vote.

Nevertheless, radical political groups fostered the strike to achieve more than just "bread and butter" demands and the closed shop (unionization of all workers in a factory) to safeguard their gains. The strike was a tool for the education of workers. It was through the experience of making the strike, it was claimed, that the worker would see the true nature of the conflict between bosses and workers. Through the consciousness that came from such practice, the worker would understand class struggle and the proletariat's role in bringing about an industrial democracy in which factories and services would be owned by the very people who labored in them. So while the strike was the enactment of labor's power, it also served as a crucible for the development of a new social identity: the revolutionary worker.

Class Struggle

At the turn of the century, almost all labor activist groups, including the AFL, conceptualized the labor struggle as between an oppressor class and oppressed workers, with their central goal to protect and further the economic well-being of the labor force. Political groups influenced by Marxist thought viewed class difference as class struggle not just for economic gain, but also for political power. For them, the proletariat that emerged with industrialization had a clearer understanding of the unequal relations between capital and labor because they experienced exploitation of their labor every day. Moreover, when workers acted on their own behalf through their only recourse—refusal to work—the ensuing police repression and legal punishments exposed the collaboration of the state and the law with industry. The working class had extensive personal experience of industrial labor's theft of their full humanity by turning them into "hands" to increase the profits of business; the working class, therefore, were the only ones who could dismantle this unjust economic structure and, in its place, build a political and economic system designed to benefit all the people rather than the few.

Although the many political groups on the left shared this utopian goal, they differed vigorously on how they would achieve their ideal. Anarchism, a nineteenth-century movement that was still powerful in agrarian Europe, asserted that human beings would construct a good society if they were free to act without the coercive forces of the state, the church, or the family. Socialists, on the other hand, turned to the state, albeit a democratic people's state, to organize and carry out the policies that were to improve their lives. Some progressives in the U.S. watched intently as revolutionary groups in Russia planned to implement Karl Marx's ideals. Yet many American socialists, heartened by their electoral successes and popularity among temperance unions, Populists, **Fabian societies**, and a newly organized Socialist Party of America (1901) cautioned that real change would come only through a slow, steady transformation of society by the established social structures: political reform, legislative change, and the ballot box.

The **Fabian Society** was a socialist, reformist British organization with branches in the U.S., dedicated to the investigation of social problems and the improvement of "society in accordance with the highest moral possibilities."

THE INDUSTRIAL WORKERS OF THE WORLD

Arise, ye prisoners of starvation!
Arise, ye wretched of the earth!
For Justice thunders condemnation.
A better world's in birth.
No more tradition's chains shall bind us;
Arise, ye slaves! No more in thrall!
The earth shall stand on new foundations;
We have been *naught*—We shall be All!
'Tis the final conflict!
Let each stand in his place.
The Industrial Union
Shall be the Human Race.[7]

INDUSTRIAL WORKERS OF THE WORLD'S VERSION, "THE INTERNATIONALE"

Elizabeth Gurley Flynn (1890–1964), daughter of staunch socialists, recalled that in her youth the Socialist Party seemed dull, even tame, in comparison to the fiercely independent and flamboyant "working stiffs" of the Industrial Workers of the World (IWW), affectionately nicknamed the Wobblies. Migrant workers, unskilled laborers, and hobos: these were the rough-and-ready whose militant songs called for class struggle and whose rhetoric defied "bushwa" (bourgeois) law and order.

The IWW had developed out of the organizing efforts of Western miners, who resisted the profound changes in their working conditions once the mining industry became heavily capitalized at the end of the nineteenth century. Attracted to Colorado, Montana, Idaho, and the territory of Arizona after the gold rush of the 1850s, these prospectors who once went looking for surface ore now faced a mining of refractory ores (gold and silver) as well as base metals (especially copper) that made use of new technologies, smelting facilities, and railroad transportation in order to become hugely profitable. The new mining industries that arose in the middle of mountain ranges, forests, and deserts had no use for skilled workers; the miners thus were hired for unskilled tasks or replaced by machinery altogether. Although they joined together to form the Western Federation of Miners (WFM) in 1893, demanding better wages and safety conditions, they soon realized that the new corporations would not negotiate with them. To the contrary, the businesses intended to crush the union's strength and isolate miners from their once supportive local communities. In the violent conflicts that arose in Coeur d'Alene, Idaho (1892) as well as in Cripple Creek and Telluride, Colorado (1903), mine owners established private armies, infiltrated unions with their spies, and hired agents provocateurs to spark the violence that they then could repress. State governments called for federal troops to quell labor unrest, sent militia to break strikes, and even declared martial law. In response, the WFM stockpiled arms and ammunition, torches and dynamite, seeing class warfare as a response to a capitalism that valued the market over human lives.

In 1905, a group of Western miners, socialists, and labor organizers met secretly in Chicago at a "Continental Congress of the Working Class" to form the Industrial Workers of the World, dedicated to creating a "great brotherhood" through industrial unionism. Its goals, set forth by "Big" Bill Haywood (1869–1928), were threefold:

1. "We are here to confederate the workers of this country into a working class movement that shall have for its purpose the emancipation of the working class from the slave bondage of capitalism";

2. "The aims and objects of this organization should be to put the working class in possession of the economic power, the means of life, in control of the machinery of production and distribution, without regard to capitalist masters";

3. "This organization will be formed, based, and founded on the class struggle, having in view no compromise and no surrender."

Unlike the AFL, the IWW did not separate members by craft nor did it ignore the masses of unskilled workers that were entering the labor force: immigrants in the East, African Americans in the South, and Midwestern small farmers turned migrant workers when they could not compete in newly capitalized agriculture. The Wobblies persuaded "the least of all workers" that they were responsible for the wealth of the nation, but had been robbed of this value by the capitalist class. They would, someday, rise up and destroy this enemy, then use their knowledge of industry to seize power and use it to benefit humanity. Industries run by the workers themselves would take the place of the state in this utopian future.

In spite of its revolutionary fervor, however, the IWW acted primarily to improve working conditions in the present and generally cautioned against the use of violence. After considerable internal struggle, it reaffirmed its identity as a labor union outside of "politics," understood as the parties and movements that vied for power. In choosing syndicalism over affiliation with a political party, the Wobblies affirmed that the American political system could not represent them, not even the Socialist Party, which was increasing in popularity. As migrants, disenfranchised blacks, women, and foreigners, many Wobs had no access to the vote. Yet even the majority of the IWW, those English-speaking white male laborers of northern European descent, saw no possibility of emancipation in what Wobbly-priest Father Thomas J. Hagerty called "dropping pieces of paper into a hole in a box." The power of labor, they argued, was to come from the solidarity of the working class. Once one craft or sex or race could not be played against another, the working class as a whole would triumph using "direct action" (strikes, passive resistance, sabotage, and the general strike) which would eventually destroy the capitalist system.

The IWW in the East: Paterson, New Jersey

The IWW's organizing efforts turned to Paterson, New Jersey, the center of American silk production in 1913 and only seventeen miles away from New York City. Long an industrial town known as "Red City" for its rebellious spirit, Paterson at this time had absorbed new populations of Italian and Jewish immigrants, adding them to the Old World artisans who were weaving and dying fabric in some three hundred mills. As in other towns dominated by the textile industries, strong competition among small shops kept wages down and imposed an erratic work schedule: overtime in peak seasons followed by slowdowns and layoffs. It was an industry-wide change in technology, however, that brought about a worker revolt. Factories could now adopt a new high-speed loom that could turn out silk, albeit of inferior quality, at a much faster pace. Since the new looms required little skill, they could be operated easily by untrained women, who could tend up to four looms at a time and for far lower wages than those earned by the skilled Paterson weaver who tended two looms and produced a high-quality product. The big manufacturers hoped to bring the new looms to New Jersey as well as to set up "annexes" in Pennsylvania with its cheaper workforce, thereby threatening workers not only with a speed-up that would physically exhaust them, but also with a possible cut in wages and increased unemployment in the industry.

On January 27, 1913, eight hundred workers spontaneously walked out of the Doherty Silk Mill. As others joined them, strikers turned to the IWW, fresh from its success in Lawrence, Massachusetts, to organize a general strike demanding an end to the four-loom system, an eight-hour day, and a minimum wage for the dyers, who received starvation wages in spite of their daily contact with toxic chemicals. Responding to the Wobblies' call to starve while fighting rather than while working, over twenty-five thousand went out on strike, around twelve hundred per day, leaving the factories until all silk production in Paterson was shut down. Yet this was not a strike to the IWW's liking, for it was to drag on for six months—so long that supportive radical Greenwich Villagers could make weekly treks to enjoy the speeches and weekend entertainments in nearby Haledon, a tiny town that welcomed the strikers and their activities. The IWW believed that only short and focused strikes could positively affect negotiations. Strike organizers, including Bill Haywood, worried as the $60,000 strike fund was forced to stretch alarmingly, providing only fifty cents a month to support each striker.

In addition, mill owners and town officials were determined to get the IWW out of Paterson, defeat the strike, and curtail any further attempts at unionization. They warned other manufacturers that they too would be affected by the strikes unless the Wobblies could be defeated; they hired armed detectives, the hated O'Brien Agency men, who escorted strikebreakers to the factories. The press threatened IWW organizers with violence, even death. Mill owners accused the IWW of teaching un-American ideas to ignorant workers and turned to the AFL as an unpleasant but lesser evil. Their goal, according to a concerned town rabbi, was to starve workers into submission. Unfortunately, a press blackout in New York City kept many outsiders from learning about Paterson as the strike settled into a tense stalemate.

Bill Haywood, who frequented Greenwich Village and was well known in bohemian circles, hoped to break the press censorship, build working-class solidarity with the strike, and add some much-needed cash to the strike fund. The workers of New York City and their allies could do just that. As the story goes, Haywood was explaining this goal one night at a Village party, when someone—Mabel Dodge asserts that it was she—suggested that the IWW should put on a pageant staging significant moments in the strike. The strikers could play themselves, giving immediacy to the scene. If it were performed in the City, at some place as famous as Madison Square Garden, it could draw thousands of supporters. All it would take would be a few weeks of planning to become a "living newspaper" that would represent working-class experience from a working-class point of view. They say that Jack Reed jumped with enthusiasm upon hearing the idea; a former cheerleader and Drama Society member at Harvard College, he offered to design and direct the pageant. His Harvard pal Bobby Jones (Robert Edmund Jones, later a famous stage designer) could create the scenery. John Sloan, art director for the radical magazine *The Masses*, could paint the backdrop. The ideas were set into motion.

Parades and Pageants, 1900–1920

"Nothing is more likely to cement the sympathies of our people and to accentuate our homogeneity than a cultivation of pageants."　　　　　　　　　　Century, July 1910

During the first two decades of the twentieth century, parades and pageants flourished in big cities and in small towns throughout the United States, particularly during the Fourth of July and local holiday celebrations such as Founders' Days, town anniversaries, and commemorations of other important moments in the life of a community. At the center of these festivities was a speech by a prominent civic leader extolling the nation's or community's many successes, its sacred destiny, and the moral principles that had been guiding its people since the beginning. What historian David Glassberg calls "community relics" were often placed on public display: a piece of ancient flag, a hero's sword, artifacts from the daily life. A monument—statue, tree, tablet—was commonly erected to suggest movement into a prosperous future.

Members of the community could participate in the events by marching toward the speaker's stand in groups that represented their civic, fraternal, religious, and labor organizations. Some put on historical dress to represent their connection to the past. Others reenacted these moments through the popular **tableaux vivants** set on wagons (later, floats) that were pulled through the streets. In these "living pictures," costumed but silent and motionless people depicted famous scenes from history as well as abstract ideals such as justice, liberty, and brotherhood. Municipal governments supported these ceremonies as a way to boost local economies, but also to build community identity and civic virtues.[8]

Yet large celebrations also worried local authorities who responded to the inevitable "rowdyism": drinking, gambling, the arrival of hucksters, gunshots into the air, and fireworks. Containing a boisterous crowd of merrymakers became a key concern of social elites who were horrified at such widespread "desecration" of patriotic holidays. Some town leaders turned to more sedate fare, reviving English medieval and Elizabethan festivities—such as morris dances, maypoles, and minuets—as well as the everyday customs of a New England colonial past in order to reinforce Anglo-American identity, social hierarchy, and decorum.

Towns and organizations often hired pageant masters (professional designers of pageants) who would recreate a homogeneous history—placing Native peoples, African Americans, the working class, and immigrants in secondary roles or excluding them entirely—and convey this imagined past as a model of social order and moral behavior for the future. By mounting extravaganzas that routinely included hundreds of townspeople as amateur actors, these spectacles were meant to appeal to a mass audience seeking affirmation of its identity at a time when urbanization, industrialization, and immigration were transforming the lives of all Americans. Festivals that portrayed a town's harmonious progress from wilderness to modern greatness (or utopian future) sought to relieve anxieties about social change and thereby strengthen community life.

Progressive Era reformers had yet another use for pageants and parades when faced with large groups of urban youth who had little time and few facilities for recreation, or with rural villages suffering from a declining economic base in agriculture: play. Well-known educators such as John Dewey insisted that children needed play and physical education in order to develop their imagination, sociability, and, ultimately, citizenship. Playground Associations were formed. Interactive pedagogies involving dance, crafts, and song were suggested. Extracurricular activities such as scouting were planned. Pageantry, the reformers believed, would engage interest in the past and provide structured, wholesome activity for children as well as adults; the ritual play of historical pageantry could heal the antagonisms emerging from class and ethnic differences as well as the social

Tableaux vivants ("living pictures") were popular parlor entertainments during the nineteenth century, in which women would enact famous literary characters, artworks, and historical moments. Though the tableaux are often seen as domestic activities that reinforced women's domestic roles, physical charm, and silence, Professor Mary Chapman argues that the tableaux allowed nineteenth-century women to particulate in the cultural debates of the day.[9]

wounds of poverty and economic exploitation. Festivals were designed to emphasize democratic ideals, establishing a shared history and values for the nation. As such, they often highlighted American folk dances and ethnic heroes as well as the traditional enjoyments of early country life, such as the county fair, husking bee, and picnics.

By 1910, *American Homes and Gardens* could proclaim that the country had gone "pageant mad." Participants and audiences flocked to commemorations of a town's founding, Christmas pageants, college May Day festivities, and celebrations by private organizations of religious, political, and even commercial endeavors. Pageant structure evolved to include six episodes in chronological sequence that celebrated the central theme with music, dance, costumes, and props. Pageantry became a profession, including pageant masters to design them; the American Pageant Association to set guidelines; and universities to offer courses on how to plan them. What excited the imagination was the potent affirmation of community life through a participatory art form that included hundreds, even thousands, of amateur actors. Rich and poor, factory owners and laborers, men and women, all would be incorporated into the spectacle of harmony and goodwill.

Though pageantry was primarily used to assert patriotic spirit and reduce social conflict, it was also adapted by groups that wished to challenge that dominant view. Labor organizations were the first to take to the streets in celebratory parades to make their presence known, to proclaim their ideals on banners, and to demonstrate, indirectly, their political power.

In 1911, for example, New York suffragists adapted the parade to demand for women's full political equality. It was a bold challenge to the prevailing belief that women should remain in the home, as well as a public refusal to follow class-based norms that required ladies to avoid being "conspicuous." The parades, which included suffragists on horseback, suffrage colors, floats, and banners, demanded the attention of onlookers and created an audience of spectators. As such, the parade initially frightened NAWSA leaders, who could imagine success only insofar as suffragists maintained their respectability and seriousness of purpose. Many refused to march in those early years. Yet by 1913, the suffrage parade had become commonplace, a carnival of color as well as a show of force.

When Alice Paul called for a national parade, she deliberately proclaimed women's right to occupy the streets of the nation's capital. Moreover, she planned an allegorical pageant to follow the parade on the very steps of the U.S. Treasury Building, appropriating a male political space to affirm women's beauty, femininity, and connection to the most cherished values of the country, what historian Mary Chapman has called "America's democratic mythology." The pageant *Allegory*, designed by Hazel MacKaye (1880–1944) who lived in Greenwich Settlement and avidly supported suffrage, turned to the ancient tradition of using female figures to embody civic virtues. As described by theater scholar Karen Blair, on that day in 1913:

The action in Allegory began when the massive doors swung open before the crowds to feature the figure of Columbia, who descended a flight of stairs, as a gigantic American flag was unfurled. In the course of an hour, she summoned a series of symbolic figures representative of the virtues of American womanhood: first Justice, in purple robes, accompanied by female attendants in violet, all making their obeisance to the majestic strains of the "Pilgrim's Chorus"; (sic) then Charity, preceded by little girls strewing her path with roses; next a statuesque Liberty, who raced down the stairs followed by "brave" girls decked with red and gold scarves. Next Peace entered, dressed in silver and white, sending a dove to the White House nearby. She was followed by Plenty, surrounded by maidens carrying cornucopias of fruit. And finally Hope, shyly venturing forth, accompanied by girls dressed in rainbow colors, dancing and releasing bouquets of balloons.[10]

Such a pageant, designed to bedazzle the audience and win converts to the cause, demonstrated that political power could be compatible with womanhood.

The story of African Americans, generally either entirely ignored in mainstream pageantry or dismissed though the buffoonery of the minstrel tradition, was presented in the huge pageant designed by W.E.B. Du Bois to commemorate the fiftieth anniversary of the Emancipation Proclamation. With more than one thousand participants, *The Star of Ethiopia* reenacted black history from prehistoric times to the present, at which point black progress won over the "Furies" of intolerance, idleness, and intemperance. Nor did the pageant, which premiered in New York in 1913, ignore the "Valley of Humiliation" of slavery, instead following scenes of toil and sorrow with those of slave rebellion, abolition movements, and revolt, leading to the awakening of "Ethiopia." So popular was *The Star* that Du Bois was able to mount all-black productions of the pageant in Washington D.C. as well as in Philadelphia in the following years.

The Paterson Pageant, as planned by the IWW and various Villagers, took the conservative origins of the spectacle to still more radical ends. This theatrical event did not seek to convey timeless, universal concepts or replay heroic history; rather it was going to reenact moments of an ongoing strike, using real strikers and real organizers to play themselves. As Rose Pastor Stokes commented in her review for the *New York Call*, this was to be history "fresh from the hands of its makers."[11] The pageant would be theater, using the stage sets, music, costumes, and amateur acting that people had come to expect of pageantry. However, it was not going to separate the actor and spectator. To the contrary, there was to be no curtain isolating a dramatic space; actors would march through the aisles of the old Madison Square Garden, recreating Paterson and turning the audience into participant strikers. This was an event to celebrate the power of the working class to determine the

> **IN 1912**
>
> 2 percent of all Americans controlled 60 percent of the wealth of the nation.

country's future. It was revolutionary theater, what historian Leslie Fishbein would later call "docudrama as a weapon in the class struggle," a new genre that emerged out of workers' lives and spoke to their deepest feelings.[12] As Bill Haywood saw it, this was an example of a truly proletarian art that could combat the alienation of industrial labor; it would inspire and emotionally move its audience toward a greater class consciousness and a more fully human existence.

BOHEMIA: THE SPIRIT OF THE NEW

Chronology

1903   W.E.B. Du Bois asserts that the twentieth century will focus on the problem of the "color line" in his collection of essays, *The Souls of Black Folk*.

1909   Sigmund Freud lectures on *The Interpretation of Dreams* at Clark University in the U.S., asserting the existence of the unconscious.

1909   National Association for the Advancement of Colored People (NAACP) established.

1910   Hutchins Hapgood's *Types from City Streets* introduces readers to marginalized social groups on the Lower East Side.

1911   Franz Boas publishes *The Mind of Primitive Man*, challenging the widespread belief in a racial hierarchy topped by those of Anglo-Saxon/Nordic ancestry.

1911   May White Ovington publishes *Half a Man: The Status of the Negro in New York*, focusing attention on the growing African American population.

1911   Publication of the English translation of Ellen Key's *Love and Marriage*, which suggests that motherhood should not be confined to marriage.

1912   Marie Jenny Howe starts Heterodoxy, a women's luncheon/conversation club to discuss the issues of the day.

1912   Italian Maria Montessori challenges prevailing ideas on child development as well as primary education, showing how children thrive in the freedom of her Montessori Method.

1912   Max Eastman accepts offer to be the editor of *The Masses*.

1913   International Exhibition of Modern Art opens on February 7 at the 69th Regiment Armory.

1913   The term "feminism" is first used in the United States.

1913   French philosopher Henri Bergson lectures on "Spirituality and Liberty" at Columbia University, presenting the view that reality is reached through intuition rather than reason.

1913 Elsie Clews Parsons uses anthropological methods to attack essentialist notions of sex in *The Old-Fashioned Woman: Primitive Fancies about the Sex*. She includes a spoof on her own society.

1913 First of the "white slave" or "vice" films, *Traffic in Souls*, marks the rise of cinema for mass audiences and reveals social anxiety over women's sexuality and new social freedoms. The term *white slavery* used to refer to the abduction of girls for prostitution.

The Spirit of the New

"There seems to be a vague but real relationship between all the real workers of our day. Whether in literature, plastic art, the labor movement . . . we find an instinct to blow up the old forms and traditions, to dynamite the baked and hardened earth so that fresh flowers can grow." —HUTCHINS HAPGOOD, JANUARY 1913

On February 17, 1913, the 69th Regiment Armory opened its doors to the International Exhibition of Modern Art, a monthlong exhibit of the latest works of postimpressionist painting and sculpture. To be sure, Alfred Steiglitz had brought works by Pablo Picasso and Paul Cézanne to his tiny gallery at 291 Fifth Avenue previously, but that was nothing compared to the more than one thousand pieces that were to astonish the throngs of New Yorkers who clamored to see them. There they saw works by American painters, including New York realists, who had recently caused a stir by portraying everyday lives, even squalor, lived out on the city streets. Known later as the Ashcan School, these artists, including Robert Henri and his students, spurned academic art and its insistence on idealized beauty. Their work surprised audiences with its social commentary. John Sloan's *Sunday, Girls Drying Their Hair* was there, as was his *McSorley's Ale House*.

The **Immortal Eight** were a group of eight American artists, under the leadership of Robert Henri, who rebelled against the artistic demands and economic control of the American Academy of Design. The eight men, dubbed the Immortal Eight by the press, abandoned the Academy to show their work at Macbeth Gallery in New York (1908). Because of their interest in depicting everyday life without idealization, they were called the "apostles of ugliness" and later categorized as the Ashcan School. The eight are Arthur B. Davies, William J. Glackens, Robert Henri, Ernest Lawson, George Luks, Maurice B. Prendergast, Everett Shinn, and John Sloan.

But it was not the **Immortal Eight's** rejection of the spiritual uplift and exaltation of the heroic that staggered visitors at the Armory Show, but rather the European revolution in form and color. Cubism, especially Marcel Duchamp's *Nude Descending a Staircase*, was singled out by critics as an affront to representational art, a joke, and even an insult to the viewer who was expected to value this incompetence. The Cubist Room, with its works by Duchamp, Picasso, Georges Braque, and Francis Picabia, was dubbed a "Chamber of Horrors." Then too, Henri Matisse shocked viewers with his use of distortion and color. The "ugliness" of his fauvism with its "primitive" or childlike drawing, as well as the physicality of his nudes, was deemed indecent, vulgar, and degenerate. The art offended the public's sensibilities and mocked its intelligence. This "guerrilla warfare" of aesthetic modernism, this "French invasion," marked new ways of seeing that, beyond provoking controversy about the nature of art, sparked an emerging American modernism.

Art was not the only dynamite blowing up old forms. By 1910, Americans had been introduced to the ideas of Sigmund Freud and were absorbing a popularized notion of psychoanalysis. In Greenwich Village particularly, bohemian writer Susan Glaspell mused that "one couldn't go out for buns" without encountering a conversation on the subject.[13] Freud's lectures at Clark University in 1909—attended by Emma Goldman—and his *Interpretation of Dreams*, translated into English in 1911, astounded the public with the idea that the rational self, which appeared to direct one's will, could be undermined by intricate and unseen motivations, and particularly by sexual drives that demanded to be gratified. Indeed, a common understanding of Freud's ideas concluded that civilization's sexual repression led to individual neurosis, to the intellectual inferiority of women, and to a general weakening of society. Americans, more than Freud himself, were optimistic that analysis could "cure" them, unlocking the "traumas" of childhood that limited adult life. Thus arose the fad of "psyching out": analyzing one's dreams, jokes, and slips of the tongue to reveal a "true self" obscured by the manners and practices of everyday life.

French philosopher Henri Bergson also asserted that there was a "living spark" (*élan vital*) flowing beneath the formalities of civilized life. When he came to lecture at Columbia University in 1913, Bergson caused one of the city's first traffic jams as intellectuals and socialites alike clamored to hear his speech "Spirituality and Liberty." Bergson believed that rational thought provided a knowledge flawed by self-interest, whereas intuition allowed one to perceive an object, a person, and even oneself with a deeper understanding.

These ideas mattered to the moderns—those who embraced the destabilizing of the observable world. As their surroundings had changed dramatically—by 1913 the New York subway system was transporting millions, the sixty-story Woolworth building had changed the city's skyline, and Henry Ford's mass production was filling the streets with automobiles—the moderns turned to ideas to catalyze similar changes within themselves. With intellectual and artistic currents urging them to break loose from the confinement of conventional social roles and beliefs, they hoped to liberate an inner vision, a waiting Self, forging an autobiography through the deed. Turning to the iconoclastic poet of an earlier generation for inspiration, the moderns of Greenwich Village saw themselves as traveling down an open road:

> ONE'S-SELF I sing, a simple separate person,
> Yet utter the word Democratic, the word En-Masse.
> Of physiology from top to toe I sing,
> Not physiognomy alone nor brain alone is worthy for the Muse, I say.
> The Form complete is worthier far,

The Female equally with the Male I sing.

Of Life immense in passion, pulse, and power,

Cheerful, for freest action form'd under the laws divine,

The Modern Man I sing.

WALT WHITMAN, LEAVES OF GRASS (1882)

Bohemia and "The New Woman"

Take a walk down MacDougal or any other narrow street in Greenwich Village in the early years of the twentieth century and you would immediately notice the presence of women. Some of these would be factory girls going to work in the shops filling the tall buildings on the east side of Washington Square. Grabbing their lunches from pushcarts, these girls would laugh and talk in loud voices, calling your attention to the strange rhythms and accents of their English. Some wouldn't speak English at all: you'd hear rapid-fire Italian and singsong Yiddish instead. Others would be obviously "American," but instead of the dress and behavior you had come to expect of ladies, these women would shock you by their appearance. Not only missing hats and gloves, they'd also have replaced a proper dress with a formless sack, with flat sandals instead of heeled leather shoes. Moreover, you see them walking around town freely, popping into tearooms and tiny hole-in-the-wall restaurants making up for their small size with a lively atmosphere. If you followed them inside the Pepper Pot or the Samovar, you'd see them sitting at tables in ardent conversation with young men who are clearly neither brothers nor cousins! At night, you could look through the windows of the Liberal Club to see couples in an embrace, dancing to the syncopated tunes coming from a pianola.

Today such a scene would not elicit a second glance. But in 1913, it marked a sea change in women's lives as well as in relationships between the sexes. By the turn of the century, native-born white women across the U.S. had gained a freedom unheard of by their mothers and grandmothers. The elaborate costumes that had confined their elders in corsets and pounds of skirting were streamlined, allowing these New Women to engage in physical activity, such as the popular activities of bicycling, golf, and tennis. The automobile and the telephone had given them a privacy hitherto unknown to women. Increasing numbers of universities opened their doors to women, allowing them to enroll in the same educational program demanded of male students. By 1910 almost 40 percent of the nation's undergraduates were women, and the pursuit of advanced degrees was also possible. A large percentage of these college-educated women did not marry or married later in life. Birth rates dropped for all white women, from over 7 to just 3.5 children per family. Divorce rates, too, were increasing, leaving many women to raise their children alone. More than ever, women of all social groups joined the workforce. Although the legal and medical professions remained notoriously resistant to women, the college-educated carved out careers in teaching, social work, nursing, and journalism as immigrant women by necessity flocked to the factories. As early as 1910, women made up over 27 percent of the entire workforce in New York City. No longer confined to the home, women appeared to be "everywhere."

Such rapid changes in the experiences and expectations of American women did not occur without provoking anxiety over their newfound public presence and independent purchasing power. One early response was reflected in the popularity of the Gibson Girl, an ideal feminine type of New Woman expressed in the cartoon drawings of Charles Dana Gibson from the 1890s through the 1910s. Tall and slim, with a small, upturned nose and piles of shining hair, this beauty assuaged concerns that the active young woman at the turn of the century would no longer want or need men—the Gibson Girl used her charms to find a suitable husband. At a time of massive immigration from eastern and southern Europe as well as the great migration of Southern blacks to Northern cities, her image, broadcast in the popular press as well as in advertising campaigns, presented as uniquely American a northern European, "white" womanhood that excluded from the national imagination any other ethnic or racial presence. Moreover, the Gibson Girl's jokes about seeking the right kind of man could, in the context of increased nativist sentiment, be interpreted as a wink at "natural selection" of the fittest, an emerging eugenics movement that was to counter widespread fears of an impending "**race suicide**."

Concerns about women's new freedoms also surfaced in the heightened debates over prostitution at the beginning of the twentieth century. In the early nineteenth century, the prostitute had been seen as depraved, a female whose natural modesty had been corrupted, a "fallen" woman who must be cast out of society lest she contaminate the pure. In contrast, women's rights advocates tended to view the prostitute as the prey of evil men, an innocent who had succumbed to male lust and who could be redeemed, often by the curing powers of female friendship. At the turn of the century, prostitution was reframed as "white slavery," part of a narrative in which young white girls were imagined to be carried off into brothels after being injected with drugs while on streetcars or in other public places. The furor over "white slave traffic," amplified by the popularity of the new feature-length "vice films," responded to the visible presence of wage-earning girls who sought out entertainment at the nickelodeons, dance halls, and amusement parks, accepting "treats" from men in a frank challenge to middle-class norms of courtship and propriety. There was no longer a clear difference between a "good girl" and a streetwalker, or between a professional prostitute and a poor woman who might sell sex to supplement her income in times of need.

Yet the New Woman had become a favored symbol of modern sensibility in bohemia. Indeed, Hutchins Hapgood credited women with establishing places where both men and women could abandon their prescribed social roles and forge a new subjectivity, new selves conceived in freedom to enhance the "life force" that had been extinguished by

At the beginning of the century, many white Americans were becoming alarmed by the influx of immigrants and the growth of non-white communities. They feared that whites would be outnumbered and so urged elite and middle class white women to produce large families in order to avoid "**race suicide**."

The term **feminism**, taken from the French *feminisme*, emerged in the 1910s to describe a modern movement for women's rights. According to historian Christine Stansell, "feminism betokened not just a claim to the vote or to making mother's roles in society more honored but rather to economic independence, sexual freedom, and psychological exemption from the repressive obligations of wifehood, motherhood, and daughterhood—a jettisoning of family duties for a heightened female individualism."[15]

middle-class conformity: "[w]hen the world began to change, the restlessness of women was the main cause of the development called Greenwich Village, which existed not only in New York but all over the country."[14] Many were to seek in women's emancipation from social restrictions a new kind of revolution that some were beginning to call "feminist." It was to be a movement to eliminate all the remaining limitations to women's activities—including social customs, legal restraints, and political marginalization—but its primary focus was to challenge the way individuals lived their daily lives: their emotions, sexual desires, and romantic relationships as well as how they dressed, ate, and set up their homes. It was to question the very nature of woman, to defy assumptions of her natural domesticity, and to scoff at the ideal of her purity. "Feminism" was a bold stance—"an awakening of conscience" (*Harper's Weekly,* 1913)—that embraced the personal as a source of social change.

The Old in the New

Although bohemias became havens for those who craved personal freedom, they were not the first "spiritual zones of mind" to galvanize change in American heterosocial and heterosexual relationships. The nineteenth century saw many utopian

---

FEMINISM IN 1913

"The removal of all social, political, economic, and other discriminations which are based upon sex, and the award of all rights and duties in all fields on the basis of individual capacity alone."

HENRIETTA RODMAN[16]

"The attempt of women to grow up, to accept the responsibilities of life, to outgrow those characteristics of childhood—selfishness and cowardliness—that we require our boys to outgrow, but that we permit and by our social system encourage our girls to retain."

HENRIETTA RODMAN[17]

"The state of mind of women who realize that their whole position in the social order is antiquated, as a woman cooking over an open fire with heavy iron pots would know that her entire housekeeping was out of date."

RHETA CHILDE DORR[18]

"The awakening and liberation of women is a revolution in the very process of life. It is not an event in any class or an issue between classes. It is an issue for all humanity."   MAX EASTMAN[19]

"Feminism is going to make it possible for the first time for men to be free."   FLOYD DELL[20]

communities that attempted to address the equality of women by transforming the ways in which men and women related to one other. As early as the 1820s, visionaries, basing their ideas on both evangelical Christianity and the social ideals of utopian pioneer Charles Fourier and his American followers, looked to communal living to perfect social life and to hasten what one such group described as the "Good Time Coming." Utopian communities throughout the country included New Harmony (Indiana), Brook Farm and Fruitlands (Massachusetts), Equity and Berlin Heights (Ohio), Modern Times and Oneida (New York), the Shakers, and an emerging national "sex radical" movement centered in the farmlands of the Midwest. Nevertheless, these experiments, isolated in rural areas, were short, albeit intensely, lived.[21]

Although they differed widely—the Shakers demanded celibacy, whereas the Oneida established complex marriage in which all men were considered married to all women—these groups attempted to purify male-female relationships by eliminating what they saw as the flaws of traditional marriage: women's legal subordination, criticized as "sex slavery"; the sexual abuse of women; and the sexual repression of women deprived of their "sex hunger." Reformers tended either to emphasize social purity and abstinence—often aided by vegetarianism and teetotalism—or to espouse "free love," a sexual relationship between a man and woman who had found their "spiritual affinity," their divinely assigned soul mate. The "true marriage" of this couple, whose sexual encounters were to be entirely mutual, lifted them to a higher spiritual plane and, therefore, did not need to submit to the authority of state or church. The issue of sexual expression, be it the attempt to control desire or encourage it, was central to the social movements that sought the emancipation of women and tried to imagine the paths that a new freedom might take.

Nevertheless, sex radicals were seen as highly disreputable throughout the nineteenth and early twentieth centuries. A whiff of support for "free lover" Victoria Woodhull by Elizabeth Cady Stanton turned the suffrage movement toward the platforms of social purity and temperance. Shortly thereafter, the first wave of "New Women," college-educated and born in the 1850s and '60s, skirted the issue of sexuality altogether, seeking independence and self-reliance in meaningful work, often in the areas newly opened to them: government, social reform, and education. As they united the American ideal of individual achievement and assertions of women's natural morality, innovators like Jane Addams and Florence Kelley entered the male domains of politics and the professions to enact what they called "public housekeeping," a strategy that allowed them to take leadership in public life without direct confrontation and competition with men. These New Women meant to "sweep out" corruption and bring their spiritual purity and nurturing to the young and the poor as well as into the workplace. This generation sought alternatives to the marriage that was expected of them, finding emotional and intellectual sustenance in all-female communities such as women's colleges and settlement houses. Some individuals also entered into "Boston marriages," long-term female couples whose relationship was based on profound, but not necessarily physically intimate, friendship. Thus the first New Women gained personal autonomy and often remarkable success, but only by avoiding male control of their projects as well as of themselves.

The next generation of New Women, however, rejected the all-female communities in order to seek equality alongside men. These women asked themselves what it might mean to see oneself primarily as an individual rather than as a member of a family, someone's daughter, or someone's wife. Middle-class women, barred from most professions and discriminated against in almost all others, sought economic independence as a starting point to equality. Many even envied the "wage-earning girl," assuming that her tiny salary gave her a self-sufficiency that they lacked. Moreover, these New Women saw entry into the labor force as particularly important because it gave them the opportunity to work with male colleagues (although rarely as equals in status or salary), allowing them to "do things that mattered" and to take their place, as Floyd Dell described it, as "world-builders."

Full emancipation called for more than suffrage or equity in the workplace, however; it would require middle-class women to reject both the norms of ladylike behavior that they had been taught since birth and the female enclaves that had promised autonomy at the price of celibacy. Legions of women, asserted writer Mary Heaton Vorse, sought "to hurt their mothers" in order to claim a place for themselves in the modern world. Smoking became a sign of asserting masculine prerogatives, while hard drinking and wild behavior at "pagan rout" parties affirmed their equality with men on men's own terms. Free love became a crusade. As the Heterodoxy club founder Marie Jenney Howe affirmed, these newest of New Women no longer valued their "little female selves," but strove instead to embrace their "whole, big human selves," insisting on inclusion in the "human sex."[22]

> ### HITTING THE SHELVES AT BONI'S BOOKSTORE (UPSTAIRS FROM POLLY'S) IN 1913
>
> Marcel Proust's *Swann's Way*
> Thomas Mann's *Death in Venice*
> D.H. Lawrence's *Sons and Lovers*
> Sigmund Freud's *Totem and Taboo*

"It's Sex O'Clock in America," *Current Opinion*, August 1913

Village women assumed that sexual freedom would facilitate their transformation into independent adults. They rebelled against social norms of virginity before marriage, not only engaging in the practice of "petting" so popular among college students at the time, but also taking and living with a series of lovers, even fighting off the impulse to marry. It was marriage rather than heterosexual sex that emerged as a problem for women bohemians. Although divorce was possible—indeed 33 percent of Heterodoxy had been divorced at a time when divorce was experienced by about 3 percent of the national population—marriage brought with it both legal restrictions on a woman's life, such as the ban on married women teachers in New York City schools, and cultural demands of subservience. Ida Rauh, for instance, received hate mail when a newspaper published the fact that she did not use her married name, Mrs. Max Eastman, on her mailbox. Henrietta Rodman briefly hid her marriage to keep her job as a high school English teacher. The older Mary Heaton Vorse worried that her marriage might somehow make her too respectable, thereby undermining her reputation as a radical. Marriage, for these moderns, was equated with emotional confinement, dreary domestic life that would extinguish the spark of sexual passion, and male ownership of women's lives.

Nevertheless, most male and female Villagers sooner or later sought out the intimacy of a companionate marriage as a union of sexual partners founded on the principles of honesty and equality. Indeed, it was with some pride that a woman would "marry like a man." The moderns toyed with the conventions of marriage, trying to change the institution from within. Hutchins Hapgood, for instance, hoped to seduce his wife through long letters describing his desires and affairs with other women, an attempt to give voice to a sexuality that had no language outside of the medical or the pornographic. Crystal Eastman sought to establish separate apartments for husbands and wives so that their encounters would be fresh, exciting, and voluntary. Flamboyant suffragist Inez Milholland taunted her husband with details of her flirtations and masturbation, a subject unmentionable even in bohemia.

Yet even amid the celebrations of pre- and extra marital relationships, fidelity to one's lover or spouse became an increasing concern. Many of the female Villagers could support "varietism" (non-monogamy) theoretically, but emotionally it could be hurtful, confusing, and damaging to one's friendships within a small bohemian circle that socialized together winter and summer. From the first, Henrietta Rodman created a schism in the Liberal Club by espousing free love and urging a fellow member to set up a ménage à trois in his home. While this may have been brash even by Village standards, the commonplace pairings, breakups, and changing of partners could leave a feeling of meaninglessness and futility. Floyd Dell would later see his fascination with sexual pleasure as adolescent, while the Villagers who were to form the Provincetown Players wrote many short plays that expressed their conflicts over such sexual explorations. Even less understanding were those who fell in love with Villagers; many, like Margaret Sanger's husband, would tire of their sexual rebellion, rejecting it as promiscuity and selfishness. Yet for all of their personal flaws and uncritical experimentations, the bohemian moderns articulated their understanding that sex was not only a physical act but also an intimate part of an emerging subjectivity, thereby affirming the existence of a "sexuality" that formed an integral part of the self.

The twin pursuits of a free heterosexual sexuality and "work that mattered" asked women to control their fertility at a time when artificial methods of birth control were illegal and the taboo on pregnancy and lactation demanded that pregnant women and new mothers be hidden from public view. Villagers, of course, strongly supported family limitation both to protect middle-class women's autonomy and to help poor women safeguard their health and precarious economic standing. Although most of the middle classes already knew about postcoital douching, cots (condoms), and the pessary (an early kind of diaphragm), the working classes had no access either to information on birth control or to contraceptive devices. Both were legally categorized as obscene and made illegal by a 1873 law that continued in force until well into mid-century. Birth control campaigner Margaret Sanger faced long jail sentences for her distribution of birth control pamphlets, her newspaper *The Woman Rebel*, and her clinic to aid working women. Emma Goldman, an outspoken supporter of women's sexual freedom and another pioneer for birth control, was arrested along with Ida Rauh and other Villagers while passing out flyers on the subject.

Yet most Villagers accepted the existence of a maternal instinct. Indeed, they flocked to read the translation of Swedish writer Ellen Key's *Love and Marriage* (1911), which affirmed a female drive to motherhood so strong that it need not be confined to marriage. Most Village women had at least one child of their own or raised the children of others. Perhaps even more than instinct, they saw in children the hope of the future, raised in freedom to grow to adulthood without the repressions, social conventions, and emotional distortions that characterized their own upbringing. Children, they thought, were thoroughly natural and spontaneous creatures, each with his or her own potential that was just awaiting the right moment to emerge and thrive. As the Italian educator Dr. Maria Montessori had asserted, the child was not a blank slate to be imprinted with the rules of a society, but rather an individual reacting to his or her environment. Indeed, the Montessori method of teaching, which asked teachers to stand aside and permit the natural process of self-education to occur, aligned with the hopes that Villagers placed on the "new child" whom they would "let arise." Women Villagers in particular were fascinated by education and child development both in and out of school system. Dr. Sara Josephine ("Jo") Baker (1873–1945) headed the Division of Child Hygiene for the Department of Public Health, establishing health education to improve infant and child mortality in New York City; Elisabeth Irwin (1880–1942) pioneered the pedagogy of experiential learning, establishing a progressive Little Red Schoolhouse within the public school system; Caroline Pratt (1867–1954) founded the City and Country School that valued children's play as a source for learning. By 1915, Mabel Dodge (1879–1962) too would establish a school in Croton-on-Hudson for Elizabeth Duncan (1871–1948), sister of famous modernist dancer Isadora Duncan, to teach children creativity through the freedom of movement and spirit.

Yet it remained unquestioned that children would grow up in the care of their mothers, which created yet another problem for women Villagers, who generally did not employ domestic help. Some, like Margaret Sanger and Mary Heaton Vorse, left their children with friends or nannies while they pursued their activism and traveled. Others, like Neith Boyce, found themselves isolated doing household chores in the newly developing suburbs of New York. It was Henrietta Rodman, inspired by the work of Charlotte Perkins Gilman, who between 1913 and 1915 designed an apartment house for professional women. Her "Paradise Palace" was to have a communal kitchen in the basement staffed by cooks and a Montessori school on the roof to care for small children, thereby freeing women to have families while avoiding the everyday burdens of domesticity. An idea ahead of its time, the apartment house did not receive financial backing and was never constructed, but it did focus attention on the conflict facing the new woman who was trying to reconcile her desire for work and self-expression with a husband, home, and family.

As the initiators of a new kind of social movement, the women of 1913 had few examples to follow. They therefore struck out wherever they felt constrained, campaigning for dress reform, economic independence, freedom from small town life, and emancipation from the traditional home, seeking alternatives to constrictive sexual arrangements, and rejecting subservience in marriage. Theirs was what historian Christine Stansell has called a "willed equality," a belief that they could live "big, whole human selves" outside of established female roles by means of spunk, education, and dreams alone.[23] In an era when progressives believed that big ideas would change the world, these New Women embodied the hope that women could develop their unique potential unfettered either by law or by social custom. They could not yet see that their stabs at freedom were not reflected in structural change that would support the long-term transformation of their lives.

For the most part, male bohemians were only too happy to support this new femininity, for they too were rebelling against Victorian mores for men. Max Eastman established the Men's League in support of suffrage, Randolph Bourne celebrated intellectual intimacy with close female friends, and Jig Cook and Jack Reed championed their wives' writing careers. Although early twentieth-century society tolerated sexual freedom for men, it prohibited the same for women of the middle and upper classes. In contrast, male bohemians demanded independent companions and social equals as their sexual partners. The New Woman, self-supporting and sexually free, permitted bohemian men multiple liaisons with few responsibilities. For this reason perhaps, Floyd Dell went so far as to claim that feminism primarily served men because it freed them from the manipulations of the dependent woman of the past.

Turning away from prescribed male roles—the patriarchal autocrat and the hardworking family man—these bohemians were dreamers, trying to fashion an adult masculinity that permitted social freedoms without the traditional constraints of family or work. John Reed abandoned his lover Mabel Dodge to follow

Pancho Villa's troops in Mexico, and later left his wife Louise Bryant to report on the Russian revolution. Max Eastman did not engage in such derring-do, but he did leave Ida Rauh and their newborn baby, whom he did not see again for twenty years, feeling that his freedom had been limited by his son's birth. After three wives and two children, George Cram Cook sought his personal liberation in Greece, hoping to find in the stark countryside the primitive life forces that once inspired ancient drama. These New Men formed a transitional generation, caught between the expectations of nineteenth-century respectability and a determination to make change that was not at all clear, defined, or articulated. Their inconsistencies and contradictions mark the process that was the birth of the new.

On the Margins

Demographic changes had uprooted many Americans from their small towns of origin, while debates about women's role in the modern world pervaded the mainstream as well as bohemian press. But the actual number of men and women who found refuge in the subcultures flourishing in cities such as New York, San Francisco, and Chicago was much smaller than their cultural influence might indicate. The majority of Americans remained uneasy about changes in women's social position; conservatives proclaimed that the loss of patriarchal authority would bring about the demise of social order, while the unleashing of female sexuality would cause the moral collapse of society. Following the example of a zealous Anthony Comstock, who inspired the federal Act for the Suppression of Trade in and Circulation of Obscene Literature and Articles of Immoral Use (1873), many town leaders closed theaters that showed "sex dramas," created boards of censorship to regulate the popular "vice films," controlled dance halls with public licenses, and passed laws to arrest women who wore immodest clothing such as the split skirt or provocative "X-Ray" dress. The press, moreover, warned of the evils of personal liberation with stories of sex crimes, opium dens, and murders. Even supporters of change, such as the reformer Frederic C. Howe, husband of Marie Jenney Howe, revealed that his political ideals were at odds with his feelings: "I have sometimes doubted whether many of the men who spoke and worked for the equality of women really desired it. Intellectually yes, but instinctively no; they clung as I did to the propertied instinct, to economic supremacy, to the old idea of marriage, in which all that a woman got she got through petitioning for it."[24]

Yet the general sexual license that many feared was welcomed by an emerging social group seeking recognition for their same-sex relationships and desires. Although the formation of a neighborhood with a critical mass of homosexual men and women did not begin until a decade later, there was a homosexual presence in lower Manhattan by the end of the nineteenth century. Several "concert saloons," drinking spots with lewd entertainment that catered only to men, featured male performers and "waiter-girls" performing in drag. Male prostitutes were not uncommon on the streets or in the many brothels that lined working-class neighborhoods. Popular songs of the 1910s refer to a "Fairyland" near Washington Square, and several male bohemians who might have visited Polly's or the Liberal Club were known to have liaisons with other men. Mabel Dodge, for instance, referred obliquely to the sexuality of Carl Van Vechten, a music critic for the *New York Times*, as involving "close relationships with other men." However, it is unclear how Van Vechten and others understood their same-sex desire.

In the first decades of the twentieth century, Americans looked to sexology, a study of sexuality that had emerged from nineteenth-century European science, to understand same-sex desire. Like other scientists of their time, nineteenth-century sexologists based their knowledge on careful scrutiny of empirical evidence—in this case, the human body—as well as increasingly detailed categorization of sexual fantasies, acts, and fears. How, they asked, did sexual difference come about? As men of science, they rejected earlier notions of same-sex desire as a moral flaw or sin, theorizing that it stemmed from physical or mental abnormalities. After exhaustive collection of case studies, sexologists concluded that homosexuality (a clinical term they had coined for same-sex desire) was due to congenital defects that existed to greater or lesser degrees within the population. This they called "inversion" because they saw the homosexual as a man who rejects masculinity rather than one who looks to other men as objects of desire. Absorbing these scientific theories in the early twentieth century, men who identified as "pansies" or "queer," in the slang of the 1910s, might adopt a feminine demeanor, clothing, and makeup, while those who maintained a masculine appearance and a dominant role in sexual acts might consider themselves "straight" or "husbands."

Sexologists did not pay much attention to female sexuality until the late nineteenth and early twentieth centuries. Until that time, women were assumed to have a passive sexual nature ignited by men's passion. Therefore women were allowed, even expected, to engage in intimate friendships, have crushes on one another, and use highly erotic language to speak of their affection, in what historian Carroll Smith-Rosenberg has described as the "female world of love and ritual."[25] Yet when the New Woman emerged to claim social and sexual freedoms, sexologists like the British Havelock Ellis found "inversion" in those who dressed and acted like men. Moreover, sexologists suggested that there existed another kind of woman, of feminine appearance, who had a vulnerability toward the invert and could easily be corrupted by her advances. By the 1910s, female enclaves such as women's colleges and settlement houses were becoming suspect as places that might harbor "mannish lesbians" who would prey on their susceptible victims.

Several women in Heterodoxy were known to have assumed masculine attire. Dr. "Jo" Baker, for instance, claimed that she wore men's clothes, including trousers, in order to assert her professional competence. Novelist Helen R. Hull, a professor of creative writing at Columbia University, wrote about women loving women. Others, Heterodites as well as working-class labor organizers such as Rose Schneiderman and Pauline Newman, had long-term relationships with women that were treated in the Village as marriages or families. The cross-dressing Jane Heap and her lover Margaret Anderson would soon bring their *Little Review* and a lesbian identity to New York, but even in 1913 female Villagers seem to have had a variety of same-sex relationships: they "kept house together," had flirtations with other women, and enjoyed sexual liaisons with both women and men. However, it is not certain that any of these individuals saw themselves as representatives of the newly created categories of "lesbian," "invert," or her potential partner. Some might have joined in Village spoofs to laugh at popular theories of deeply hidden sexual drives; some might have tried to articulate a female sexuality outside of a heterosexual framework; others might have followed an earlier generation's tradition of female love, even in these times of heightened interest in sex. It is clear, however, that all manner of relationships and dress were tolerated, although not directly discussed. It was still heterosexual experiences that dominated Heterodoxy's and the Village's conversations of a Saturday afternoon.

The Color Line in American Life

Even groups that were excluded from or ignored in white bohemian circles transformed the new spirit to suit their own goals. A decade before the Harlem Renaissance blossomed, the "New Negro" movement sought to develop an urban African American identity free of racist stereotypes and independent of the rural culture of the previous generation. Like whites, African Americans faced enormous changes in the new century, including the "Great Migration" from the South to the urban North between 1910 and 1930. Yet unlike white Americans, these new city dwellers did not generally turn to individualism but rather to the advancement of their race as a mark of their freedom. The "new," to them, meant racial progress. Debates in the black community during the first decades of the century pitted Booker T. Washington's accommodationist strategies, which urged blacks to better their lives through industrial education and acceptance of segregation, and the ideas proposed by W.E.B. Du Bois, a Harvard-educated college professor who demanded political agitation to achieve black civil rights. In contrast to Washington's *Up from Slavery* (1901), Du Bois's *The Souls of Black Folk* (1903) asserted that the problem of the new century was to be the "problem of the color line."

Race was indeed a central concern in American life during the last decade of the nineteenth century and the beginning of the twentieth. Sometimes the term "race" was used to refer to all humanity, as in "the human race"; at other times,

New York City's black population grew 66.3 percent between 1910 and 1920 and migrated from the Minettas (in the Ninth Ward—Greenwich Village) uptown through the Tenderloin and into Harlem.

race was equated with nationality, allowing references to an Italian or Jewish race. Nevertheless, as Du Bois has predicted, racism fueled the development of an invisible yet powerful "color line" between those seen as white or Northern European in origin and those of a "darker hue," predominately but not exclusively African Americans.

For a short time after the Civil War, proponents of abolition had reason to believe that the United States could develop into an integrated society. Yankee matrons went South to teach literacy to former slaves in Freedman's schools. Military troops from the North were sent to "reconstruct" the South, and integrated legislative bodies were established in the Southern states. But these changes met significant resistance. The Ku Klux Klan, a vigilante group that set out to terrorize newly freed slaves and their allies, emerged in 1866. Once Northern armies left in 1877, the white South pushed even more forcefully toward "Redemption," reasserting its former dominance and reestablishing segregation. State by state, the South added poll taxes, literacy requirements, and physical intimidation to limit black men's right to vote. Segregation also seeped into law as the states imposed "Jim Crow" legislation to regulate the social status, social presence, and opportunities available to all those they classified as black, establishing separate accommodations in all areas of public life.

The most decisive moment in this process to reestablish a racially based caste system came in 1896 with the U.S. Supreme Court decision *Plessy v. Ferguson*. Civil rights groups and railroad officials in Louisiana sought to challenge the state's requirement of separate train cars for blacks and whites. They selected Homer Plessy, a young man who was seven-eighths white, to test the law by refusing to move from the white section to a "colored car." He was arrested according to plan and then brought suit against the state of Louisiana that went up to the Supreme Court of the United States. The Court's 1892 decision favored Louisiana's segregation statute, thereby asserting the legitimacy of the South's "separate but equal" treatment that divided whites from citizens of color:

> A statute which implies merely a legal distinction between the white and the colored races—a distinction which is founded in the color of the two races, and which must always exist so long as white men are distinguished from the other race by color—has no tendency to destroy the legal equality of the two races, or re-establish a state of involuntary servitude. . . . (*Plessy v. Ferguson*, U.S. Supreme Court, 1892)

Many white Americans who would see themselves as "Old Stock" defenders of a Protestant nation not only feared that the "Negro problem" and the "alien menace" would bring about "race suicide" and the demise of the country's most cherished principles, they also believed that they represented the highest level of civilization in the world, a culture invigorated by "manly" endeavors of empire: war, sport, hunting, and courageous industry. Teddy Roosevelt—Rough Rider and president—was their ideal. A popularized understanding of Charles Darwin's theory of evolution led them to assume that civilizations evolved from the primitive stage to the civilized. Scholars sought to classify the distribution of mankind into races, to place cultures into a hierarchical system, and to assert the vigor of the dominant Anglo-Saxons. Some suggested that there was a "white man's burden," a duty to bring their political order and culture to primitive peoples. As European nations consolidated their empires, the United States also exerted its "manifest destiny" in the Western frontier and then in the Americas through the Spanish-American War (1898), extending its control into Cuba, Puerto Rico, and the Philippines.

It was in this intellectual climate that the New Negro—described by civil rights activist A. Philip Randolph as "educated, radical and fearless"—turned to black pride and nationalism to build economic and social self-determination and to face an American society increasingly distorted by racist violence. There were 2,522 documented cases of lynching between 1889 and 1918, primarily in rural areas. Cities and towns suffered from "race riots" and mass lynching that resulted in many dead and wounded: Wilmington, North Carolina, in 1898; Atlanta, Georgia, in 1906; and Springfield, Illinois, in 1908. As the riots spread to the North, black and white political activists joined to form the National Association for the Advancement of Colored People (1909). Tensions continued to worsen, leading to the fatal "Red Summer" of 1919 with over twenty-six white attacks on African American neighborhoods in both the North and South. One of the foremost fearless crusaders against this violence was African American Ida B. Wells-Barnett (1862–1931), who gathered and published data on racist killings and attempted to publicly disprove the common assertion—and justification for lynching—that black men sought to rape white women. A newspaperwoman and political activist, Wells-Barnett formed strategic alliances with the white-dominated suffrage movement and the male-dominated National Equal Rights League to advance her campaign for racial justice.

Sex was to be found at the heart of the dilemma facing African American women in the first decades of the century. Popular culture fanned white racism by stoking fears of black men's relationships with white women. Postcards with festive photographs of lynching, the outpourings of writers such as Thomas Dixon Jr. who celebrated the Klu Klux Klan in his romantic fiction, and the immensely influential film *Birth of a Nation* (1915), which received public praise for its veracity by no less a personage than President Woodrow Wilson, contributed to a glorification of vigilante violence to save white womanhood from sexual assault and the white race from miscegenation. This climate of intolerance and aggression threatened the entire African American community with destruction of property and loss of lives. Black women, stereotyped as lewd and promiscuous and facing harassment, sexual coercion, and sexual assault, could find little emancipation in sexual freedom. To the contrary, they asserted their dignity as ladies through a "politics of respectability" involving proper dress, refined manners, modern housekeeping, and childrearing.

Many Villagers, almost all of whom were white and of wealthy or middle-class origin, celebrated urban black life just as they sought out other outcasts from the American mainstream—immigrants, Jews, tramps, prostitutes, thieves, and urban gangs—fantasizing that these groups were primitive, closer to nature, free of civilization's power to repress human instinct, and worthy of emulation. Jack Reed interviewed prostitutes, Hutchins Hapgood ambled through Jewish ghettos, John Sloan painted daily life in the Irish Tenderloin district, and Carl Van Vechten chronicled the development of Harlem. A few years later, Mabel Dodge, followed by several bohemian artists and writers, went to the Southwest to seek in American Indian cultures a spirituality that seemed to be lacking in urban life. Villagers possessed little understanding of the complexities of these lives and social conditions; they were primarily searching for a group that embodied their ideals of freedom. Indeed, Villagers, like other Anglo-Saxon Americans, slipped easily into insensitive parodies of "Paddy's" drunken speech, comments on the uncultured behaviors of "dagos," and even anti-Semitic and racist name-calling. Nevertheless, the bohemians' contact with those marginalized in American society led to increasing awareness, deeper analysis, and more powerful activism on their behalf. Mary White Ovington, after conducting several reform studies on African Americans in New York City, became a founding member of the National Association for the Advancement of Colored People. Elsie Clews Parsons, a student of anthropologist Franz Boas, dedicated her research in ethnography and folklore to the indigenous and black peoples of the Americas. Villagers' efforts to understand the diversity in American life and to value cultural difference built bridges toward a future ideal of a multiracial and multicultural society.

PART 3: THE GAME

"THE SOCIALIST AND THE SUFFRAGIST"

Said the Socialist to the Suffragist:
"My cause is greater than yours!
You only work for a Special Class
We for the gain of the General Mass,
Which every good ensures!"

Said the Suffragist to the Socialist:
"You underrate my Cause!
While women remain a Subject Class,
You can never move the General Mass,
With your Economic Laws!"

Said the Socialist to the Suffragist:
"You misinterpret facts!
There is no room for doubt or schism
In Economic Determinism—
It governs all our acts!"

Said the Suffragist to the Socialist:
"You men will always find
That this old world will never move
More swiftly in its ancient groove
While women stay behind!"

"A lifted world lifts women up,"
The Socialist explained.
"You cannot lift the world at all
While half of it is kept so small,"
The Suffragist maintained.

The world awoke, and tartly spoke:
"Your work is all the same:
Work together or work apart,
Work, each of you with all your heart—
Just get into the game!"

—Charlotte Perkins Gilman (1912)

MAJOR ISSUES FOR DEBATE

As members of the Suffrage and Labor factions come to Polly's restaurant, they will try to persuade bohemian Villagers and their friends to vote to participate in a suffrage parade or to plan a workers' pageant. These acts are simply outward signs of complex, even contradictory, views on what makes a good, just, and modern society: should women's political participation be our priority today or should it be the transformation of our economic system in favor of workers? Like others in 1913, Villagers find themselves in a world on the verge of change: small town America now faces cities that boast of immense, ostentatious wealth side by side with poverty of hitherto unimaginable levels; people who once believed in common American values are challenged by the arrival of immigrants in unprecedented numbers; men and women who once conformed to the norms that shaped their gender and class see their stable social positions undermined by a new fascination with the Self, a unique and complex identity meant to be discovered, nourished, even created.

In this game, bohemians and friends will have to decide which faction makes the best case about their particular goals taking priority in 1913. If bohemians can agree on one thing, it will be the importance of conversation in making sense of all these changes. Indeed, they believe that free speech, in private exchanges as well as public oratory, can create a truly democratic community in which the sexes, social classes, and ethnicities can come together. This game, therefore, values acts of communication as well as the ideas expressed. You are encouraged to cross faction lines, talk with those who have different views than those of your role, and use conversation to clarify your own position on the issues that were debated hotly in 1913 and long thereafter. These include:

Suffrage Issues

- What does it mean to be the citizen of a nation?

- What does it mean to have the vote?

- Would suffrage change the lives of individual women?

- Would suffrage change women as a group?

- Would suffrage change relationships between men and women?

- Would suffrage change the nation? How?

- Is women's political equality the starting point for a New Woman? A New America?

Labor Issues

- What is an economically just society?

- How can a society build an economically just nation?

- What is work? An exchange of labor for wages? Wage slavery? Self-development?

- Are women workers just "workers who happen to be female"?

- Or do women who work have unique characteristics or conditions?

- How could all workers improve the conditions of their labor?

- Do we need a revolution and overturning of capitalism?

- Can we reform U.S. capitalism to create a just society?

Bohemian Issues

- What is the New Woman? Does our society really want her?

- How can the New Woman come into existence? What does she need?

- How could the New Woman change relationships between men and women?

- Would the New Woman change the family, everyday life, the nation?

- What is America now? How has it been changing?

- What could it become if we nurture its potential?

- How could we nurture its potential?

- Could we start a revolution of our national values and identities?

Issues for All Players

- How does a group make lasting social change?

- How do you gain supporters for your cause?

- Do you stick to your principles even at the risk of failure?

- Should you compromise in order to make some gains?

- How might a cause change over time and under new social conditions?

RULES AND PROCEDURES

Victory Objective: Win the Vote in Game Session 8

Villagers will vote for either the:

Suffrage faction, supporting suffragists in the parade that will take place down Pennsylvania Avenue in Washington D.C. on the eve of Woodrow Wilson's inauguration **and affirming the priority of women's participation in the political life of the nation**

or

Labor faction, joining the Industrial Workers of the World and strikers in a reenactment of the Paterson strike in a pageant at Madison Square Garden, **and affirming the priority of labor's demands for change in the economic life of the nation**

How to Win the Vote

Each Villager/Indeterminate Friend has an opportunity to vote for the faction of his/her choice in the final session of the game. She or he must have 15 Personal Influence Points (PIPs) in order to vote. (See below). She or he passes all of the accrued PIPs to the faction of his or her choice. The faction with the most PIPs wins *Greenwich Village, 1913*.

How to Gather Personal Influence Points (PIPs)

Players with the most influence control the game. They gain influence through their actions.

All of the following political strategies were common in the 1910–1917 period. Players may imitate some of these tried-and-true strategies to build support for their causes, but you may also want to invent your own.

NOTE: Players must earn at least one PIP per game session.

One suggestion for the collection of PIPs is as follows:

Players prepare a three-by-five-inch index card for each game session. Each card states:

1. the player's role and the game session

2. the PIP activity and the estimated number of PIPs assigned to it

Example:

> Susan Glaspell, Feminist Mass Meeting, Game Session 6
> Designed and wore a button expressing my support for X.
> **1 PIP**

You may repeat an activity, but you may not count it for PIPs more than once. Activities conducted outside of class must be documented (photo, video, recording, testimony by others, etc.).

Polly Holladay, owner of Polly's, will collect PIP cards at the beginning of each game session. Polly and the Gamemaster (GM) determine the number of PIPs awarded to any innovative strategies, using the guidelines below.

PIPS WORTH 1 POINT

Display your interest through dress, decoration, simple acts of affiliation.

Bohemians:

- Wear a bohemian outfit of sack dress, brown socks, and sandals (women).

- Wear garish colors, especially magenta (women).

- Bob your hair (women).

- Dress in the Paris fashion of 1913 (women).

- Wear corduroy pants and plaid flannel shirts (men).

- Imitate Max Eastman's signature bright orange sweater; pick a bright color and wear it every day (men).

- Play a game of chess in a public place.

- Play poker or bridge at Polly's after class.

- Decorate Polly's (the classroom) in a bohemian style.

- Publicize your bohemian identity by taking a photograph of your new self.

- Gather five men's signatures to start a Men's League for Sex Equality.

- Bring ragtime music to Polly's.

- Teach the latest dance craze at Polly's.

Suffrage:

- Wear suffrage colors: sunflower yellow and white.

- Decorate a hat to show support for suffrage.

- Design and wear a "Votes for Women" button.

- Distribute "suffrage jonquils" to Villagers.

- Release or distribute pro-suffrage balloons.

- Fly a kite with pro-suffrage slogans.

- Attend a suffrage tea and collect a suffrage pamphlet.

- Write suffrage graffiti on the sidewalk with chalk.

- Design a pro-suffrage postcard or Valentine.

- Design and wear a sandwich board bearing a suffrage slogan.

- Ride public transportation holding a poster that calls for Votes for Women.

- Lead the class in a suffrage song.

- Write a suffrage slogan.

- Organize two women to stand as silent "Votes for Women" sentinels outside Polly's.

Labor:

- Wear an IWW T-shirt.

- Design and wear a "One Big Union" pin.

- Design and carry a red union card.

- Wear a red armband with a union slogan.

- Wear something red to Polly's (red bowtie or red hair ribbon).

- Wear Dutch wooden shoes (*sabots*) as a symbol of sabotage.

- Distribute red carnations to Villagers.

- Distribute stickers of a black cat, the symbol of the IWW.

- Play a recording of a song by IWW member Joe Hill.

- Write a slogan for the industrial union.

- Lead the class in an IWW song (see *The Little Red Songbook*).

- Sing "The Internationale" in class, in any language.

- Sing "La Marseillaise" in class, in French.

PIPS WORTH 5 POINTS

Show your support by drawing, designing, doing.

Bohemians:

- Make and distribute birth control information at Polly's.

- Draw a cartoon poking fun at some social belief or practice.

- Draw a stinging political cartoon.

- Start a Feminism Club that meets at least twice during the *Greenwich Village, 1913* game.

- Start a "Conversation Table" in the cafeteria to discuss a bohemian topic of your choice.

- Create and distribute flyers on an issue of vital importance.

- Hold a poetry reading.

- Run a Heterodoxy meeting.

- Present a tableau vivant on a bohemian ideal of your choice.

- Make a photographic essay on "Greenwich Village Today."

- Create a tearoom on campus where people meet and talk at least twice during this game.

- Act in a one-act play written for this class.

- Design an eye-catching poster for a Bohemian Ball.

Suffrage:

- Design a poster on women's rights and hang it somewhere on campus.

- Sew a banner that combines womanly needlework and a militant message.

- Make a banner that will be noticed for its wit.

- Make and distribute a suffrage pamphlet.

- Draw a pro-suffrage cartoon that mocks the antis.

- Draw a pro-suffrage cartoon that woos the working class.

- Present an allegorical tableau vivant on campus (topics: heroines from the past, the suffrage movement, women today).

- Write suffrage-themed lyrics to a popular song and sing it in class or on campus.

- Sell lemonade and sandwiches (wrapped in yellow paper) for the Collegiate Equal Suffrage League.

- Set up a Suffrage Shop at Polly's.

- Canvas one residence hall, going door-to-door to encourage political participation by women.

- Bring a map of the U.S. to Polly's and highlight the states with woman suffrage.

Labor:

- Design a poster that encourages class awareness and solidarity.

- Design and distribute leaflets on the IWW door-to-door.

- Design a flyer that calls people to a mass rally for the IWW.

- Hold a meeting to explain the goals of organized labor.

- Write and distribute a pamphlet on an issue of labor or class.

- Write and distribute a pamphlet on *Rules for Pickets*.

- Give a soapbox speech on campus urging students to support workers.

- Rewrite the speech using words and concepts that a recent non-English-speaking immigrant would understand, and deliver it.

- Translate and give this speech in Yiddish.

- Translate and give this speech in Italian.

PIPS WORTH 10 POINTS

Win over hearts as well as minds through spectacle, stunts, and art.

Bohemians:

- Write and direct a one-act play in your living room or at Polly's.

- Hold a Bohemian Forum on a vital topic of the day.

- Create a Greenwich Village Art Gallery to show works by Villagers.

- Go into psychotherapy; write about your new insights.

- Write an essay on your favorite painting from the Armory Show.

- Write a short review of one of the latest books at Boni's (Washington Square Bookstore owned by Albert Boni).

- Draw or paint something in the Cubist style introduced at the Armory Show.

- Conduct a "scientific investigation" on women's lives in 1913. Gather the necessary data from the players at Polly's.

- Hold a masquerade ball to make money for the Liberal Club's activities.

Suffrage:

- Write and present a one-act play on suffrage.

- Write and film a short movie on suffrage to show in class.

- Write a newspaper article that urges women to vote.

- Give a soapbox speech on campus urging women to claim their political rights.

- Conduct a "trolley tour" on campus with speeches on suffrage/women's political voice.

- Present a slide show (lantern slides are most historically accurate) on women's achievements.

- Write and present on campus a "silent speech" on a suffrage topic (imparting the speech through posters while remaining silent.)

- Compose a humorous rhyme about life on the stump.

- Write the story of your conversion to the cause.

- Organize a torchlit parade through campus at night in support of women's rights.

- Enter an all-male enclave and convince the men to support women's rights.

- Hold a pro-suffrage auto parade with all cars draped in yellow banners.

- Design a float for suffrage.

- Create and sell a suffrage cookbook.

- Develop a suffrage card game or board game.

- Hold a suffrage bazaar with handmade foods and crafts.

Labor:

- Reenact a moment in labor history in a public space on campus.

- Create a short comic book on the importance of the strike.

- Write an investigative report of the conditions of labor in a single industry, time period, or social group.

- Organize a "mass picket" (waves of picketers who keep moving).

- Form a committee, plan how to build a strike fund, get money for Paterson strikers.

- Sponsor a rally to support unskilled workers.

- Host a morale-boosting picnic for "friends of labor."

- Convene a study group with at least three members to read and discuss "Marx today."

- Create a Speaker's Bureau with at least three members. Each writes a short speech on a specific topic pertaining to the working class.

- Write a "one-column" short story on life in the slums, showing the inner beauty of the working class.

- Plan a publicity campaign for the Paterson Pageant.

Special Ways to Accrue PIPs

Three "wild card" players in *Greenwich Village, 1913* can help you accrue points in a different way:

Wild card Mabel Dodge. "Lady Mabel," a Village celebrity famous for hosting provocative conversations in her Fifth Avenue apartment, will extend a secret written invitation to the protégé or protégée of her choice to speak at her Evening. She asks her speaker to put forth his or her arguments in the most interesting way. She wants to see the intellectual sparks fly as people debate their views.

The speaker has ten minutes to present her or his views and to elicit questions and comments from the other guests. Although **Mabel keeps all her personal influence points**, she can "give away" a like number to the speaker at her Evening according to the following rules:

1. If Mabel thinks the performance has been exciting, she will give the speaker the same number (100 percent) of her PIPs.

2. If Mabel deems the presentation good but not inspiring, she will award the equivalent of 50 percent of her PIPs.

3. If the speaker has not created controversy or sparks, he or she receives zero PIPs.

Mabel Dodge will set up a mailbox on campus for those players who want to contact her privately. A decorated shoe box placed in a public area or campus office allows for small bribes and gifts.

TIP

All players should cultivate Mabel's favor throughout the game. She can make you a celebrity!

Wild card Max Eastman. Brilliant rebel Max is equally at home with bohemians, suffragists, and labor organizers. His main goal is to solicit material from players for his first issue of *The Masses*. As editor "without pay," Max is seeking a new image for the magazine. His vision is "a revolutionary and not a reform magazine; a magazine with a sense of humor and no respect for the respectable; frank, arrogant, impertinent, searching for the true causes; a magazine directed against rigidity and dogma wherever it is found; printing what is too naked or true for a money-making press; a magazine whose final policy is to do as it pleases and conciliate nobody, not even its readers."

The submission guidelines are as follows:

1. All materials selected **must** conform to the general editorial policy outlined above. They may include essays, stories, songs, poems, drawings, and cartoons.

2. Max will include only those submissions of high quality; a poorly designed and badly written magazine may drag him into another bankruptcy and loss of influence.

TIP

Players should make every effort to submit material to *The Masses*. But remember: submission does not mean automatic publication.

3. Max gives 5 points to each player whose work he selects for inclusion in *The Masses*.

Wild card Emma Goldman. The anarchist nicknamed "Red Emma" does not stoop for PIPs. A political agitator, she will not tolerate such artificial incentives for her life's work. Emma builds her personal influence in other ways: she takes detailed notes at each game session, listening intently for the theoretical assumptions underlying the factions' arguments. She prepares a brief commentary on the debates at Polly's for her own journal, *Mother Earth*. Her commentary always includes a serious critique of the views: clarifying the ideas, teasing out the assumptions upon which they are based, demonstrating the impact of such ideas on society or on individuals. She will distribute her commentaries at Polly's, but she will have to do so secretly in order to avoid possible censorship from the authorities.

At the time of the vote, Emma will present an overall critique of the debates.

WARNING ! *If Emma favors a faction, she can double its total points. All Villagers need to take note of "this dangerous woman."*

Develop a "Winning Plan" for *Greenwich Village, 1913*

Find Your Allies. Use the "conversation time," usually 5 to 10 minutes built into the beginning of each class meeting, to find your allies. Each role sheet includes information about the character's life, his or her ideas, and the historical period. Let the conversations teach you about the debates and experiences of the era.

Know Your Opponents and Their Arguments. If you hope to win *Greenwich Village 1913*, you will have to know your opponents' ideas and figure out a way to respond to them. You will have to read beyond the basic material assigned to you.

Build a Following. The Personal Influence Points included in this game replicate the strategies used in the first decades of the twentieth century to "win hearts and minds" for social movements. Remember that you are witnessing the birth of publicity, celebrity culture, radio, and film as well as the heyday of pageantry, parades, and political spectacle.

You do not have to follow the list of possible activities listed in this game book—they are included to give you information about what was done between 1910 and 1917—but you do have to build excitement for your cause if you hope to win.

Write Your Speeches and Know Them by Heart. Max Eastman gives a wonderful example of what *not* to do in a formal presentation. When he first started on the suffrage speaking circuit, he planned a 45-minute speech for a suffrage convention in Ontario, New York. It was to be long and peppered with citations:

> It occupied, in mere geometric outline, five large pages each containing two columns of script. It might, if I talked fast and left no time for rhetorical pauses, have been compressed to the size of a small college education. Of course I didn't expect to go through it all: my idea was to be thoroughly prepared and trust the inspiration of the moment. The moment brought panic instead of inspiration, and I plunged and floundered around in that thorough preparation like man trying to find his way out of a swamp. I never did find my way out. I just kept talking slower and slower until finally I stopped through sheer lack of momentum.[26]

Eastman learned from this embarrassing experience and, when asked to address the 1909 suffrage convention in Troy, New York, he was ready:

> A speech has only one dimension; it starts at the beginning and flows to the end. You can not spread it out, or carry it back and forth, or take it here and there. You can not dig around under it. A speech should be rapid, clear and energetic, and make but one main point. It should run like a river between high banks, the flood of emotion adding to its force, but never widening the territory it covers. This can

not be accomplished extemporaneously except once or twice in a lifetime; it can not be accomplished by taking successive starts from a series of penciled notes. The more impassioned the language, the more it will in these circumstances tend to expatiate and meander. All great orators have known this, and all great orators, from Deuteronomy and Demosthenes to Daniel Webster and Mark Twain, have written their speeches and learned them by heart whenever they could. A great orator is both a dramatist and an actor; he can write as though he were speaking, and he can speak as though he had not written; he can act the part of himself. . . . This obvious, yet for some strange reason this esoteric piece of good sense is what I learned in that purgatory at Ontario. . . . [27]

STRATEGIES

For All Players: Mabel Dodge's Mailbox

Mabel Dodge will place her mailbox somewhere on campus. Personal notes and small gifts may capture her attention, lead to an invitation to speak at her Evening, and bring you great influence.

For Most Players:

(see your role sheet for exceptions)

- Build PIPs in the Game Sessions.

- Earn a minimum of 1 PIP per session.

- You will need a minimum of 15 PIPS to vote.

For All Faction Members:

Cultivate the favor of those Villagers who have many PIPs. Encourage Villagers to gather PIPs for your cause and not to show support for the other faction.

For the Labor Faction: Haledon, New Jersey

Haledon was a refuge for strikers in Paterson, New Jersey. The socialist mayor of this nearby town permitted gatherings, social activities, and strike planning in his town.

Any member of the Labor faction may call for time in Haledon, but it may be called only once in the game. In the event that debate becomes heated and you feel that the faction should regroup, you may call for "Haledon." This means that other players may not interrupt or heckle Labor for a specific amount of time. The GM usually allows 5 minutes for this freedom from attack. Labor may use this time to speak freely.

For Faction Members: Jumping Ship

If you are genuinely convinced by the other side, you may secretly leave your faction and surreptitiously gather points for the new affiliation. You have thereby turned into an "indeterminate" unbeknownst to former faction-mates, whom you can undermine by giving incorrect information and bad advice.

A shift in views can happen at any time in the game, but it is only at the time of the vote that you reveal your true beliefs. If you jump ship, you lose all the PIPs gathered for the faction you rejected.

You may not have a frivolous change of heart. You must gather a minimum of 15 *new* points for the faction that has persuaded you of its superior merit. These points are likely to be gathered outside of Polly's (the classroom) and will therefore need verification (photo, witnesses, materials, etc.).

For All Indeterminates

Assert your independence by gathering Bohemian points early in the game. Do not rush to support the factions. Make them work to gain your support. Demand that the factions add your concerns to their platforms.

You may gather Bohemian, Suffrage, **and** Labor points. You are "trying out" ideas only; gathering pro-Suffrage or pro-Labor points does not require a vote for that faction. You are free to vote for any faction as long as you have the minimum of 15 points needed to vote. At the time of the vote, you will pass all of your points to the faction of your choice.

If you meet the one-point session requirement but not the 15-PIP minimum to vote, thereby revealing that neither Suffrage nor Labor has convinced you of its importance, then you must write a 3- to 5-page critique of one of these movements for publication in either the mainstream *New York World* or Emma Goldman's *Mother Earth*. You will not be able to vote and will not pass any PIPs to either faction.

For "Female" Indeterminates: Heterodoxy

Heterodoxy is a luncheon/conversation club for women (characters) only.

"We thought we discussed the whole field, but we really discussed ourselves."
—Rheta Childe Dorr

"This club was composed of women, many of them of force, character, and intelligence, but all of them shunted on the sliding path from the early suffrage movement into the passionate excesses of feminism, in which "the vital lie" was developed, that men had consciously oppressed women since the beginning of time, enslaved, and exploited them."

—Hutchins Hapgood

At any time during the game, a woman Villager or female Indeterminate Friend, members of the informal women's group Heterodoxy, can call a bimonthly meeting, stating the topic of the discussion: "I call a Heterodoxy meeting to talk about. . . ." All female characters, including faction members, leave Polly's and go to the Liberal Club upstairs (that is, they leave the classroom during class time) to discuss how the announced topic affects their own daily lives and experiences. The GM determines the numbers of minutes allowed for the meeting, usually 5 to 10.

Any woman Indeterminate can call the meeting, but it can be called only once during the game. If called well, a player can use the Heterodoxy meeting to sway more women to her views; this meeting is more likely to be called, therefore, in Sessions 6 or 7, when factions and players are seeking more influence. As was true at the time, Heterodites agree to total confidentiality on anything said at the meeting. All of the conversations look at how the abstract ideas of suffrage, bohemia, and labor play out in "real life."

The player who calls the meeting sets the initial discussion topic, presents her views, and opens the floor for responses and more conversation. However, there are many women at Polly's and the Liberal Club's rooms are quite spacious; small conversation circles may ignore or challenge the first speaker. A frivolous call could backfire.

Little Rosa Bianchi who cleans the restaurant does not join the women of Heterodoxy unless specifically invited. Several players have role sheets asking them to call a Heterodoxy meeting, but any woman Villager may choose to call a meeting. All players—male and female—may urge Village women friends to call a meeting on their behalf. Only one player can be successful. This player receives 5 PIPs for leading the discussion.

> ## TIP
>
> Emma Goldman and "female" faction members, with the exception of Elizabeth Gurley Flynn, who was a Heterodite, may not call a Heterodoxy meeting, but they do attend when one is called.

For All Indeterminates: A Bohemian Coup

Villagers who decide that they do not want to support Labor or Suffrage may stage a coup and proclaim a Republic of Greenwich Village! There must be at least three supporting Villagers with a minimum of 15 points each. The plan must remain underground until just before the vote, when the Bohemian Coup declares itself publicly. It then becomes a faction and can solicit votes.

Any faction members who want to join the coup may not pass their faction-based PIPs to the new Bohemian faction; they must procure 15 new Bohemia-supporting PIPs to vote. Coup members will need additional support (i.e., votes from other players) in order to win *Greenwich Village, 1913*. They should plan accordingly and in secret.

BASIC OUTLINE OF THE GAME

When life is very strenuous and spirits are way down
You'd better go to Polly's in little Greenwich town
For there the clans are gathered-it's there you'll find 'em all
The artists and the writers ranged along the wall.
Miss Polly takes the money and Mike says he just can't
Wait any faster on the folks in Polly's res-tau-rant.

—Jessie Tarbox Beals, Photographer

Preparatory Sessions:

SESSION 1: WOMEN'S RIGHTS AND SUFFRAGE

Reading Due:

- Historical Background: Women's Rights and Suffrage, pp. 16–30
- Elizabeth Cady Stanton, "Declaration of Sentiments" (1848), p. 101
- "The Constant," *Godey's Lady's Book* (January, 1851), p. 104

Class Activities: Discussion

- How does Stanton present women's condition at mid-century?
- Contrast Stanton's view with the presentation of womanhood in *Godey's Lady's Book*.
- Why would the call for the franchise have shocked Stanton's peers?
- What might the franchise have offered nineteenth-century women?

SESSION 2: LABOR AND LABOR MOVEMENTS

Reading Due:

- Historical Background: Labor and Labor Movements, pp. 31–50
- Karl Marx, "Bourgeois and Proletarians," *The Manifesto of the Communist Party* (1848), p. 153

Class Activities: Discussion

- What is social class? How might it differ from caste or clan?

- How did the bourgeoisie come into being according to Marx's analysis?

- What is the world that it created?

- Why does Marx think that the proletariat has revolutionary promise?

SESSION 3: THE SPIRIT OF THE NEW

Reading Due:

- The Game, pp. 68–84

- Historical Background: Parades and Pageants, p. 46–50

- Historical Background: The Spirit of the New, pp. 51–67

- Hutchins Hapgood, "The Bohemian, The American and the Foreigner," *Types from City Streets* (1910), p. 210

- Randolph Bourne, "Youth," *The Atlantic Monthly* (1912), p. 220

- Walter Lippmann, "Introduction," *Drift and Mastery* (1914), p. 222

Class Activities: Discussion

- What is the "New" sensibility?

- What is the "Old" that is being challenged or defeated?

- What social changes seem to interest Villagers the most? Why?

Overview:

- *Greenwich Village, 1913* and how it works in this course

- Distribution of roles

- Faction meetings: Villagers seek out those with common interests and concerns.

- The GM meets with players to discuss their roles and contributions.

Game Sessions:

SESSION 4: THE SUFFRAGE CAUSE

Reading Due for All Players:

- Elizabeth Cady Stanton, "Solitude of Self," (1892), p. 104

- Rheta Childe Dorr, "American Women and the Common Law," *What Eight Million Women Want* (1910), p. 112

- Ida M. Tarbell, "On the Ennobling of the Woman's Business," *The Business of Being a Woman* (1912), p. 120

Writing Assignment Due for the Suffrage Faction:

- Each suffragist will write a 3- to 5-page speech expressing her particular views on why "Suffrage Must Be Our Priority Today."

Formal Speeches by the Suffrage Faction:

- Each suffragist will present her views based on the writing assignment. She may not read the speech. A three-by-five-inch card may be used for an outline or notes.

Class Activities:

- The Game Session begins informally as Polly walks around, greets patrons, and makes note of their PIPs. During this time, players make alliances, try to impress Mabel Dodge and Max Eastman, and strategize.

- Presentations take place at the "cash register" in front of the class. Polly presides over the agenda, timekeeping, questions, and answers. Each suffragist has 5 to 10 minutes to present her views.

- Villagers and Labor Activists respond with questions and comments.

- Surprises may occur.

Reading Due for All Players:

- Jane Addams, "Industrial Amelioration," *Democracy and Social Ethics* (1902), p. 168

- William Haywood, "The General Strike" (1911), p. 180

- *The Socialist Party Platform* (1912), p. 185

Writing Assignment for the Labor Faction:

- Each Labor activist will write a 3- to 5-page speech expressing her particular views on why "Labor Must Be Our Priority Today."

Formal Speeches by the Labor Faction:

- Each Labor activist will present a formal speech based on the writing assignment. She or he may not read the speech. A three-by-five-inch card may be used for an outline or notes.

Class Activities:

- Polly makes note of the points as players talk and strategize. Villagers court Mabel and seek out Max's approval.

- Labor organizers have 5 to 10 minutes each to present their views on the American economic system and the current situation of the U.S. worker.

- Villagers and Suffragists respond with questions and comments.

- Unexpected news may arrive.

Reminder to the Labor Faction: There are very few protections for labor in 1913. When you speak out, picket, and strike, you are at great risk of beatings, arrest, and harassment by hired thugs, private detectives, local police, even federal troops. You have one recourse, as did strikers in Paterson: to go to the town of Haledon (New Jersey) whose socialist mayor will protect you when things get too hot at Polly's.

Any member of the Labor faction may call "Haledon." At this moment, suffragists and Villagers must stop their questions and challenges for 5 minutes. The Labor faction can speak without interruption or fear. You may go to Haledon only once in the entire game. Make sure that you use this strategy purposefully.

Reading Due for All Players:

- Charlotte Perkins Gilman, "Chapter XIV," *Women and Economics* (1898), p. 194

- Elsie Clews Parsons, "Ethical Considerations," *The Family* (1906), p. 199

- Floyd Dell, "Charlotte Perkins Gilman," *Women as World-Builders* (1913), p. 216

Writing Assignment Due for All Villagers and Friends (except Emma Goldman):

- By now, you Villagers have heard the arguments of the people who have pushed their way into your beloved Polly's and annoyed you with their speeches and harangues. It is now your turn. Write a 3- to 5-page essay that tells them what you care about and why.

- This is not the moment to respond to their ideas, but rather to assert your own in your own style. Your role sheet will give more details.

Formal Speeches by Three Villagers:

- The GM will invite three Villagers to explain what "feminism means to me." Each will have 5 to 10 minutes to address this issue. They may not read their speeches. A three-by-five-inch card may be used for an outline or notes.

Class Activities:

- Polly mingles with players while others strategize. Players make a big push to get Mabel to send her invitation their way. They may also show off their best work to Max, hoping that he will consider them for the next issue of *The Masses*.

- The Feminist Mass Meeting: three Villagers, who have been invited to do so, present their views. Each is allowed a maximum of 10 minutes.

- Other Villagers sit in the audience and later take the floor to vie for their own cause.

Note: Villagers may support either faction, but only after trying to add their own political, literary, artistic, and personal agendas to that of the faction they favor. They use the Feminist Mass Meeting to convey their wishes to the factions in the hope that the factions will add historically appropriate bohemian and/or feminist ideas to their current positions. Woe to the factions that do not pay attention to the challenges presented today!

Villagers may find that neither faction gives them everything they want; they may have to make do with the faction that best approximates their views. The factions may have to respond by modifying their ideas or forfeiting the game. On the other hand, the Villagers may agitate to form their own faction altogether and seek to gather points for their own "Independent Republic of Greenwich Village." This Game Session may be a turning point.

Closing Activities:

- Planning Ahead: Those factions or players who want to present pageants, plays, or other spectacles in Session 7 must write a proposal that includes a short description of the activity and asks for a specific amount of time. This proposal (1-3 paragraphs) is to be submitted to Polly. She will determine if an activity has sufficient merit to be presented and, if so, will impose a time limit.

- Mabel Dodge extends a secret written invitation to speak at her Evening.

- Mabel assigns a reading for the following class. This will support the speaker at her Evening and enrich all players' understanding of the topics to be discussed. Mabel announces the assignment at the end of class.

SESSION 7: MABEL DODGE'S EVENING

Reading Due for All Players:

- Mabel's Dodge's choice of reading.

Writing Assignments Due:

- Players who wish to submit work to *The Masses* must give their work to Max Eastman on or before Session 7. Max will give you more details.

Class Activities:

- Polly gathers points. Factions put on their last big push to gather supporters.

- Mabel Dodge introduces one individual who will present her or his views on a specific subject at an Evening.

- The speaker takes the floor for up to 15 minutes and makes sure to interact with the audience. To be well received, the talk must have a clear point of view, incite conversation, and provoke controversy.

- Mabel is the one who decides how the speaker has fared at her Evening, but she bases her judgment on the "freshness" of the ideas and the speaker's future as a "mover and shaker." Mabel explains her decision and may award PIPs to the speaker.

- Festivities, pre-arranged with Polly, as well as other activities, may take place.

SESSION 8 : THUS SPEAK *THE MASSES* + THE VOTE

Class Activities:

- Polly gathers points. Players talk. Time is getting short (5 minutes).

- Max distributes *The Masses* to all players and awards PIPs to those whose work is published

- Max delivers a lecture to explain his editorial vision, the themes and goals of this issue, how the submissions advance the ideas that he wants to highlight, and how they enhance the independent perspective of *The Masses*. Max has 20 to 30 minutes to show and discuss his issue.

- The vote:

  - **Eligibility**. Polly makes sure that each Villager has a minimum of 15 PIPs to be able to vote.

  - **Call to Vote**. Faction members summarize their Calls to Vote in one to three sentences per speaker. This would be an optimal time to address any new debates or challenges to the factions' positions.

  - **Possible Ship-Jumping**. A faction member may announce that she or he is switching sides (see rules on page 82). The player must present 15 PIPs to support the favored faction. She or he distributes a written statement of true conviction and summarizes this statement in an oral presentation of one to three sentences, hoping to sway others at the last minute.

Note: A ship-jumper may not amass PIPs in support of the original faction and then transfer them to the opposition. To switch sides, she or he needs to gain new PIPs for the new faction. These could have been accrued in secret throughout the game and must be presented with documentation at this time.

  - **Possible Bohemian Coup**. If some Villagers have decided to revolt, they do so now by distributing a written platform and proving that they have sufficient PIPs. Each member of a Bohemian coup must have a minimum of 15 PIPs, and the group must have a total of 45 points in order to become a new faction.

  - **Vote**. Polly calls for the vote. Villagers make their choice to support the faction of their choice. All of each voter's points are given to the one faction that he or she supports. This calls for **a paper ballot with the Villager's signature**.

- **Emma Speaks Out**. After distribution of the ballot and before ballots are counted, Emma Goldman takes to the floor. She critiques each of the factions and describes what might happen if each faction were to gain political power. She makes sure to include what might change for women, the human spirit, the working class, and the nation. Generally, Emma will not be impressed by either faction. If she has been convinced that the political agenda of one faction may further her own goals, however, she will reveal it at this time. Such support **may** double the entire amount of points gathered in support of this faction.

- **And the winner is . . . !** The GM and Polly take the final count. The faction that has amassed the most points wins.

- Seeing into the Future: The GM distributes copies of the Village newspaper, *The Quill,* which has a special Review of the Year for 1917.

> **TIP:**
>
> Emma may not know if there will be a Bohemian coup. If a new faction has formed today, Emma is required to address its ideas as well.

SESSION 9: 1917—FACING THE FUTURE + DEBRIEFING THE GAME

Reading Due:

- *The Quill* (1917) (handout)

Four years later, the factions and Villagers are back at Polly's. Some have never left, having taken refuge in Greenwich Village. *The Quill* has brought them up to date on the war, suffrage and labor movements, and goings-on in the Village.

Class Activities: Discussion

- How do the factions and the Village respond to the U.S. entry into the Great War?

Debriefing: The Gamemaster will bring the game to a close and lead a postmortem that clarifies what happened between 1913 and 1917 for the individuals and their factions.

ASSIGNMENTS

The Gamemaster will determine how your work in *Greenwich Village, 1913* will be graded. The game includes the following components that may be included in the grade:

Writing Assignments

Formal writing assignments (3 to 5 pages):

- Faction position papers (Sessions 4 and 5)

- Villager position papers (Session 6)

- Contributions to *The Masses* (Session 7) [NOTE: Your contributions will be graded even if they are not selected by Max Eastman for inclusion in his issue.]

- Homework and in-class writing assignments as selected by the GM (Sessions 1–9)

Tests and Quizzes on the Required Readings

- Quizzes on each Historical Background as determined by the GM (Sessions 1–3)

- Test on all Historical Background materials as determined by the GM (Session 3)

Oral Presentations

Formal presentations:

- Faction presentations (Sessions 4 and 5)

- Villager presentations at the Feminist Mass Meeting (Session 6)

- Informal or spontaneous speeches

- Participation in class discussions and activities

Individual Tasks and Victory Objectives

Each player's role sheet includes individual Victory Objectives. You may be graded on how well you seek to meet these VOs. You may not be able to attain all your VOs, but you should make an effort to achieve them.

Winning the Game

The Gamemaster may award points to the final grade of those players who win the game. Consult your GM.

4

PART 4: ROLES AND FACTIONS

INTRODUCTION

You have the role of a real person who participated in social movements in 1913 or a role that is a composite of several such lives. The facts provided in your role sheet are accurate and you have been given references to auto/biographies if you wish to learn more about your character. However, you are not obliged to look for more information to complete this assignment. Rather, you will use your role sheet, the Historical Background, the Core Texts, and your conversations with other players to develop a character who is faithful to the thinking of the times. It is the intellectual debate that matters here. You will find out more about the life of your character during the postmortem.

FACTIONS

The Suffrage Faction

- *Miss Jeannie Rodgers.* 23 years old. A recent graduate of Vassar College who has joined Alice Paul's Congressional Committee. She has come up from Washington, D.C. to mobilize New Yorkers for the big Suffrage Parade.

- *Mrs. Maud Preston.* 35 years old. A longtime New York suffragist who has been working on the state level to obtain a referendum on woman suffrage. She is an Albany insider who is high up in Harriot Stanton Blatch's Women's Political Union.

- *Miss Alice Hallam.* 46 years old. An ardent member of the cross-class Women's Trade Union League who has experience in settlement work as well. She has been assigned to Greenwich Village because of her fluency in Italian. Her goal is to obtain the vote to get better working conditions for women and children.

The Labor Faction

- *"Big" Bill Haywood.* 44 years old. The former miner and leader of the Industrial Workers of the World (IWW). He and Elizabeth Gurley Flynn have come to New York to organize the Paterson workers who have recently gone on strike.

- *Elizabeth Gurley Flynn.* 23 years old. A young, New York–raised IWW agitator, "Gurley" has achieved a reputation for her ability to stir crowds.

- *Leah Schwartz*. 24 years old. A Jewish immigrant and former factory worker in New York's garment industry. She has turned to the Socialist Party and the Women's Trade Union League to work for improved wages, work hours, and social conditions for "the girls."

Wild Cards

These characters have special roles and powers in the game.

- *Mabel Dodge*. 34 years old. Wealthy socialite who has become a patron and muse of Village celebrities. Her Evenings bring celebrity to those who attend them. Currently flirting with Jack Reed.

  Role: Mabel asserts herself as the Muse of Fifth Avenue, the Mover and Shaker of Greenwich Village, the de facto Queen of Polly's Restaurant. The more PIPs Mabel has, the greater her celebrity and more widespread her fame. Her task is to spark debate and conversations, getting the intellectual sparks to fly at Polly's and her Evening.

  Powers: Mabel is so influential that she selects the reading assignment and the speaker for her Evening. Although Mabel keeps all her own PIPs, she can endow 50 or 100 percent of them if her speaker has stirred controversy, excited the audience, and provoked debate at the Evening. Of course, she can also refuse to award PIPs.

- *Max Eastman*. 30 years old. Newly appointed editor of the collective that produces the radical magazine *The Masses*. Married to Ida Rauh and brother of Crystal Eastman.

  Role: His main task is to solicit material for his edition. As editor "without pay," Max wields great influence as he selects pieces for publication. He will use this edition to highlight his point of view.

  Power: If Max selects a work for his issue, the author of that work will receive 5 PIPs for each piece of work accepted.

- *Emma Goldman*. 44 years old. Anarchist, orator, and political organizer who provides an anarchist critique of the goings-on at Polly's.

  Role: Emma takes detailed notes at each class meeting, listening intently for the theoretical assumptions underlying the factions' arguments. At the time of the vote, "Red Emma" will present an overall critique of the debates.

Power: Emma may or may not want to support a specific faction. If she does favor a faction, she can double its total number of PIPs. All Villagers need to take note of Emma.

Indeterminates: Villagers and Their Friends

Some or all of the following people will stop by Polly's for dinner and conversation:

- *Paula Holladay.* In her 30s. The anarchist owner of Polly's restaurant and mistress of ceremonies.

- *Rosa Bianchi.* 14 years old. A recent immigrant from Sicily and newly hired dishwasher at Polly's. She lives in the Italian section of Greenwich Village.

- *Randolph Bourne.* 27 years old. A young writer for the *Atlantic Monthly* who is gaining a name for his insightful comments on an emerging "youth culture." He hopes to become the spokesman for his generation.

- *Neith Boyce.* 41 years old. A New Woman, novelist, (future) playwright, and mother of four. Married to "Hutch" Hapgood.

- *George Cram "Jig" Cook.* 40 years old. A writer, rebel against middle-class conformity, and seeker of a new kind of American community. Married to Susan Glaspell.

- *Floyd Dell.* 26 years old. Recently arrived from Chicago, this young writer has already made a name for himself with his sparkling book reviews and amusing one-act plays.

- *W.E.B. Du Bois.* 45 years old. Black scholar and public intellectual. A friend of "May" Ovington and general editor of the NAACP's journal *The Crisis*, Du Bois has spoken out frequently on suffrage, labor, education, and the place of the Negro in today's America.

- *Crystal Eastman.* 32 years old. Lawyer, suffrage organizer, and feminist who is now joining the Woman's Peace Party. Sister of Max Eastman.

- *Charlotte Perkins Gilman.* 53 years old. Writer, speaker, and intellectual, Gilman has made her reputation through asserting the need to transform the home and family life for a true feminist revolution.

- *Susan Glaspell.* 37 years old. Writer of short stories and plays. Married to "Jig" Cook.

- *Hutchins Hapgood.* 44 years old. Urban flâneur and observer of New York immigrant neighborhoods. He has developed a new kind of "personal journalism" that combines objective reporting with personal commentary. Married to Neith Boyce.

- *Inez Milholland.* 27 years old. Lawyer and suffrage celebrity who will lead the parade in Washington, D.C. She is known for her "star quality," high style, and fundraising ability among the very rich. Friend of Crystal and Max Eastman.

- *Mary "May" White Ovington.* 48 years old. Settlement worker, organizer, and writer who cofounded the NAACP. Friend of Alice Hallam and W.E.B. Du Bois.

- *Elsie Clews Parsons.* 39 years old. Anthropologist and former Barnard College instructor whose cross-cultural studies of the family have caused a stir for demonstrating that the family unit changes over time and differs widely among cultures.

- *Ida Rauh.* 36 years old. Lawyer by training, actress in one-act plays performed at the Liberal Club for amusement. Married to Max Eastman. Former roommate of his sister, Crystal.

- *John "Jack" Reed.* 26 years old. Journalist looking for action: the IWW, Paterson, Mexico. Flirts with Mabel Dodge.

- *Henrietta Rodman.* 35 years old. Feminist high school teacher who joins every movement for reform and heads attacks on all forms of discrimination against women in public life.

- *Margaret Sanger.* 34 years old. Nurse, sex educator, and organizer who dares to talk about family limitation. Worked with Elizabeth Gurley Flynn and Mary Heaton Vorse at the Lawrence Strike in 1912.

- *John Sloan.* 42 years old. Painter and member of the New York realists called "the Eight" and later the Ashcan School for their interest in portraying everyday life in the city. Art director and cartoonist for *The Masses.*

- *Rose Pastor Stokes.* 34 years old. "The Jewish Cinderella," an immigrant and former stogie-maker who married a millionaire but has dedicated her life to the welfare of the working class. Outspoken public speaker.

- *Mary Heaton Vorse.* 39 years old. Journalist who follows the labor movement and writer of light fiction, her "lollipops," for popular women's magazines. One of the founders of *The Masses.* Friend of Elizabeth Gurley Flynn.

Gamemaster

Your instructor, the Gamemaster (GM), will serve as consultant to all players. He or she may take on the temporary role of a police officer or other Village character.

A note of caution: the ideas that are debated in *Greenwich Village, 1913* can sometimes seem remarkably close to those that we still discuss today: the self, sexuality, freedom, immigration, social justice, women's social roles, war, and national security. Nevertheless, to play the game well you cannot use present-day perspectives and knowledge to construct your argument. You must situate yourself in 1913 at the very beginning of these debates, using the knowledge and the dreams of that era. It is only in this way that you will be able to feel the excitement—as well as the disappointments—of the New.

Similarly, because the debates in *Greenwich Village, 1913* can seem so fresh, you may feel that you are being asked to adopt ideas and beliefs that challenge or undermine your own. This is not the case. You are being asked to take on a role, to inhabit a way of thinking and living from the past in order to understand a perspective in its own context.

Other players have been asked to take on roles as well. Some of these characters might be people whom you could admire. Others may exhibit values, personality traits, and behaviors that you might want to condemn. Indeed, this game is designed to place you in intellectual conflict with others. It is important to pay attention to these "in-role" rivalries or animosities and to make sure that they are placed to one side once you leave Polly's.

5

 **PART 5: CORE TEXTS**

ELIZABETH CADY STANTON

"Declaration of Sentiments," *Report of the Women's Rights Convention*, Seneca Falls, New York, 1848

Obtain a copy of the Declaration of Independence and compare it with Stanton's Declaration of Sentiments. What has Stanton taken verbatim? What has she added? While Stanton clearly argues to grant women the franchise (the vote), does her Declaration of Sentiments suggest even more extensive changes to the American way of life? Make a list of any additional demands that may be stated or suggested in this speech.

SOURCE: *Ann D. Gordon, ed.* Selected Papers of Elizabeth Cady Stanton and Susan B. Anthony. Vol I., In the School of Anti-Slavery, 1840 to 1866. *New Brunswick, N.J.: Rutgers University, 1997. ecssba.rutgers.edu/docs/seneca.html*

When, in the course of human events, it becomes necessary for one portion of the family of man to assume among the people of the earth a position different from that which they have hitherto occupied, but one to which the laws of nature and of nature's God entitle them, a decent respect to the opinions of mankind requires that they should declare the causes that impel them to such a course.

We hold these truths to be self-evident: that all men and women are created equal; that they are endowed by their Creator with certain inalienable rights; that among these are life, liberty, and the pursuit of happiness; that to secure these rights governments are instituted, deriving their just powers from the consent of the governed. Whenever any form of government becomes destructive of these ends, it is the right of those who suffer from it to refuse allegiance to it, and to insist upon the institution of a new government, laying its foundation on such principles, and organizing its powers in such form, as to them shall seem most likely to effect their safety and happiness. Prudence, indeed, will dictate that governments long established should not be changed for light and transient causes; and accordingly all experience hath shown that mankind are more disposed to suffer, while evils are sufferable, than to right themselves by abolishing the forms to which they were accustomed. But when a long train of abuses and usurpations, pursuing invariably the same object, evinces a design to reduce them under absolute despotism, it is their duty to throw off such government, and to provide new guards for their future security. Such has been the patient sufferance of the women under this government, and such is now the necessity which constrains them to demand the equal station to which they are entitled.

The history of mankind is a history of repeated injuries and usurpations on the part of man toward woman, having in direct object the establishment of an absolute tyranny over her. To prove this, let facts be submitted to a candid world.

He has never permitted her to exercise her inalienable right to the elective franchise.

He has compelled her to submit to laws, in the formation of which she had no voice.

He has withheld from her rights which are given to the most ignorant and degraded men—both natives and foreigners.

Having deprived her of this first right of a citizen, the elective franchise, thereby leaving her without representation in the halls of legislation, he has oppressed her on all sides.

He has made her, if married, in the eye of the law, civilly dead.

He has taken from her all right in property, even to the wages she earns.

He has made her, morally, an irresponsible being, as she can commit many crimes with impunity, provided they be done in the presence of her husband. In the covenant of marriage, she is compelled to promise obedience to her husband, he becoming to all intents and purposes, her master—the law giving him power to deprive her of her liberty, and to administer chastisement.

He has so framed the laws of divorce, as to what shall be the proper causes, and in case of separation, to whom the guardianship of the children shall be given, as to be wholly regardless of the happiness of women—the law, in all cases, going upon a false supposition of the supremacy of man, and giving all power into his hands.

After depriving her of all rights as a married woman, if single, and the owner of property, he has taxed her to support a government which recognizes her only when her property can be made profitable to it.

He has monopolized nearly all the profitable employments, and from those she is permitted to follow, she receives but a scanty remuneration.

He closes against her all the avenues to wealth and distinction which he considers most honorable to himself.

As a teacher of theology, medicine, or law, she is not known.

He has denied her the facilities for obtaining a thorough education, all colleges being closed against her.

He allows her in Church, as well as State, but a subordinate position, claiming Apostolic authority for her exclusion from the ministry, and, with some exceptions, from any public participation in the affairs of the Church.

He has created a false public sentiment by giving to the world a different code of morals for men and women, by which moral delinquencies which exclude women from society, are not only tolerated, but deemed of little account in man.

He has usurped the prerogative of Jehovah himself, claiming it as his right to assign for her a sphere of action, when that belongs to her conscience and to her God.

He has endeavored, in every way that he could, to destroy her confidence in her own powers, to lessen her self-respect, and to make her willing to lead a dependent and abject life.

Now, in view of this entire disfranchisement of one-half the people of this country, their social and religious degradation—in view of the unjust laws above mentioned, and because women do feel themselves aggrieved, oppressed, and fraudulently deprived of their most sacred rights, we insist that they have immediate admission to all the rights and privileges which belong to them as citizens of the United States.

In entering upon the great work before us, we anticipate no small amount of misconception, misrepresentation, and ridicule; but we shall use every instrumentality within our power to effect our object. We shall employ agents, circulate tracts, petition the State and National legislatures, and endeavor to enlist the pulpit and the press in our behalf. We hope this Convention will be followed by a series of Conventions embracing every part of the country.

Note the "action plan" that Stanton sets forth in this Declaration. What can women do to reach the goal of the franchise?

"The Constant," *Godey's Lady's Book*, 1851

Godey's Lady's Book, a magazine produced by Louis A. Godey, was an "arbiter of good taste" from 1830 to 1878. See if you can piece together a story from the scenes depicted in this illustration. What does it tell you about the society's ideal of a "lady," the important moments in her life, and the values and expectations that she might embrace? Pay attention to the scenes in the corners as well as the central figures.

SOURCE: Godey's Lady's Book. *Vol. 42. January, 1851. Courtesy Project Gutenberg. http://www.gutenberg.org/files/15080/15080-h/15080-h.htm*

ELIZABETH CADY STANTON

"Solitude of Self," January 18, 1892

Now seventy-seven years old, Stanton leaves the public stage with the following speech given before the Congressional Judiciary Committee as well as to the NAWSA convention of 1892. What changes do you see in her argument for suffrage from her first Declaration of Sentiments in 1848?

Consider how Stanton emphasizes woman as an individual. How is this an important shift in understanding women's social role? What might be the benefits to women of being seen as individuals? What might be the burdens?

SOURCE: *http://memory.loc.gov*

*M*r. Chairman and gentlemen of the Committee: We have been speaking before Committees of the Judiciary for the last twenty years, and we have gone over all the arguments in favor of a sixteenth amendment which are familiar to all you gentlemen; therefore, it will not be necessary that I should repeat them again.

The point I wish plainly to bring before you on this occasion is the individuality of each human soul; our Protestant idea, the right of individual conscience and judgment—our republican idea, individual citizenship. In discussing the rights of woman, we are to consider, first, what belongs to her as an individual, in a world of her own, the arbiter of her own destiny, an imaginary Robinson Crusoe with her woman Friday on a solitary island. Her rights under such circumstances are to use all her faculties for her own safety and happiness.

Secondly, if we consider her as a citizen, as a member of a great nation, she must have the same rights as all other members, according to the fundamental principles of our Government.

Thirdly, viewed as a woman, an equal factor in civilization, her rights and duties are still the same—individual happiness and development.

Fourthly, it is only the incidental relations of life, such as mother, wife, sister, daughter, that may involve some special duties and training. In the usual discussion in regard to woman's sphere, such a man as Herbert Spencer, Frederic Harrison, and Grant Allen uniformly subordinate her rights and duties as an individual, as a citizen, as a woman, to the necessities of these incidental relations, some of which a large class of woman may never assume. In discussing the sphere of man, we do not decide his rights as an individual, as a citizen, as a man by his duties as a father, a husband, a brother, or a son, relations some of which he may never fill. Moreover he would be better fitted for these very relations and whatever special work he might choose to do to earn his bread by the complete development of all his faculties as an individual.

Note how Stanton relegates marriage and motherhood to "incidental relations of life," a radical challenge to beliefs in women's social role and separate sphere.

Just so with woman. The education that will fit her to discharge the duties in the largest sphere of human usefulness will best fit her for whatever special work she may be compelled to do.

The isolation of every human soul and the necessity of self-dependence must give each individual the right to choose his own surroundings. The strongest reason for giving woman all the opportunities for higher education, for the full development of her faculties, forces of mind and body; for giving her the most enlarged freedom of thought and action; a complete emancipation from all forms of bondage, of custom, dependence, superstition; from all the crippling influences of fear, is the solitude and personal responsibility of her own individual life. The strongest reason why we ask for woman a voice in the government under which she lives; in the religion she is asked to believe; equality in social life, where she is the chief factor; a place in the trades and professions, where she may earn her bread, is because of her birthright to self-sovereignty; because, as an individual, she must rely on herself. No matter how much women prefer to lean, to be protected and supported, nor how much men desire to have them do so, they must make the voyage of life alone, and for safety in an emergency they must know something of the laws of navigation. To guide our own craft, we must be captain, pilot, engineer; with chart and compass to stand at the wheel; to match the wind and waves and know when to take in the sail, and to read the signs in the firmament over all. It matters not whether the solitary voyager is man or woman.

Nature having endowed them equally, leaves them to their own skill and judgment in the hour of danger, and, if not equal to the occasion, alike they perish.

To appreciate the importance of fitting every human soul for independent action, think for a moment of the immeasurable solitude of self. We come into the world alone, unlike all who have gone before us; we leave it alone under circumstances peculiar to ourselves. No mortal ever has been, no mortal ever will be like the soul just launched on the sea of life. There can never again be just such environments as make up the infancy, youth and manhood of this one. Nature never repeats herself, and the possibilities of one human soul will never be found in another. No one has ever found two blades of ribbon grass alike, and no one will ever find two human beings alike. Seeing, then, what must be the infinite diversity in human character, we can in a measure appreciate the loss to a nation when any large class of the people uneducated and unrepresented in the government. We ask for the complete development of every individual, first, for his own benefit and happiness. In fitting out an army we give each soldier his own knapsack, arms, powder, his blanket, cup, knife, fork and spoon. We provide alike for all their individual necessities, then each man bears his own burden.

What is Stanton's understanding of the "solitude of self?" How does it challenge prevailing ideas about women as a separate sex (what today we might call gender)? What are the implications of the "solitude of self" for how society should view and treat the women of the future?

Again we ask complete individual development for the general good; for the consensus of the competent on the whole round of human interest; on all questions of national life, and here each man must bear his share of the general burden. It is sad to see how soon friendless children are left to bear their own burdens before they can analyze their feelings; before they can even tell their joys and sorrows, they are thrown on their own resources. The great lesson that nature seems to teach us at all ages is self-dependence, self-protection, self-support. What a touching instance of a child's solitude; of that hunger of heart for love and recognition, in the case of the little girl who helped to dress a Christmas tree for the children of the family in which she served. On finding there was no present for herself she slipped away in the darkness and spent the night in an open field sitting on a stone, and when found in the morning was weeping as if her heart would break. No mortal will ever know the thoughts that passed through the mind of that friendless child in the long hours of that cold night, with only the silent stars to keep her company. The mention of her case in the daily papers moved many generous hearts to send her presents, but in the hours of her keenest sufferings she was thrown wholly on herself for consolation.

In youth our most bitter disappointments, our brightest hopes and ambitions are known only to otherwise, even our friendship and love we never fully share with another; there is something of every passion in every situation we conceal. Even so in our triumphs and our defeats.

The successful candidate for Presidency and his opponent each have a solitude peculiarly his own, and good form forbid either in speak of his pleasure or regret. The solitude of the king on his throne and the prisoner in his cell differs in character and degree, but it is solitude nevertheless.

We ask no sympathy from others in the anxiety and agony of a broken friendship or shattered love. When death sunders our nearest ties, alone we sit in the shadows of our affliction. Alike mid the greatest triumphs and darkest tragedies of life we walk alone. On the divine heights of human attainments, eulogized and worshiped as a hero or saint, we stand alone. In ignorance, poverty, and vice, as a pauper or criminal, alone we starve or steal; alone we suffer the sneers and rebuffs of our fellows; alone we are hunted and hounded thro dark courts and alleys, in by-ways and highways; alone we stand in the judgment seat; alone in the prison cell we lament our crimes and misfortunes; alone we expiate them on the gallows. In hours like these we realize the awful solitude of individual life, its pains, its penalties, its responsibilities; hours in which the youngest and most helpless are thrown on their own resources for guidance and consolation. Seeing then that life must ever be a march and a battle, that each soldier must be equipped for his own protection, it is the height of cruelty to rob the individual of a single natural right.

To throw obstacles in the way of a complete education is like putting out the eyes; to deny the rights of property, like cutting off the hands. To deny political equality is to rob the ostracized of all self-respect; of credit in the market place; of recompense in the world of work; of a voice among those who make and administer the law; a choice in the jury before whom they are tried, and in the judge who decides their punishment. Shakespeare's play of Titus and Andronicus contains a terrible satire on woman's position in the nineteenth century—"Rude men" (the play tells us) "seized the king's daughter, cut out her tongue, cut off her hands, and then bade her go call for water and wash her hands." What a picture of woman's position. Robbed of her natural rights, handicapped by law and custom at every turn, yet compelled to fight her own battles, and in the emergencies of life to fall back on herself for protection.

The girl of sixteen, thrown on the world to support herself, to make her own place in society, to resist the temptations that surround her and maintain a spotless integrity, must do all this by native force or superior education. She does not acquire this power by being trained to trust others and distrust herself. If she wearies of the struggle, finding it hard work to swim upstream, and allow herself to drift with the current, she will find plenty of company, but not one to share her misery in the hour of her deepest humiliation. If she tried to retrieve her position, to conceal the past, her life is hedged about with fears lest willing hands should tear the veil from what she fain would hide. Young and friendless, she knows the bitter solitude of self.

How the little courtesies of life on the surface of society, deemed so important from man towards woman, fade into utter insignificance in view of the deeper tragedies in which she must play her part alone, where no human aid is possible.

The young wife and mother, at the head of some establishment with a kind husband to shield her from the adverse winds of life, with wealth, fortune and position, has a certain harbor of safety, occurs against the ordinary ills of life. But to manage a household, have a desirable influence in society, keep her friends and the affections of her husband, train her children and servants well, she must have rare common sense, wisdom, diplomacy, and a knowledge of human nature. To do all this she needs the cardinal virtues and the strong points of character that the most successful state man possesses.

An uneducated woman, trained to dependence, with no resources in herself must make a failure of any position in life. But society says women do not need a knowledge of the world, the liberal training that experience in public life must give, all the advantages of collegiate education; but when for the lack of all this, the woman's happiness is wrecked, alone she bears her humiliation; and the attitude of the weak and the ignorant is indeed pitiful in the wild chase for the price of life they are ground to powder.

In age, when the pleasures of youth are passed, children grown up, married and gone, the hurry and hustle of life in a measure over, when the hands are weary of active service, when the old armchair and the fireside are the chosen resorts, then men and women alike must fall back on their own resources. If they cannot find companionship in books, if they have no interest in the vital questions of the hour, no interest in watching the consummation of reforms, with which they might have been identified, they soon pass into their dotage. The more fully the faculties of the mind are developed and kept in use, the longer the period of vigor and active interest in all around us continues. If from a lifelong participation in public affairs a woman feels responsible for the laws regulating our system of education, the discipline of our jails and prisons, the sanitary conditions of our private homes, public buildings, and thoroughfares, an interest in commerce, finance, our foreign relations, in any or all of these questions, here solitude will at least be respectable, and she will not be driven to gossip or scandal for entertainment.

The chief reason for opening to every soul the doors to the whole round of human duties and pleasures is the individual development thus attained, the resources thus provided under all circumstances to mitigate the solitude that at times must come to everyone. I once asked Prince Krapotkin, the Russian nihilist,[1]

---

1. Nihilism, from the Latin nihil (nothing), refers to a philosophical movement that asserts that there is no intrinsic truth or meaning in the world.

how he endured his long years in prison, deprived of books, pen, ink, and paper. "Ah," he said, "I thought out many questions in which I had a deep interest. In the pursuit of an idea I took no note of time. When tired of solving knotty problems I recited all the beautiful passages in prose or verse I have ever learned. I became acquainted with myself and my own resources. I had a world of my own, a vast empire, that no Russian jailor or Czar could invade." Such is the value of liberal thought and broad culture when shut off from all human companionship, bringing comfort and sunshine within even the four walls of a prison cell.

As women of times share a similar fate, should they not have all the consolation that the most liberal education can give? Their suffering in the prisons of St. Petersburg; in the long, weary marches to Siberia, and in the mines, working side by side with men, surely call for all the self-support that the most exalted sentiments of heroism can give. When suddenly roused at midnight, with the startling cry of "fire! fire!" to find the house over their heads in flames, do women wait for men to point the way to safety? And are the men, equally bewildered and half suffocated with smoke, in a position to more than try to save themselves?

At such times the most timid women have shown a courage and heroism in saving their husbands and children that has surprised everybody. Inasmuch, then, as woman shares equally the joys and sorrows of time and eternity, is it not the height of presumption in man to propose to represent her at the ballot box and the throne of grace, do her voting in the state, her praying in the church, and to assume the position of priest at the family altar.

Nothing strengthens the judgment and quickens the conscience like individual responsibility. Nothing adds such dignity to character as the recognition of one's self-sovereignty; the right to an equal place, every where conceded; a place earned by personal merit, not an artificial attainment, by inheritance, wealth, family, and position. Seeing, then that the responsibilities of life rest equally on man and woman, that their destiny is the same, they need the same preparation for time and eternity. The talk of sheltering woman from the fierce storms of life is the sheerest mockery, for they beat on her from every point of the compass, just as they do on man, and with more fatal results, for he has been trained to protect himself, to resist, to conquer. Such are the facts in human experience, the responsibilities of individual. Rich and poor, intelligent and ignorant, wise and foolish, virtuous and vicious, man and woman, it is ever the same, each soul must depend wholly on itself.

Whatever the theories may be of woman's dependence on man, in the supreme moments of her life he can not bear her burdens. Alone she goes to the gates of death to give life to every man that is born into the world. No one can share her fears, no one mitigate her pangs; and if her sorrow is greater than she can bear, alone she passes beyond the gates into the vast unknown.

From the mountain tops of Judea, long ago, a heavenly voice bade His disciples, "Bear ye one another's burdens," but humanity has not yet risen to that point of self-sacrifice, and if ever so willing, how few the burdens are that one soul can bear for another. In the highways of Palestine; in prayer and fasting on the solitary mountain top; in the Garden of Gethsemane; before the judgment seat of Pilate; betrayed by one of His trusted disciples at His last supper; in His agonies on the cross, even Jesus of Nazareth, in these last sad days on earth, felt the awful solitude of self. Deserted by man, in agony he cries, "My God! My God! why hast Thou forsaken me?" And so it ever must be in the conflicting scenes of life, on the long weary march, each one walks alone. We may have many friends, love, kindness, sympathy and charity to smooth our pathway in everyday life, but in the tragedies and triumphs of human experience each moral stands alone.

But when all artificial trammels are removed, and women are recognized as individuals, responsible for their own environments, thoroughly educated for all the positions in life they may be called to fill; with all the resources in themselves that liberal thought and broad culture can give; guided by their own conscience and judgment; trained to self-protection by a healthy development of the muscular system and skill in the use of weapons of defense, and stimulated to self-support by the knowledge of the business world and the pleasure that pecuniary independence must ever give; when women are trained in this way they will, in a measure, be fitted for those hours of solitude that come alike to all, whether prepared or otherwise. As in our extremity we must depend on ourselves, the dictates of wisdom point to complete individual development.

Stanton argues that women are already equal to men by Nature; the differences between men and women have been imposed by social norms. Note how she dismisses them as "artificial trammels."

In talking of education how shallow the argument that each class must be educated for the special work it proposed to do, and all those faculties not needed in this special walk must lie dormant and utterly wither for want of use, when, perhaps, these will be the very faculties needed in life's greatest emergencies! Some say, Where is the use of drilling girls in the languages, the Sciences, in law, medicine, theology? As wives, mothers, housekeepers, cooks, they need a different curriculum from boys who are to fill all positions. The chief cooks in our great hotels and ocean steamers are men. In large cities men run the bakeries; they make our bread, cake, and pies. They manage the laundries; they are now considered our best milliners and dressmakers. Because some men fill these departments of usefulness, shall we regulate the curriculum in Harvard and Yale to their present necessities? If not why this talk in our best colleges of a curriculum for girls who are crowding into the trades and professions; teachers in all our public schools rapidly hiring many lucrative and honorable positions in life? They are showing too, their calmness and courage in the most trying hours of human experience. You have probably all read in the daily papers of the terrible storm in the Bay of Biscay when a tidal wave made such havoc on the shore, wrecking vessels, un-roofing houses and carrying destruction everywhere. Among other buildings the woman's prison was demolished. Those who escaped saw men struggling to reach the shore. They promptly by clasping hands made a chain of themselves and pushed out into the sea, again and again, at the risk of their lives until they had brought six men to shore, carried them to a shelter, and did all in their power for their comfort and protection.

What special school of training could have prepared these women for this sublime moment of their lives. In times like this humanity rises above all college curriculums and recognizes Nature as the greatest of all teachers in the hour of danger and death. Women are already the equals of men in the whole of realm of thought, in art, science, literature, and government. With telescope vision they explore the starry firmament, and bring back the history of the planetary world. With chart and compass they pilot ships across the mighty deep, and with skillful finger send electric messages around the globe. In galleries of art the beauties of nature and the virtues of humanity are immortalized by them on their canvas and by their inspired touch dull blocks of marble are transformed into angels of light.

In music they speak again the language of Mendelssohn, Beethoven, Chopin, Schumann, and are worthy interpreters of their great thoughts. The poetry and novels of the century are theirs, and they have touched the keynote of reform in religion, politics, and social life. They fill the editor's and professor's chair, and plead at the bar of justice, walk the wards of the hospital, and speak from the pulpit and the platform; such is the type of womanhood that an enlightened public sentiment welcomes today, and such the triumph of the facts of life over the false theories of the past.

Is it, then, consistent to hold the developed woman of this day within the same narrow political limits as the dame with the spinning wheel and knitting needle occupied in the past? No! no! Machinery has taken the labors of woman as well as man on its tireless shoulders; *Here is Stanton's call to action. What does she ask her audience to do and for what reason?* the loom and the spinning wheel are but dreams of the past; the pen, the brush, the easel, the chisel, have taken their places, while the hopes and ambitions of women are essentially changed.

We see reason sufficient in the outer conditions of human being for individual liberty and development, but when we consider the self dependence of every human soul we see the need of courage, judgment, and the exercise of every faculty of mind and body, strengthened and developed by use, in woman as well as man.

Whatever may be said of man's protecting power in ordinary conditions, mid all the terrible disasters by land and sea, in the supreme moments of danger, alone, woman must ever meet the horrors of the situation; the Angel of Death even makes no royal pathway for her. Man's love and sympathy enter only into the sunshine of our lives. In that solemn solitude of self, that links us with the immeasurable and the eternal, each soul lives alone forever. A recent writer says:

> I remember once, in crossing the Atlantic, to have gone upon the deck of the ship at midnight, when a dense black cloud enveloped the sky, and the great deep was roaring madly under the lashes of demoniac winds. My feeling was not of danger or fear (which is a base surrender of the immortal soul), but of utter desolation

and loneliness; a little speck of life shut in by a tremendous darkness. Again I remember to have climbed the slopes of the Swiss Alps, up beyond the point where vegetation ceases, and the stunted conifers no longer struggle against the unfeeling blasts. Around me lay a huge confusion of rocks, out of which the gigantic ice peaks shot into the measureless blue of the heavens, and again my only feeling was the awful solitude.

And yet, there is a solitude, which each and every one of us has always carried with him, more inaccessible than the ice-cold mountains, more profound than the midnight sea; the solitude of self. Our inner being, which we call our self, no eye nor touch of man or angel has ever pierced. It is more hidden than the caves of the gnome; the sacred adytum of the oracle; the hidden chamber of Eleusinian mystery, for to it only omniscience is permitted to enter. Such is individual life. Who, I ask you, can take, dare take, on himself the rights, the duties, the responsibilities of another human soul?[2]

---

2. The adytum was the inner sacred space of ancient Greek temples where only priests were permitted to enter. The Eleusinian mysteries, part of an ancient Greek cult of the goddess Demeter, were secret rites that promised followers special benefits in the afterlife.

RHETA CHILDE DORR

"American Women and the Common Law," *What Eight Million Women Want*, 1910

Writing for Hampton's Magazine, *journalist, suffragist, and future Heterodoxy member Rheta Childe Dorr provides a series of articles on the state of American women in 1910, later collected into her book,* What Eight Million Women Want. *Here she examines women's legal status and alerts us to some "disagreeable surprises" that women's clubs found when they examined the laws of their states: "American women have been so accustomed to their privileges that they have taken their rights for granted, and they are usually astonished when they find how limited their rights actually are."*

What surprises you about women's legal position in 1910? How would this information influence your role's arguments in this game?

SOURCE: What Eight Million Women Want. *Boston: Small, Maynard and Co., 1910. 75–114.*

    *J*n America some women have all the rights they want. Your wife and the wives of the men you associate with every day usually have all the rights they want, sometimes a few that they do not need at all. Is the house yours? The furniture yours? The motor yours? The income yours? Are the children yours? If you are the average fond American husband, you will return the proud answer: "No, indeed, they are *ours*."

This is quite as it should be, assuming that all wives are as tenderly cherished, and as well protected as the women who live on your block. For a whole big army of women there are often serious disadvantages connected with that word "ours." . . .

American law, except in Louisiana and Florida, is founded on English common law, and English common law was developed at a period when men were of much greater importance in the state than women. The state was a military organization and every man was a fighter, a king's defender. Women were valuable only because defenders of kings had to have mothers.

English common law provided that every married woman must be supported in as much comfort as her husband's estate warranted. The mothers of the nation must be fed, clothed, and sheltered. What more could they possibly ask? In return for permanent board and clothes, the woman was required to give her husband all of her property, real and personal. What use had she for property? Did she need it to support herself? In case of war and pillage could she defend it?

Husband and wife were one—and that one was the man. He was so much the one that the woman had literally no existence in the eyes of the law. She not only did not possess any property; she could possess none. Her husband could not give her any, because there could be no contract between a married pair. A contract implies at least two people, and husband and wife were one. The husband could, if he chose, establish a trusteeship, and thus give his wife free use of her own. But you can easily imagine that he did not very often do it.

A man could, also, devise property to his wife by will. Often this was done, but too often the sons were made heirs, and the wife was left to what tender mercies they owned. If a man died intestate the wife merely shared with other heirs. She had no preference.

Under the old English common law, moreover, not only the property, but also the services of a married woman belonged to her husband. If he chose to rent out her services, or if she offered to work outside the home, it followed logically that her wages belonged to him. What use had she for wages?

On the other hand, every man was held responsible for the support of his wife. He was responsible for her debts, as long as they were necessities of life. He was also responsible for her conduct. Being property-less, she could not be held to account for wrongs committed. If she stole, or destroyed property, or injured the person of another, if she committed any kind of misdemeanor in the presence of her husband, and that also meant if he were in her neighborhood at the time, the law held him responsible. He should have restrained her. . . .

You may well imagine that, in these circumstances, husbands were interested that their wives should be very good. The law supported them by permitting "moderate correction." A married woman might be kept in what Blackstone calls "reasonable restraint" by her husband. But only with a stick no larger than his thumb.[1]

The husbandly stick was never imported into the United States. Even the dour Puritans forbade its use. The very first modification of the English common law, in its application to American women, was made in 1650, when the General Court of Massachusetts Bay Colony decreed that a husband beating his wife, or, for that matter a wife beating her husband, should be fined ten pounds, or endure a public whipping.

The Pilgrim Fathers and the other early colonists in America brought with them the system of English common law under which they and their ancestors had for centuries been governed. From time to time, as conditions made them necessary, new laws were enacted and put into force. In all cases not specifically covered by these new laws, the old English common law was applied. It did not occur to any one that women would ever need special laws. The Pilgrim Fathers and their successors, the Puritans, simply assumed that here, as in the England they had left behind, woman's place was in the home, where she was protected, supported, and controlled.

But in the new world woman's place in the home assumed an importance much greater than it had formally possessed. Labor was scarce, manufacturing and trading were undeveloped. Woman's special activities were urgently needed. Woman's hands helped to raise the roof-tree, her skill and industry, to a very large extent, furnished the house. She spun and wove, cured meat, dried corn, tanned skins, made shoes, dipped candles, and was, in a word, almost the only manufacturer in the country. But this did not raise her from her position as an inferior. Woman owned neither her tools nor her raw materials. These her husband provided. In consequence, husband and wife being one, that one, in America, as in England, was the husband. . . .

No legislature in the United States has deliberately made laws placing women at a disadvantage with men. Whatever laws are unfair and oppressive to women have just happened—just grown up like weeds out of neglected soil.

The first struggle made by women in their own behalf was against this condition of marital slavery. Elizabeth Cady Stanton, Lucretia Mott, Lydia Maria Child, and others of that brave band of rebellious women, were active for years, addressing legislative committees in New York and Massachusetts, circulating petitions, writing to newspapers, agitating everywhere in favor of married women's property rights. Finally it began to dawn on the minds of men that there might be a certain public advantage, as well as private justice, attaching to separate ownership by married women of their own property.

---

1. William Blackstone (1723–1780), a jurist and judge, wrote the Commentaries on the Laws of England (1766), the basics of common law that were adapted in the United States.

In 1839 the Massachusetts State Legislature passed a cautious measure giving married women qualified property rights. It was not until 1848 that a really effective Married Women's Property Law was secured, by action of the New York State Assembly. . . .

Men of property stood for the Married Women's Property Act, because they perceived plainly that their own wealth, devised to daughters who could not control it, might easily be gambled away, or wasted through improvidence, or diverted to the use of strangers. In other words, they knew that their property, when daughters inherited it, became the property of their sons-in-law. They had no guarantee that their own grandchildren would ever have the use of it, unless it was controlled by their mothers.

There are some states in the Union where women are on terms of something like equality with men. There is one State to which all intelligent women look with a sort of envious, admiring, questioning curiosity, Colorado, which is literally the woman's paradise. In Colorado it would be difficult to find even the smallest inequality between men and women. . . .

Contrast Colorado with Louisiana, possibly the last State in the Union a well-informed woman would choose for a residence. The laws of Louisiana were based, not on the English common law, but on the Code Napoleon, which regards women merely as a working, breeding, domestic animal.

"There is one thing that is not *French*," thundered the great Napoleon, closing a conference on his famous code, "and that is that a woman can do as she pleases." . . .

Between these two extremes, Colorado and Louisiana, women have the other forty-six States to choose. None of them offers perfect equality. Even in Idaho, Wyoming, and Utah—the three states besides Colorado where women vote—women are in such a minority that their votes are powerless to remove all their disabilities. . . .

In most of the older States the property rights of married women are now fairly guaranteed, but the proud boast that in America no woman is the slave of her husband will have to be modified when it is known that in at least seventeen States these rights are still denied.

The husband absolutely controls his wife's property and her earnings in Texas, Tennessee, Louisiana, California, Arizona, North Dakota, and Idaho. He has virtual control—that is to say, the wife's rights are merely provisional—in Alabama, New Mexico, and Missouri.

Women to control their own business property must be registered as traders on their own account in these States: Georgia, Montana, Nevada, Massachusetts, North Carolina, Oregon, and Virginia.

Nor are women everywhere permitted to work on equal terms with men.

There is a current belief, often expressed, that in the United States every avenue of industry is open to women on equal terms with men. This is not quite true. In some States a married woman may not engage in any business without permission from the courts. In Texas, Louisiana, and Georgia this is the case. In Wyoming, where women vote, but where they are in such minority that their votes count for little, a married woman must satisfy the court that she is under the necessity of earning her living.

* * *

If you are a woman, married or unmarried, and wish to practice law, you are barred from seven of the United States. The legal profession is closed to women in Alabama, Georgia, Virginia, Arkansas, Delaware, Tennessee, and South Carolina.

In some States they discourage women from aspiring to the learned professions by refusing them the advantages of higher education which they provide for their brothers.

Four state universities close their doors to women, in spite of the fact that women's taxes help support the universities. These states are Georgia, Virginia, Louisiana, and North Carolina. The last-named admits women to post-graduate courses.

You can hold no kind of an elective office, you cannot be even a country superintendent of schools in Alabama or Arkansas, if you are a woman. In Alabama, indeed, you may not be a minister of the gospel, a doctor of medicine, or a notary public. Florida likewise will have nothing to do with a woman doctor.

Only a few women want to hold office or engage in professional work. Every woman hopes to be a mother. What then is the legal status of the American mother? When the clubwomen began the study of their position before the law they were amazed to find, in all but ten of the States and territories, that they had absolutely no control over the destinies of their own children. In ten States only, and in the District of Columbia, are women co-guardians with their husbands of their children.

In Pennsylvania if a women supports her children, or has money to contribute to their support, she has joint guardianship. Under somewhat similar circumstances Rhode Island women have the same right.

In all the other States and territories children belong to their fathers. They can be given away, or willed away, from the mother. That this almost never happens is due largely to the fact that, as a rule, no one except the mother of a child is especially keen to possess it. . . .

Many times these unjust laws have been protested against. In every State in the Union where they exist they have been protested against by organized groups of intelligent women. But their protests have been received with apathy, and, in some instances, with contempt by legislators. Only last year a determined fight was made by the women of California for a law giving them equal guardianship of their children. The women's bill was lost in the California Legislature, and lost by a large majority.

What arguments did the California legislators use against the proposed measure? Identically the same that were made in Massachusetts and New York a quarter of a century ago. If women had the guardianship of their children, would anything prevent them from taking the children and leaving home? What would become of the sanctity of the home, with its lawful head shorn of his paternal dignity? . . .

At one time the law which made the husband the head of the home guaranteed to the family support by the husband. It does not do that now. There are laws on many States obliging the wife to support her husband if he is disabled, and the children, if the husband defaults. There are no laws compelling the husband to support his wife. The husband is under an assumed obligation to support his family, but there exists no means of forcing him to do his duty. Family desertion has become one of the commonest and one of the most baffling of modern social problems. Everybody is appalled by its prevalence, but nobody seems to know what to do about it. . . .

Women, far more law abiding than men, insist that a system which evolved out of feudal conditions, and has for its very basis the assumption of the weakness, ignorance, and dependence of women, has no place in twentieth century civilization.

American women are no longer weak, ignorant, dependent. The present social order, in which military force is subordinated to industry and commerce, narrows the gulf between them, and places men and women physically on much the same plane. As for women's intellectual ability to decide their own legal status, they are, taken the country over, rather better educated than men. There are more girls than boys in the high schools of the United States; more girls than boys in the higher grammar grades. Fewer women than men are numbered among illiterate. As for the great middle class of women, it is obvious that they are better read than their men. Their specific knowledge of affairs may be less, but their general intelligence is not less than men's.

Increasingly women are ceasing to depend on men for physical support. Increasingly even married women are beginning to think of themselves as independent human beings. Their work of bearing and rearing children, of managing the household, begins to assume a new dignity, a real value, in their eyes. . . .

EMMA GOLDMAN

"Woman Suffrage," *Anarchism and Other Essays,* 1910

Although anti-suffrage perspectives most often came from a conservative world view, Goldman here critiques the suffrage movement from the perspective of her anarchist convictions: the state (government) itself oppresses human freedom. What, she asks, is the good of bringing women into a political system that is fundamentally flawed?

SOURCE: *Emma Goldman, Hippolyte Havel.* Anarchism and Other Essays with Biographic Sketch by Hippolyte Havel. *New York: Mother Earth Publishing Association, 1910. 201–218.*

WE BOAST of the age of advancement, of science, and progress. Is it not strange, then, that we still believe in fetish worship? True, our fetishes have different form and substance, yet in their power over the human mind they are still as disastrous as were those of old.

Our modern fetish is universal suffrage. Those who have not yet achieved that goal fight bloody revolutions to obtain it, and those who have enjoyed its reign bring heavy sacrifice to the altar of this omnipotent deity. Woe to the heretic who dare question that divinity!

Woman, even more than man, is a fetish worshipper, and though her idols may change, she is ever on her knees, ever holding up her hands, ever blind to the fact that her god has feet of clay. Thus woman has been the greatest supporter of all deities from time immemorial. Thus, too, she has had to pay the price that only gods can exact,—her freedom, her heart's blood, her very life. . . .

Religion, especially the Christian religion, has condemned woman to the life of an inferior, a slave. It has thwarted her nature and fettered her soul, yet the Christian religion has no greater supporter, none more devout, than woman. Indeed, it

Goldman points to the values that Americans and particularly American women hold as holy. What are they?

is safe to say that religion would have long ceased to be a factor in the lives of the people, if it were not for the support it receives from woman. The most ardent church workers, the most tireless missionaries the world over, are women, always sacrificing on the altar of the gods that have chained her spirit and enslaved her body.

The insatiable monster, war, robs woman of all that is dear and precious to her. It exacts her brothers, lovers, sons, and in return gives her a life of loneliness and despair. Yet the greatest supporter and worshiper of war is woman. She it is who instills the love of conquest and power into her children; she it is who whispers the glories of war into the ears of her little ones, and who rocks her baby to sleep with the tunes of trumpets and the noise of guns. It is woman, too, who crowns the victor on his return from the battlefield. Yes, it is woman who pays the highest price to that insatiable monster, war.

Then there is the home. What a terrible fetish it is! How it saps the very life-energy of woman,—this modern prison with golden bars. Its shining aspect blinds woman to the price she would have to pay as wife, mother, and housekeeper. Yet woman clings tenaciously to the home, to the power that holds her in bondage.

It may be said that because woman recognizes the awful toll she is made to pay to the Church, State, and the home, she wants suffrage to set herself free. That may be true of the few; the majority of suffragists repudiate utterly such blasphemy. On the contrary, they insist always that it is woman suffrage which will make her a better Christian and home keeper, a staunch citizen of the State. Thus suffrage is only a means of strengthening the omnipotence of the very Gods that woman has served from time immemorial. . . .

What are the arguments that suffragists make to demand political equality and how does Goldman refute them?

Woman's demand for equal suffrage is based largely on the contention that woman must have the equal right in all affairs of society. No one could, possibly, refute that, if suffrage were a right. Alas, for the ignorance of the human mind, which can see a right in an imposition. Or is it not the most brutal imposition for one set of people to make laws that another set is coerced by force to obey? Yet woman clamors for that "golden opportunity" that has wrought so much misery in the world, and robbed man of his integrity and self-reliance; an imposition which has thoroughly corrupted the people, and made them absolute prey in the hands of unscrupulous politicians.

The poor, stupid, free American citizen! Free to starve, free to tramp the highways of this great country, he enjoys universal suffrage, and, by that right, he has forged chains about his limbs. The reward that he receives is stringent labor laws prohibiting the right of boycott, of picketing, in fact, of everything, except the right to be robbed of the fruits of his labor. Yet all these disastrous results of the twentieth-century fetish have taught woman nothing. But, then, woman will purify politics, we are assured.

Needless to say, I am not opposed to woman suffrage on the conventional ground that she is not equal to it. I see neither physical, psychological, nor mental reasons why woman should not have the equal right to vote with man. But that cannot possibly blind me

What, according to Goldman, are the flaws of the U.S. suffrage movement?

to the absurd notion that woman will accomplish that wherein man has failed. If she would not make things worse, she certainly could not make them better. To assume, therefore, that she would succeed in purifying something which is not susceptible of purification, is to credit her with supernatural powers. Since woman's greatest misfortune has been that she was looked upon as either angel or devil, her true salvation lies in being placed on earth; namely, in being considered human, and therefore subject to all human follies and mistakes. Are we, then, to believe that two errors will make a right? Are we to assume that the poison already inherent in politics will be decreased, if women were to enter the political arena? The most ardent suffragists would hardly maintain such a folly. . . .

The American suffrage movement has been, until very recently, altogether a parlor affair, absolutely detached from the economic needs of the people. Thus Susan B. Anthony, no doubt an exceptional type of woman, was not only indifferent but antagonistic to labor; nor did she hesitate to manifest her antagonism when, in 1869, she advised women to take the places of striking printers in New York. I do not know whether her attitude had changed before her death.

There are, of course, some suffragists who are affiliated with working women—the Women's Trade Union League, for instance; but they are a small minority, and their activities are essentially economic. The rest look upon toil as a just provision of Providence. What would become of the rich, if not for the poor? What would become of these idle, parasitic ladies, who squander more in a week than their victims earn in a year, if not for the eighty million wage-workers? Equality, who ever heard of such a thing?

Few countries have produced such arrogance and snobbishness as America. Particularly is this true of the American woman of the middle class. She not only considers herself the equal of man, but his superior, especially in her purity, goodness, and morality. Small wonder that the American suffragist claims for her vote the most miraculous powers. In her exalted conceit she does not see how truly enslaved she is, not so much by man, as by her own silly notions and traditions. Suffrage can not ameliorate that sad fact; it can only accentuate it, as indeed it does. . . .

It is just sixty-two years ago since a handful of women at the Seneca Falls Convention set forth a few demands for their right to equal education with men, and access to the various professions, trades, etc. What wonderful accomplishments, what wonderful triumphs! Who but the most ignorant dare speak of woman as a mere domestic drudge? Who dare suggest that this or that profession should not be open to her? For over sixty years she has molded a new atmosphere and a new life for herself. She has become a world-power in every domain of human thought and activity. And all that without suffrage, without the right to make laws, without the "privilege" of becoming a judge, a jailer, or an executioner.

Yes, I may be considered an enemy of woman; but if I can help her see the light, I shall not complain.

The misfortune of woman is not that she is unable to do the work of a man, but that she is wasting her life-force to outdo him, with a tradition of centuries which has left her physically incapable of keeping pace with him. Oh, I know some have succeeded, but at what cost, at what terrific cost! The import is not the kind of work woman does, but rather the quality of work she furnishes. She can give suffrage or the ballot no new quality, nor can she receive anything from it that will enhance her own quality. Her development, her freedom, her independence, must come from and through herself. First, by asserting herself as a personality, and not as a sex commodity. Second, by refusing the right to anyone over her body; by refusing to bear children, unless she wants them; by refusing to be a servant to God, the State, society, the husband, the family, etc., by making her life simpler, but deeper and richer. That is, by trying to learn the meaning and substance of life in all its complexities, by freeing herself from the fear of public opinion and public condemnation. Only that, and not the ballot, will set woman free, will make her a force hitherto unknown in the world, a force for real love, for peace, for harmony; a force of divine fire, of life-giving; a creator of free men and women.

IDA M. TARBELL

"On the Ennobling of the Woman's Business," *The Business Of Being A Woman*, 1912

Ida M. Tarbell (1857–1944), one of the nation's first women investigative journalists, gained fame as a "muckracker," one of the Progressive Era reformists who exposed social injustice and corruption. She is most famous for her investigation of the trusts, Standard Oil, and John D. Rockefeller in her groundbreaking History of Standard Oil *(1904).*

In spite of her own independence and professional standing, Tarbell was a strong opponent of woman suffrage. In this chapter from her collection of essays on women's role in society, she presents a contemporary argument against the women's movement for more direct political participation. How does she respond to suffragists' critiques of the "women's sphere"? What does Tarbell present as her ideal for women in the twentieth century?

Imagine a conversation between the Stanton of the 1892 "Solitude of Self" and Tarbell on women's nature and their role in society. What would they agree on? What would cause the biggest disagreement?

SOURCE: The Business of Being a Woman. *New York: Macmillan, 1912. 216–242.*

... *T*he movement for a fuller life for American women has always suffered from the disregard of some of its noblest followers, both for things as they are and for things as they have been. The persistent belittling for campaign purposes of the Business of Being a Woman I have repeatedly referred to in this little series of essays; indeed, it has been founded on the proposition that the Uneasy Woman of to-day is to a large degree the result of the belittlement of her natural task and that her chief need is to dignify, make scientific, professionalize, that task.

I doubt if there is to-day a more disintegrating influence at work—one more fatal to sound social development—than that which belittles the home and the position of the woman in it. As a social institution nothing so far devised by man approaches the home in its opportunity, nor equals it in its successes.

The woman's position at its head is hard. The result of her pains and struggles are rarely what she hopes, either for herself or for any one connected with her, but this is true of all human achievement. There is nothing done that does not mean self-denial, routine, disillusionment, and half realization. Even the superman goes the same road, coming out at the same halfway-up house! It is the meaning of the effort, not the half result, that counts.

The pain and struggle of an enterprise are not what takes the heart out of a soldier; it is telling him his cause is mean, his fight in vain. Show him a reason, and he dies exultant. The woman is the world's one permanent soldier. After all war ceases she must go daily to her fight with death. To tell her this giving of her life for life is merely a "female function," not a human part, is to talk nonsense and sacrilege. It is the clear conviction of even the most thoughtless girl that this way lies meaning and fulfillment of life, that gives her courage to go to her battle as a man-in-line to his, and like him she comes out with a new understanding. The endless details of her life, its routine and its restraints, have a reason now, as routine and discipline have for a soldier. She sees as he does that they are the only means of securing the victory bought so dearly—of winning others.

From this high conviction the great mass of women never have and never can be turned. What does happen constantly, however, is loss of joy and courage in their undertaking. When these go, the vision goes. The woman feels only her burdens, not the big meaning in them. She remembers her daily grind, not the possibilities of her position. She falls an easy victim now to that underestimation of her business which is so popular. If she is of gentle nature, she becomes apologetic, she has "never done anything." If she is aggressive, she becomes a militant. In either case, she charges her dissatisfaction to the nature of her business. What has come to her is a common human experience, the discovery that nothing is quite what you expected it to be, that if hope is to be even halfway realized, it will be by courage and persistency. It is not the woman's business that is at fault; it is the faulty handling of it and the human difficulty in keeping heart when things grow hard. What she needs is a strengthening of her wavering faith in her natural place in the world, to see her business as a profession, its problems formulated and its relations to the work of society, as a whole, clearly stated.

Quite as great an injustice to her as the belittling of her business has been the practice, also for campaigning purposes, of denying her a part in the up-building of civilization. There was a time "back of history," says one of the popular leaders in the Woman's movement, "when men and women were friends and comrades—but from that time to this she (woman) has held a subsidiary and exclusively feminine position. The world has been wholly in the hands of men, and they have believed that men alone had the ability, felt the necessity, for developing civilization, the business, education, and religion of the world."

Tarbell challenges the assertion that women have been isolated from public life.

Women's present aim she declares to be the "re-assumption of their share in human life." This is, of course, a modern putting of the List of Grievances with which the militant campaign started in this country in the 40's, re-enforced by the important point that women "back of history" enjoyed the privileges which the earlier militants declared that man, "having in direct object the establishment of an absolute tyranny over her," had always usurped.

Just how the lady knows that "back of history" women and men were more perfect comrades than to-day, I do not know. Her proofs would be interesting. If this is true, it reverses the laws which have governed all other human relations. Certainly, since history began, the only period where I can pretend to judge what has happened, the records show that comradeship between men and women has risen and fallen with the rise and fall of cultivation and of virtue. The general level is probably higher to-day than ever before.

Moreover, from these same records one might support as plausibly—and as falsely—the theory of a Woman-made World as the popular one of a Man-made World. There has been many a teacher and philosopher who has sustained some form of this former thesis, disclaiming against the excessive power of women in shaping human affairs. The teachings of the Christian Church in regard to women, the charge that she keep silent, that she obey, that she be meek and lowly—all grew out of the fear of the power she exercised at the period these teachings were given—a power which the saints believed prejudicial to good order and good morals. There is more than one profound thinker of our own period who has arraigned her influence—Strindberg and Nietzsche among them. You cannot turn a page of history that the woman is not on it or behind it. She is the most subtle and binding thread in the pattern of Human Life!

For the American Woman of to-day to allow woman's part in the making of this nation to be belittled is particularly unjust and cowardly. The American nation in its good and evil is what it is, as much because of its women as because of its men. The truth of the matter is, there has never been any country, at any time, whatever may have been their social limitations or political disbarments, that women have not ranked with the men in actual capacity and achievement; that is, men and women have risen and fallen together, whatever the apparent conditions. The failure to recognize this is due either to ignorance of facts or to a willful disregard of them; usually it is the former. For instance, one constantly hears to-day the exultant cry that women finally are beginning to take an interest and a part in political and radical discussions. But there has never been a time in this country's history when they were not active factors in such discussion. The women of the American Revolutionary Period certainly challenge sharply the women of to-day, both by their intelligent understanding of political issues and by their sympathetic cooperation in the struggle. It was the letters of women which led to that most important factor in centralizing and instructing pre-revolutionary opinion in New England, the Committee of Correspondence. There were few more powerful political pamphleteers in that period than Mercy Warren. We might very well learn a lesson which we need very much to learn from the way women aided the Revolutionary cause through their power as consumers. As for sacrifice and devotion, that of the woman loses nothing in nobility when contrasted with that of the man.

If we jump fifty years in the nation's history to the beginning of the agitation against slavery, we find women among the first and most daring of the protestants against the institution. It was for the sake of shattering slavery that they broke the silence in public which by order of the Christian Church they had so long kept—an order made, not for the sake of belittling women, but for the sake of establishing order in churches and better insuring the new Christian code of morality. The courage and the radicalism of women of the 30's, 40's, and 50's in this country compare favorably with that of the men and women in any revolutionary period in any country that we may select.

The American woman has played an honorable part in the making of our country, and for this part she should have full credit. If she had been as poor a stick, as downtrodden and ineffective as sometimes painted, she would not be a fit mate for the man beside whom she has struggled, and she would be as utterly unfit for the larger life she desires as the most bigoted misogynist pictures her to be.

Tarbell, "On the Ennobling of the Woman's Business," 1912

How does Tarbell account for the apparent injustices that women have faced and are now challenging?

Moreover, all things considered, she has been no greater sufferer from injustice than man. I do not mean in saying this that she has not had grave and unjust handicaps, legal and social; I mean that when you come to study the comparative situations of men and women as a mass at any time and in any country you will find them more nearly equal than unequal, all things considered. Women have suffered injustice, but parallel have been the injustices men were enduring. It was not the fact that she was a woman that put her at a disadvantage so much as the fact that might made right, and the physically weaker everywhere bore the burden of the day. Go back no further than the beginnings of this Republic and admit all that can be said of the wrong in the laws which prevented a woman controlling the property she had inherited or accumulated by her own efforts, which took from her a proper share in the control of her child,—we must admit, too, the equal enormity of the laws which permitted man to exploit labor in the outrageous way he has. It was not because he was a man that the labor was exploited—it was because he was the weaker in the prevailing system. Woman's case was parallel—she was the weaker in the system. It had always been the case with men and women in the world that he who could took and the devil got the hindermost. The way the laborer's cause has gone hand in hand in this country the last hundred years with the woman's cause is a proof of the point. In the 30's of the nineteenth century, for illustration, the country was torn by a workingman's party which carried on a fierce agitation against banks and monopolies.[1]

Many of its leaders were equally ardent in their support of Women's Rights as they were then understood. The slavery agitation was coupled from the start with the question of Women's Rights. It was injustice that was being challenged—the right of the stronger to put the weaker at a disadvantage for any reason—because he was poor, not rich; black, not white; female, not male,—that is, there has been nothing special to women in the injustice she has suffered except its particular form. Moreover, it was not man alone who was responsible for this injustice. Stronger women have often imposed upon the weak—men and women—as strong men have done. In its essence, it is a human, not a sex, question—this of injustice.

Tarbell challenges the assertion that women have been refused education.

The hesitation of this country in the earlier part of the nineteenth century to accord to women the same educational facilities as to men is often cited as a proof of a deliberate effort to disparage women. But it should not be forgotten that the wisdom of universal male education was hotly in debate. One of the ideals of radical reformers for centuries had been to give to all the illumination of knowledge. But to teach those who did the labor of the world, its peasants and its serfs, was regarded by both Church and State as a folly

---

1. The first organizations by skilled tradesmen and artisans, from the late 1820s to the mid 1830s, were Workingmen's Parties in Northern cities. These groups sought labor and social reforms in city governments.

and a menace. It was the establishment of a pure democracy that forced the experiment of universal free instruction in this country. It has met with opposition at every stage, and there is to-day a Mr. Worldly Wiseman at every corner bewailing the evils it has wrought. He must, too, be a hopeless Candide who can look on our experiment, wonderful and inspiring as it is, and say its results have been the best possible.[2]

It was entirely logical, things beings as they were, that there should have been strong opposition to giving girls the same training in schools as boys. That objection holds good to-day in many reflective minds. He again must be a hopeless optimist who believes that we have worked out the best possible system of education for women. But that there was opposition to giving women the same educational facilities as men was not saying that there was or ever had been a conspiracy on foot to keep her in intellectual limbo because she was a woman. The history of learning shows clearly enough that women have always shared in its rise. In the great revival of the sixteenth century they took an honorable part. "I see the robbers, hangmen, adventurers, hostlers of to-day more learned than the doctors and preacher of my youth," wrote Rabelais, and he added, "why, women and girls have aspired to the heavenly manna of good learning." Whenever aspiration has been in the air, women have responded to it as men have, and have found, as men have found, a way to satisfy their thirst.

To come down to the period which concerns us chiefly, that of our own Republic, it is an utter misrepresentation of the women of the Revolution to claim that they were uneducated. All things considered, they were quite as well educated as the men. The actual achievements of the eminent women produced by the system of training then in vogue is proof enough of the statement. Far and away the best letters by a woman, which have found their way into print in this country, are those of Mrs. John Adams, written late in the eighteenth century and early in the nineteenth. They deserve the permanent place in our literature which they have. But it was a period of good letter writing by women—if weak spelling and feminine spelling was, on the whole, quite as strong as masculine!

Out of that early system of education came the woman who was to write the book which did more to stir the country against slavery than all that ever had been written, Harriet Beecher Stowe. That system produced the scientist, who still represents American women in the mind of the world, Maria Mitchell, the only American woman whose name appears among the names of the world's great scholars inscribed on the Boston Public Library. It produced Dorothea Dix, who for twenty years before the Civil War carried on perhaps the most remarkable investigation of conditions that has ever been made in this country by man or woman,—the one which required the most courage, endurance, and persistency,—her investigation of the then barbaric system for caring—or not caring—for the insane. State after

2. *Candide* or *Optimism*, a novel written in 1759 by French philosopher of the Enlightenment Voltaire, satirizes those who believe that everything happens for good.

state enacted new laws and instituted new methods solely on the showing of this one woman. If there were no other case to offer to the frequent cry that women have never had an influence on legislation, this would be enough. Moreover, this is but the most brilliant example of the kind of work women had been doing from the beginning of the Republic.[3]

To my mind there is no phase of their activities which reveals better the genuineness of their training than the initiative they took in founding schools of advanced grades for girls, and in organizing primary and secondary schools on something like a national scale. Mary Lyon's work for Mt. Holyoke College and Catherine Beecher's for the American Woman's Education Association are the most substantial individual achievements, though they are but types of what many women were doing and what women in general were backing up. It was work of the highest constructive type—original in its conception, full of imagination and idealism, rich in its capacity for growth—a work to fit the aspiration of its day and so full of the future![4]

Now, when conditions are such that a few rise to great eminence from the ordinary ranks of life, it means a good general average. The multitude of women of rare achievements, distinguishing the Revolutionary and post-Revolutionary periods of American history are the best evidences of the seriousness, idealism, and intelligence of the women in general. Their services in the war are part of the traditions of every family whose line runs back to those days. Loyal, spirited, ingenious, and uncomplaining, they are one of the finest proofs in history of the capacity of the women of the mass to respond whole-heartedly to noble ideals,—one of the finest illustrations, too, of the type of service needed from women in great crises. But the rank and file which conducted itself so honorably in the Revolution was not a whit more noble and intelligent than the rank and file of the succeeding period. It would have been impossible ever to have established as promptly as was done the higher and the general schools for girls if women had not given them the support they did, had not been willing, as one great educator of the early part of the nineteenth century has recorded—"to rise up early, to sit up late, to eat the bread of the most rigid economy, that their daughters might be favored with means of improvement superior to what they themselves possessed." And back of this self-denial was what? A desire that life be made easier for the daughter? Not at all—a desire that the daughter be better equipped to "form the character of the future citizen of the Republic."

3. Harriet Beecher Stowe (1811–1896) wrote *Uncle Tom's Cabin* (1852). Maria Mitchell (1816–1889) was an astronomer who discovered a comet, now called Miss Mitchell's comet. Dorothea Dix (1802–1887) was a nurse and activist for humane treatment of the insane.

4. Mary Lyon (1797–1849) established the Mount Holyoke Female Seminary in 1837, now Mount Holyoke College. Catherine Beecher (1800–1878), elder sister of Harriet Beecher Stowe, another advocate for female education, established the Hartford Female Seminary.

It is not alone that justice is wounded by denying women a part in the making of the civilized world—a more immediate wrong is the way the movement for a fuller, freer life for all human beings is hampered. A woman with a masculine chip on her shoulder gives a divided attention to the cause she serves. She complicates her human fight with a sex fight. However good tactics this may have been in the past, and I am far from denying that there were periods it may have been good politics, however poor morals, surely in this country to-day there is no sound reason for introducing such complications into our struggles. The American woman's life is the fullest in its opportunity, all things considered, that any human beings harnessed into a complicated society have ever enjoyed. To keep up the fight against man as the chief hindrance to the realization of her aspiration is merely to perpetuate in the intellectual world that instinct of the female animal to be ever on guard against the male, save in those periods when she is in pursuit of him!

But complicating her problem is not the only injury she does her cause by this ignoring or belittling of woman's part in civilization. She strips herself of suggestion and inspiration –a loss that cannot be reckoned. The past is a wise teacher. There is none that can stir the heart more deeply or give to human affairs such dignity and significance. The meaning of woman's natural business in the world—the part it has played in civilizing humanity—in forcing good morals and good manners, in giving a reason and so a desire for peaceful arts and industries, the place it has had in persuading men and women that only self-restraint, courage, good cheer, and reverence produce the highest types of manhood and womanhood,—this is written on every page of history.

Women need the ennobling influence of the past. They need to understand their integral part in human progress. To slur this over, ignore, or deny it, cripples their powers. It sets them at the foolish effort of enlarging their lives by doing the things man does—not because they are certain that as human beings with a definite task they need—or society needs—these particular services or operations from them, but because they conceive that this alone will prove them equal. The efforts of woman to prove herself equal to man is a work of supererogation. There is nothing he has ever done that she has not proved herself able to do equally well. But rarely is society well served by her undertaking his activities. Moreover, if man is to remain a civilized being, he must be held to his business of producer and protector. She cannot overlook her obligation to keep him up to his part in the partnership, and she cannot wisely interfere too much with that part. The fate of the meddler is common knowledge!

A few women in every country have always and probably always will find work and usefulness and happiness in exceptional tasks. They are sometimes women who are born with what we call "bachelor's souls"—an interesting and sometimes even charming, though always an incomplete, possession! More often they are women who by the bungling machinery of society have been cast aside. There is no reason why these women should be idle, miserable, selfish, or antisocial. There are rich lives for them to work out and endless needs for them to meet.

But they are not the women upon whom society depends; they are not the ones who build the nation. The women who count are those who outnumber them a hundred to one—the women who are at the great business of founding and filling those natural social centers which we call homes. Humanity will rise or fall as that center is strong or weak. It is the human core.

CORNELIA BARNS

"United We Stand," *The Masses*, 1914

Barns (1888–1941) was a political cartoonist for The Masses, *famous for her biting wit. She has called this cartoon "United We Stand. Anti-Suffrage Meeting." What is she saying here about those now deemed worthy of the franchise? Where does she place them?*

SOURCE: *"United We Stand: Anti-Suffrage Meeting," by Cornelia Barns,* The Masses, *November 1914.*

W.E.B. DU BOIS

"Woman Suffrage," Editorial, *The Crisis*, 1915

*The journal of the National Association for the Advancement of Colored People
(NAACP), The Crisis, also included debates over woman suffrage. The following edito-
rial, written in response to a forum on suffrage in an earlier issue, attacks anti positions.
Contrast the anti arguments with those that Du Bois uses to contradict them.*

SOURCE: The Crisis. *Vol. 11, No. 1, 1915. 29–30.*

*T*his month 200,000 Negro voters will be called upon to vote on the question of giving the right of suffrage to women. THE CRISIS sincerely
trusts that everyone of them will vote Yes. But THE CRISIS would not
have them go to the polls without having considered every side of the question.
Intelligence in voting is the only real support of democracy. For this reason we
publish with pleasure Dean Kelly Miller's article against woman suffrage.[1] We trust
that our readers will give it careful attention and that they will compare it with that
marvelous symposium which we had the pleasure to publish in our August number.
Meantime, Dean Miller will pardon us for a word in answer to his argument.

Briefly put, Mr. Miller believes that the bearing and rearing of the young
is a function which makes it practically impossible for women to take any large
part in general, industrial and public affairs; that women are weaker than men;
that women are adequately protected under man's suffrage; that no adequate
results have appeared from woman suffrage and that office-holding by women is
"risky."

All these arguments sound today ancient. If we turn to easily available statistics we find that instead of the women of this country or of any other country
being confined chiefly to childbearing they are as a matter of fact engaged and
engaged successfully in practically every pursuit in which men are engaged. The
actual work of the world today depends more largely upon women upon men.
Consequently this man-ruled world faces an astonishing dilemma: either Woman

---

1. Kelly Miller (1863–1939), a professor of both mathematics and sociology, was Dean of the
College of Arts and Sciences at Howard University at the time of this essay. Like Du Bois,
Miller became a well-known public intellectual, explaining his views in numerous magazines
and journals.

the Worker is doing the world's work successfully or not. If she is not doing it well why do we not take from her the necessity of working? If she is doing it well why not treat her as a worker with a voice in the direction of work?

The statement that woman is weaker than man is sheer rot: It is the same sort of thing that we hear about "darker races" and "lower classes." Difference, either physical or spiritual, does not argue weakness or inferiority. That the average woman is spiritually different from the average man is undoubtedly just as true as the fact that the average white man differs from the average Negro; but this is no reason for disenfranchising the Negro or lynching him. It is inconceivable that any person looking upon the accomplishments of women today in every field of endeavor, realizing their humiliating handicap and the astonishing prejudices which they face and yet seeing despite this that in government, in the professions, in sciences, art and literature and the industries they are leading and dominating forces and growing in power as their emancipation grows, it is inconceivable that any fair-minded person could for a moment talk about a "weaker" sex. The sex of Judith, Candace, Queen Elizabeth, Sojourner Truth and Jane Addams was the merest incident of human function and not a mark of weakness and inferiority.

To say that men protect women with their votes is to overlook the flat testimony of the facts. In the first place there are millions of women who have no natural men protectors: the unmarried, the widowed, the deserted and those who have married failures. To put this whole army incontinently out of court and leave them unprotected and without voice in political life is more than unjust, it is a crime.

There was a day in the world when it was considered that by marriage a woman lost all her individuality as a human soul and simply became a machine for making men. We have outgrown that idea. A woman is just as much a thinking, feeling, acting person after marriage as before. She has opinions and she has a right to have them and she has a right to express them. It is conceivable, of course, for a country to decide that its unit of representation should be the family and that one person in that family should express its will. But by what possible process of rational thought can it be decided that the person to express that will should always be the male, whether he be genius or drunkard, imbecile or captain of industry? The meaning of the twentieth century is the freeing of the individual soul; the soul longest in slavery and still in the most disgusting and indefensible slavery is the soul of womanhood. God give her increased freedom this November!

Mr. Miller is right in saying that the results from woman suffrage have as yet been small but the answer is obvious: the experiment has been small. As for the risks of allowing women to hold office: Are they nearly as great as the risks of allowing working men to hold office loomed once in the eyes of the Intelligent Fearful?

MAX EASTMAN

"Confession of a Suffrage Orator," *The Masses*, 1915

In the following article, Eastman explains his reasons for supporting woman suffrage. For him, the debate goes to the heart of human freedom and development. How, according to Eastman, do debates on suffrage extend beyond women's citizenship to the very foundation of a democratic society?

Activists take note: Eastman has become an experienced "propagandist" for many causes; here he gives you suggestions on how and how not to win followers.

SOURCE: The Masses. *Vol. 7, No. 1, November–December, 1915. Woman's Citizenship Number. 7–9.*

*I*t was never a question of making people believe in the benefits of women's freedom, it was a question of making them *like the idea.* And all the abstract arguments in the world furnished merely a sort of auction ground upon which the kindly beauties of the thing could be exhibited. Aristotle, in his hopeful way, defined man as a "reasonable animal," and the schools have been laboring under that delusion ever since. But man is a voluntary animal, and he knows what he likes and what he dislikes, and that is the greater part of his knowledge. Especially is this true of his opinion upon questions involving sex, because in these matters his native taste is so strong. He will have a multitude of theories and abstract reasons surrounding it, but these are merely put on for the sake of gentility, the way clothes are. Most cultivated people think there is something indecent about a naked preference. I believe, however, that propagandists would fare better, if they were boldly aware that they are always moulding wishes rather than opinions.

There is something almost ludicrous about the attitude of a professional propagandist to his kit of arguments—and in the suffrage movement especially, because the arguments are so many and so old, and so classed and codified, and many of them so false and foolish too. I remember that during the palmiest days of the abstract argument (before California came in and spoiled everything with a big concrete example) I was engaged in teaching, or endeavoring to teach, Logic to a division of Sophomores at Columbia. And there was brought to my attention at that time a book published for use in classes like mine, which contained a codification in logical categories of all the suffrage arguments, both pro and con, and *a priori* and *a posteriori,* and *per accidens* and *per definitionem,* that had ever been advanced since Socrates first advocated the strong-minded woman as a form of moral discipline for her husband. I never found in all my platform wanderings but one suffrage argument that was not in this book, and that I discovered on the lips of an historical native of Troy, New York. It was a woman, she said, who first invented the detachable linen collar, that well-known device for saving a man the trouble of changing his shirt, and though that particular woman is probably dead, her sex remains with its pristine enthusiasm for culture and progress.[1]

But the day of the captious logician, like the day of the roaring orator, is past. What our times respond to is the propagandist who knows how to respect the wishes of other people, and yet show them in a sympathetic way that there is more fun for them, as well as for humanity in general, in the new direction. *Give them an hour's exercise in liking something else*—that is worth all the proofs and refutations in the world. Take that famous proposition that "woman's sphere is the home." A canvass was made at a women's college a while ago to learn the reasons for opposing woman suffrage, and no new ones were found, but among them all this dear old saying had such an overwhelming majority that it amounted to a discovery. It is the eternal type. And how easy to answer, if you grab it crudely with your intellect, imagining it to be an opinion.

"Woman's sphere is the home!" you cry. "Do you know that according to the census of 1910 more than one woman in every five in this country is engaged in gainful employment?

"Woman's sphere is the home! Do you know where your *soap* comes from?

"Woman's sphere is the home! Do you know that in fifty years all the work that women used to do within the four walls of her house has moved out into the—

"Woman's sphere is the home! Do you know that, as a simple matter of fact, the sphere of those women who most need the protection of the government and the laws is *not* home but the factory and the market!

"Why, to say that woman's sphere is the home after the census says it isn't, is like saying the earth is flat after a hundred thousand people have sailed round it!"

Well—such an assault and battery of the intellect will probably silence the gentle idealist for a time, but it will not alter the direction of her will. She never intended to express a statistical opinion, and the next time you see her she will be telling somebody else—for she will not talk to you any more—that "woman's *proper* sphere is the home." In other words, and this is what she said the first time, if you only had the gift of understanding, "I like women whose sphere is the home. My husband likes them, too. And we should both be very unhappy if I had to go to work outside. It doesn't seem charming or beautiful to us."

Now there is a better way to win over a person with such a gift of strong volition and delicate feeling, than to jump down her throat with a satchel full of

---

1. California voters approved woman suffrage in 1911. Eastman suggests that logical arguments do not suffice to convince others to support suffrage.

statistics. I think a propagandist who realized that here was an expression primarily of a human wish, and that these wishes, spontaneous, arbitrary, unreasoned, because reason itself is only their servant, are the divine and unanswerable thing in us all, would respond to her assertion more effectively, as well as more pleasantly.

If logical argument doesn't work, what other strategies does Eastman offer that may galvanize support for suffrage?

The truth is that any reform which associates itself with the name of liberty, or democracy, is peculiarly adapted to this more persuasive kind of propaganda. For liberty does not demand that any given person's tastes or likings as to a way of life be reformed. It merely demands that these should not be erected into a dogma, and inflicted as morality or law upon everybody else. It demands that all persons should be made free in the pursuit of their own tastes or likings.

Thus the most ardent suffragist might begin by answering our domestic idealist—"Well, I suppose it is a charming and beautiful thing for you to stay in your home, since you are happy there. I myself have a couple of neighbors who have solved their problem of life that way too, and I never have an argument with them. Why? Because they recognize that all people's problems are not to be solved in the same way. They recognize the varieties of human nature. They recognize that each one of us has a unique problem of life to solve, and he or she must be made free to solve it in her own unique way. That is democracy. That is the liberty of man. That is what universal suffrage means, and would accomplish, so far as political changes can accomplish it. Let us agree that woman's proper sphere is the home, whenever it is. But there are many women who, on account of their natural disposition perhaps, or perhaps on account of their social or financial situation, cannot function happily in that sphere; and they are only hindered in the wholesome and fruitful solution of their lives by the dogma which you and your society hold over them, and which is crystallized and entrenched as political inequality by the fundamental law."

Thus our agitation of the woman question would appear to arise, not out of our own personal taste in feminine types, but out of our very recognition of the fact that tastes differ. We would propagandize, not because we are cranks and have a fixed idea about what everybody else ought to become, and what must be done about it at once, but because we are trying to accept variety and the natural inclinations of all sorts of people as, by presumption at least, self-justified and divine. We want them all to be free.

Such is the peculiar advantage that the propaganda of liberty has over all the evangelical enthusiasms. It does not at the first gasp ask a man to mortify his nature. It merely asks him to cease announcing his own spontaneous inclinations as the type and exemplar of angelic virtue, and demanding that everybody else be like him. It tries to remove another old negative dogmatic incubus from the shoulders of life, aspiring toward variety and realization. That is what the suffrage propaganda is doing.

It would be folly to pretend, however, that the principle of equal liberty is the only motive behind the suffrage movement. I have said that it is the primary one. It is at least the broadest, the surest, the one upon which the conversion of a person whose taste opposes yours can be most graciously introduced.

But there is yet another way of changing a person's wish, and that is to show him that he himself has deeper wishes which conflict with it. And there is one deep wish in particular that almost all women, and most men possess, and that is a wish for the welfare and advancement of their children. And just as "Woman's sphere is the home" typifies the voluntary force opposing woman suffrage, so "Women owe it to their children to develop their own powers," typifies the force that favors it.

What benefits might suffrage bring American women? How might it transform them?

Universal citizenship has meant in human history universal education. That has been, next to a certain precious rudiment of liberty, its chief value. That will be its chief value to women for a long time to come. And by education I do not mean merely political education. I do not mean that it will awaken in women what we call a "civic consciousness," though it will, I suppose, and that is a good thing. Then that by giving to women a higher place in our social esteem, it will promote their universal development.

We are not educated very much by anything we study in school or see written on the blackboard. That does not determine what we grow up to be. The thing that determines what we grow up to be is the natural expectations of those around us. If society expects a girl to become a fully developed, active and intelligent individual, she will probably do it. If society expects her to remain a doll-baby all her life, she will make a noble effort to do that. In either case she will not altogether succeed, for there are hereditary limitations, but the responsibility for the main trend of the result is with the social conscience.

> "Sugar and spice and everything nice,
> That is what little girls are made of;
> Snips and snails and puppy-dogs' tails,
> That is what little boys are made of."

There is an example of what has been educating us. That kind of baby-talk has done more harm than all the dynamite that was ever let off in the history of the world. You might as well put poison in the milk.

All that is to be ended. And this is the chief thing we expect of women's citizenship. It will formulate in the public mind the higher ideal that shall develop the young girls of the future. They will no longer grow up to be, outside the years of motherhood, mere drudges or parlor ornaments. They will no longer try to satisfy their ambitions by seeing who can parade the most extreme buffooneries of contemporary fashion on the public highway. They will grow up to be interested and living individuals, and satisfy their ambitions only with the highest prizes of adventure and achievement that life offers.

And the benefit of that will fall upon us all—but chiefly upon the children of these women when they are mothers. For if we are going anywhere that a sane idealism would have us go, we must first stop corrupting the young. Only a developed and fully constituted individual is fit to be the mother of a child. Only one who has herself made the most of the present, is fit to hold in her arms the hope of the future.

We hear a good deal about "child-welfare" in these days, and we hear the business of child-welfare advanced as one of the arguments for woman suffrage. To me it is almost the heart of the arguments, but it works in my mind a little differently from what it does in the minds of the people who write the child-welfare pamphlets. I do not want women to have, for the sake of their children, the control of the milk-supply and the food laws, half so much as I want them to have, for the sake of their children, all the knowledge-by-experience that they can possibly get. That is the vital connection between child-welfare and woman suffrage—that is the deeper ideal. No woman is fit to bring children into this world until she knows to the full the rough actual character of the world into which she is bringing them. And she will never know that until we lift from her—in her own growing years—the repressive prejudice that expresses itself and maintains itself in refusing to make her a citizen.

A man who trains horses up in western New York put this to me very strongly. "If you're going to breed race-horses," he said, "you don't pick out your stallions on a basis of speed and endurance, and your mares according to whether they have sleek hides and look pretty when they hang their heads over the pasture fence. And if you're going to raise intelligent citizens you'll have to give them intelligent citizens for mothers." I do not know whether he was aware that an actual tendency to *select* the more intelligent, rather than a mere training of the intelligence of all, is the main force in racial evolution.

But that is what he said. And, either way, it is a piece of cold scientific fact. The babies of this world suffer a good deal more from silly mothers than they do from sour milk. And any change in political forms, however superficial from the standpoint of economic justice, that will increase the breadth of experience, the sagacity, the humor, the energetic and active life-interest of mothers, can only be regarded as a profound historic revolution. In these broad effects upon the progress of liberty and life, not in any political result of equal suffrage, are to be found an object of desire which can rival and replace the ideal that opposes it. They are the material for the propaganda of the will. And while we noisy orators are filling the air with syllogisms of justice, and prophecies of the purification of politics, and the end of child labor, and what women will do to wars, and the police department, and the sweat-shops, and the street-cleaning department, and the milk wagons, and the dairy farms, and how they will reform the cows when they come into their rights, we ought to remember in our sober hearts that those large warm human values, which have nothing to do with logic or politics or reform, are what will gradually bend the wishes of men toward a new age.

JANE ADDAMS

"Why Women Should Vote," *Woman Suffrage: History, Arguments, And Results*, 1916

This essay was included in Woman Suffrage, *a handbook of pro-suffrage arguments designed to help suffrage organizers plan their speeches. What is the argument that Addams provides? To whom would this argument appeal?*

Imagine a conversation between the Stanton of the 1892 "Solitude of Self" and the Addams of this pamphlet. Both favor suffrage for women. How do the reasons for their positions differ?

SOURCE: *Frances M. Bjorkman and Annie G. Porritt.* Woman Suffrage: History, Arguments and Results: A collection of six popular booklets covering practically the entire field of suffrage claims and evidence. Designed especially for the convenience of suffrage speakers and writers and for the use of debaters and libraries. *Revised edition, March 1916. New York: National Woman Suffrage Publishing Co., Inc., 1916. Hathitrust Digital Library. http://www.hathitrust.org/*

For many generations it has been believed that woman's place is within the walls of her own home, and it is indeed impossible to imagine the time when her duty there shall be ended or to forecast any social change which shall release her from that paramount obligation.

1.

This paper is an attempt to show that many women to-day are failing to discharge their duties to their own households properly simply because they do not perceive that as society grows more complicated, it is necessary that woman shall extend her sense of responsibility to many things outside of her own home if she would continue to preserve the home in its entirety. One could illustrate in many ways. A woman's simplest duty, one would say, is to keep her house clean and whole-some and to feed her children properly. Yet if she lives in a tenement house, as so many of my neighbors do, she cannot fulfill these simple obligations by her own efforts because she is utterly dependent upon the city administration for the conditions which render decent living possible. Her basement will not be dry, her stairways will not be fireproof, her house will not be provided with sufficient windows to give light and air, nor will it be equipped with sanitary plumbing, unless the Public Works Department sends inspectors who

Addams emphasizes that American society has changed with urbanization, industrialization, and immigration. How must women extend their idea of their "home" and their domestic duties?

constantly insist that these elementary decencies be provided. Women who live in the country sweep their own dooryards and may either feed the refuse of the table to a flock of chickens or allow it innocently to decay in the open air and sunshine. In a crowded city quarter, however, if the street is not cleaned by the city authorities, no amount of private sweeping will keep the tenement free from grime; if the garbage is not properly collected and destroyed a tenement house mother may see her children sicken and die of diseases from which she alone is powerless to shield them, although her tenderness and devotion are unbounded. She cannot even secure untainted meat for her household, she cannot provide fresh fruit, unless the meat has been inspected by city officials, and the decayed fruit, which is so often placed upon sale in the tenement districts, has been destroyed in the interests of public health. In short, if woman would keep on with her old business of caring for her house and rearing her children she will have to have some conscience in regard to public affairs lying quite outside of her immediate household. The individual conscience and devotion are no longer effective.

2.

Chicago one spring had a spreading contagion of scarlet fever just at the time that the school nurses had been discontinued because business men had pronounced them too expensive. If the women who sent their children to the schools had been sufficiently public-spirited and had been provided with an implement through which to express that public spirit they would have insisted that the schools be supplied with nurses in order that their own children might be protected from contagion. In other words, if women would effectively continue their old avocations they must take part in the slow upbuilding of that code of legislation which is alone sufficient to protect the home from the dangers incident to modern life. One might instance the many deaths of children from contagious diseases the germs of which had been carried in tailored clothing. Country doctors testify as to the outbreak of scarlet fever in remote neighborhoods each autumn, after the children have begun to wear the winter overcoats and cloaks which have been sent from infected city sweatshops. That their mothers charter was the unexpected enthusiasm and help which came from large groups of foreign-born women. The Scandinavian women represented in many Lutheran Church societies said quite simply that in the old country they had had the municipal franchise upon the same basis as men for many years; all the women living under the British Government, in England, Australia or Canada, pointed out that Chicago women were asking now for what the British women had long ago. But the most unexpected response came from the foreign colonies in which women had never heard such problems discussed and took the prospect of the municipal ballot as a simple device—which it is—to aid them in their daily struggle with adverse city conditions. The Italian women said that the men engaged in railroad construction were away all summer and did not know anything about their household difficulties. Some of them came to Hull-House one day to talk over the possibility of a public wash-house. They do not like to wash in their own tenements; they had never seen a washing-tub until they came to America, and find it very difficult to use it in the restricted space of their little kitchens and to hang the clothes within the house to dry. They say that in the Italian villages the women all go to the streams together; in the town they go to the public wash-house; and washing, instead of being lonely and disagreeable, is made pleasant by cheerful conversation. It is asking a great deal of these women to change suddenly all their habits of living, and their contention that the tenement house kitchen is too small for laundry work is well taken. If women in Chicago knew the needs of the Italian colony they would realize that any change bringing cleanliness and fresh air into the Italian household would be a very sensible and hygienic measure. It is, perhaps, asking a great deal that the members of the City Council should understand this, but surely a comprehension of the needs of these women and efforts toward ameliorating their lot might be regarded as matters of municipal obligation on the part of voting women.

3.

The same thing is true of the Jewish women in their desire for covered markets which have always been a municipal provision in Russia and Poland. The vegetables piled high upon the wagons standing in the open markets of Chicago become covered with dust and soot. It seems to these women a violation of the most rudimentary decencies and they sometimes say quite simply: "If women had anything to say about it they would change all that."

4.

If women follow only the lines of their traditional activities, here are certain primary duties which belong to even the most conservative women, and which no one woman or group of women can adequately discharge unless they join the more general movements looking toward social amelioration through legal enactment.

5.

The first of these, of which this article has already treated, is woman's responsibility for the members of her own household that they may be properly fed and clothed and surrounded by hygienic conditions. The second is a responsibility for the education of children: (a) that they may be provided with good books; (b) that they may be kept free from vicious influences on the street; (c) that when working they may be protected by adequate child-labor legislation.

6.

(a) The duty of a woman toward the schools which her children attend is so obvious that it is not necessary to dwell upon it. But even this simple obligation cannot be effectively carried out without some form of social organization, as the mothers' school clubs and mothers' congresses testify, and to which the most conservative women belong because they feel the need of wider reading and discussion concerning the many problems of childhood. It is, therefore, perhaps natural that the public should have been more willing to accord a vote to women in school matters than in any other, and yet women have never been members of a Board of Education in sufficient numbers to influence largely actual school curriculi. If they had been, kindergartens, domestic science courses and school playgrounds would be far more numerous than they are. More than one woman has been convinced of the need of the ballot by the futility of her efforts in persuading a business man that young children need nurture in something besides the three r's. Perhaps, too, only women realize the influence which the school might exert upon the home if a proper adaptation to actual needs were considered. An Italian girl who has had lessons in cooking at the public school will help her mother to connect the entire family with American food and household habits. That the mother has never baked bread in Italy—only mixed it in her own house and then taken it out to the village oven—makes it all the more necessary that her daughter should understand the complications of a cooking-stove. The same thing is true of the girl who learns to sew in the public school, and more than anything else, perhaps, of the girl who receives the first simple instruction in the care of little children, that skillful care which every tenement house baby requires if he is to be pulled through his second summer. The only time, to my knowledge, that lessons in the care of children were given in the public schools of Chicago was one summer when the vacation schools were being managed by a volunteer body of women. The instruction was eagerly received by the Italian girls, who had been "little mothers" to younger children ever since they could remember.

* * *

8.

(b) But women are also beginning to realize that children need attention outside of school hours; that much of the petty vice in cities is merely the love of pleasure gone wrong, the over-strained boy or girl seeking improper recreation and excitement. It is obvious that a little study of the needs of children, a sympathetic understanding of the conditions under which they go astray, might save hundreds of them. Women traditionally have had an opportunity to observe the plays of children and the needs of youth, and yet in Chicago, at least, they had done singularly little in this vexed problem of juvenile delinquency until they helped to inaugurate the Juvenile Court movement a dozen years ago. The Juvenile Court Committee, made up largely of women, paid the salaries of the probation officers connected with the court for the first six years of its existence, and after the salaries were cared for by the county the same organization turned itself into a Juvenile Protective League, and through a score of paid officers are doing valiant service in minimizing some of the dangers of city life which boys and girls encounter.

* * *

10.

(c) As the education of her children has been more and more transferred to the school, so that even children four years old go to the kindergarten, the woman has been left in a household of constantly-narrowing interests, not only because the children are away, but also because one industry after another is slipping from the household into the factory. Ever since steam power has been applied to the processes of weaving and spinning woman's traditional work has been carried on largely outside of the home. The clothing and household linen are not only spun and woven, but also usually sewed by machinery; the preparation of many foods has also passed into the factory and necessarily a certain number of women have been obliged to follow their work there, although it is doubtful, in spite of the large number of factory girls, whether women now are doing as large a proportion of the world's work as they used to do. Because many thousands of those working in factories and shops are girls between the ages of fourteen and twenty-two, there is a necessity that older women should be interested in the conditions of industry. The very fact that these girls are not going to remain in industry permanently makes it more important that some one should see to it that they shall not be incapacitated for their future family life because they work for exhausting hours and under insanitary conditions.

11.

If woman's sense of obligation had enlarged as the industrial conditions changed she might naturally and almost imperceptibly have inaugurated movements for social amelioration in the line of factory legislation and shop sanitation. That she has not done so is doubtless due to the fact that her conscience is slow to recognize any obligation outside of her own family circle, and because she was so absorbed in her own household that she failed to see what the conditions outside actually were. It would be interesting to know how far the consciousness that she had no vote and could not change matters operated in this direction. After all, we see only those things to which our attention has been drawn, we feel responsibility for those things which are brought to us as matters of responsibility. If conscientious women were convinced that it was a civic duty to be informed in regard to these grave industrial affairs, and then to express the conclusions which they had reached by depositing a piece of paper in a ballot-box, one cannot imagine that they would shirk simply because the action ran counter to old traditions.

12.

To those of my readers who would admit that although woman has no right to shirk her old obligations, that all of these measures could be secured more easily through her influence upon the men of her family than through the direct use of the ballot, I should like to tell a little story. I have a friend in Chicago who is the mother of four sons and the grandmother of twelve grandsons who are voters. She is a woman of wealth, of secured social position, of sterling character and clear intelligence, and may, therefore, quite fairly be cited as a "woman of influence." Upon one of her recent birthdays, when she was asked how she had kept so young, she promptly replied: "Because I have always advocated at least one unpopular cause." It may have been in pursuance of this policy that for many years she has been an ardent advocate of free silver, although her manufacturing family are all Republicans![1] I happened to call at her house on the day that Mr. McKinley was elected President against Mr. Bryan for the first time. I found my friend much disturbed. She said somewhat bitterly that she had at last discovered what the much-vaunted influence of woman was worth; that she had implored each one of her sons and grandsons; had entered into endless arguments and moral appeals to induce one of them to represent her convictions by voting for Mr. Bryan; that, although sincerely devoted to her, each one had assured her that his convictions forced him to vote the Republican ticket! She said that all she had been able to secure was the promise from one of the grandsons, for whom she had an especial tenderness because he bore her husband's name, that he would not vote at all. He could not vote for Bryan, but out of respect for her feeling he would refrain from voting for McKinley. My friend said that for many years she had suspected that women could influence men only in regard to those things in which men were not deeply concerned, but when it came to persuading a man to a woman's view in affairs of politics or business it was absolutely useless. I contended that a woman had no right to persuade a man to vote against his own convictions; that I respected the men of her family for following their own judgment regardless of the appeal which the honored head of the house had made to their chivalric devotion. To this she replied that she would agree with that point of view when a woman had the same opportunity as a man to register

Couldn't women use moral persuasion over male voters just as well as vote themselves?

---

1. Addams refers here to the 1896 presidential campaign between William McKinley (R) and William Jennings Bryan (D). One issue in that campaign was whether to keep the gold standard as the basis for the U.S. monetary system or shift to silver; the latter was expected to permit a greater distribution of wealth.

her convictions by vote. I believed then as I do now, that nothing is gained when independence of judgment is assailed by "influence," sentimental or otherwise, and that we test advancing civilization somewhat by our power to respect differences and by our tolerance of another's honest conviction.

13.

This is, perhaps, the attitude of many busy women who would be glad to use the ballot to further public measures in which they are interested and for which they have been working for years. It offends the taste of such a woman to be obliged to use indirect "influence" when she is accustomed to well-bred, open action in other affairs, and she very much resents the time spent in persuading a voter to take her point of view, and possibly to give up his own, quite as honest and valuable as hers, although different because resulting from a totally different experience. Public-spirited women who wish to use the ballot, as I know them, do not wish to do the work of men nor to take over men's affairs. They simply want an opportunity to do their own work and to take care of those affairs which naturally and historically belong to women, but which are constantly being overlooked and slighted in our political institutions. In a complex community like the modern city all points of view need to be represented; the resultants of diverse experiences need to be pooled if the community would make for sane and balanced progress. If it would meet fairly each problem as it arises, whether it be connected with a freight tunnel having to do largely with business men, or with the increasing death rate among children under five years of age, a problem in which women are vitally concerned, or with the question of more adequate streetcar transfers, in which both men and women might be said to be equally interested, it must not ignore the judgments of its entire adult population. To turn the administration of our civic affairs wholly over to men may mean that the American city will continue to push forward in its commercial and industrial development, and continue to lag behind in those things which make a City healthful and beautiful. After all, woman's traditional function has been to make her dwelling-place both clean and fair. Is that dreariness in city life, that lack of domesticity which the humblest farm dwelling presents, due to a withdrawal of one of the naturally co-operating forces? If women have in any sense been responsible for the gentler side of life which softens and blurs some of its harsher conditions, may they not have a duty to perform in our American cities? In closing, may I recapitulate that if woman would fulfill her traditional responsibility to her own children; if she would educate and protect from danger factory children who must find their recreation on the street; if she would bring the cultural forces to bear upon our materialistic civilization; and if she would do it all with the dignity and directness fitting one who carries on her immemorial duties, then she must bring herself to the use of the ballot—that latest implement for self-government. May we not fairly say that American women need this implement in order to preserve the home?

DORIS STEVENS

"A Militant General—Alice Paul," *Jailed For Freedom*, 1920

Stevens recalls her early years in the suffrage movement working with Alice Paul, whom she sees as the successor to Susan B. Anthony. What personal characteristics as well as political strategies does Stevens highlight to explain the success of Paul's leadership?

What strategies could you learn from Alice Paul to help you support your cause in this game?

SOURCE: Jailed for Freedom. *New York: Boni and Liveright, 1920.*

Most people conjure up a menacing picture when a person is called not only a general, but a militant one. In appearance Alice Paul is anything but menacing. Quiet, almost mouse-like, this frail young Quakeress sits in silence and baffles you with her contradictions. Large, soft, gray eyes that strike you with a positive impact make you feel the indescribable force and power behind them. A mass of soft brown hair, caught easily at the neck, makes the contour of her head strong and graceful. Tiny, fragile hands that look more like an X-ray picture of hands, rest in her lap in Quakerish pose. Her whole atmosphere when she is not in action is one of strength and quiet determination. In action she is swift, alert, almost panther-like in her movements. Dressed always in simple frocks, preferably soft shades of purple, she conforms to an individual style and taste of her own rather than to the prevailing vogue.

I am going recklessly on to try to tell what I think about Alice Paul. It is difficult, for when I begin to put it down on paper, I realize how little we know about this laconic person, and yet how abundantly we feel her power, her will and her compelling leadership. In an instant and vivid reaction, I am either congealed or inspired; exhilarated or depressed; sometimes even exasperated, but always moved. I have seen her very presence in headquarters change in the twinkling of an eye the mood of fifty people. It is not through their affections that she moves them, but through a naked force, a vital force which is indefinable but of which one simply cannot be unaware. Aiming primarily at the intellect of an audience or an individual, she almost never fails to win an emotional allegiance.

I shall never forget my first contact with her. I tell it here as an illustration of what happened to countless women who came in touch with her to remain under her leadership to the end. I had come to Washington to take part in the demonstration on the Senate in July, 1913, en route to a much-needed, as I thought, holiday in the Adirondacks.

"Can't you stay on and help us with a hearing next week?" said Miss Paul.

"I'm sorry," said I, "but I have promised to join a party of friends in the mountains for a summer holiday and . . ."

"Holiday?" said she, looking straight at me. Instantly ashamed at having mentioned such an illegitimate excuse, I murmured something about not having had one since before entering college.

"But can't you stay?" she said.

I was lost. I knew I would stay. As a matter of fact, I stayed through the heat of a Washington summer, returned only long enough at the end of the summer to close up my work in state suffrage and came back to join the group at Washington. And it was years before I ever mentioned a holiday again.

Frequently she achieved her end without even a single word of retort. Soon after Miss Paul came to Washington in 1913, she went to call on a suffragist in that city to ask her to donate some funds toward the rent of headquarters in the Capital. The woman sighed. "I thought when Miss Anthony died," she said, "that all my troubles were at an end. She used to come to me for money for a federal amendment and I always told her it was wrong to ask for one, and that besides we would never get it. But she kept right on coming. Then when she died we didn't hear any more about an amendment. And now you come again saying the same things Miss Anthony said."

Miss Paul listened, said she was sorry and departed. Very shortly a check arrived at headquarters to cover a month's rent.

A model listener, Alice Paul has unlimited capacity for letting the other person relieve herself of all her objections without contest. Over and over again I have heard this scene enacted.

"Miss Paul, I have come to tell you that you are all wrong about this federal amendment business. I don't believe in it. Suffrage should come slowly but surely by the states. And although I have been a life-long suffragist, I just want to tell you not to count on me, for feeling as I do, I cannot give you any help."

A silence would follow. Then Miss Paul would say ingenuously, "Have you a half hour to spare?"

"I guess so," would come slowly from the protestant. "Why?"

"Won't you please sit down right here and put the stamps on these letters? We have to get them in the mail by noon."

"But I don't believe . . ."

"Oh, that's all right. These letters are going to women probably a lot of whom feel as you do. But some of them will want to come to the meeting to hear our side."

By this time Miss Paul would have brought a chair, and that ended the argument. The woman would stay and humbly proceed to stick on endless stamps. Usually she would come back, too, and before many days would be an ardent worker for the cause against which she thought herself invincible.

Once the state president of the conservative suffrage forces in Ohio with whom I had worked the previous year wrote me a letter pointing out what madness it was to talk of winning the amendment in Congress "this session," and adding that "nobody but a fool would ever think of it, let alone speak of it publicly." She was wise in politics; we were nice, eager, young girls, but pretty ignorant—that was the gist of her remonstrance. My vanity was aroused. Not wishing to be called "mad" or "foolish" I sat down and answered her in a friendly spirit, with the sole object of proving that we were wiser than she imagined. I had never discussed this point with anybody, as I had been in Washington only a few months and it had never occurred to me that we were not right to talk of getting the amendment in that particular session. But I answered my patronizing friend, in effect, that of course we were not fools, that we knew we would not get the amendment that session, but we saw no reason for not demanding it at once and taking it when we got it.

When Miss Paul saw the carbon of that letter she said quietly, pointing to the part where I had so nobly defended our sagacity, "You must never say that again and never put it on paper." Seeing my embarrassment, she hastened to explain. "You see, we can get it this session if enough women care sufficiently to demand it now."

Alice Paul brought back to the fight that note of immediacy which had gone with the passing of Miss Anthony's leadership. She called a halt on further pleading, wheedling, proving, praying. It was as if she had bidden women stand erect, with confidence in themselves and in their own judgments, and compelled them to be self-respecting enough to dare to put their freedom first, and so determine for themselves the day when they should be free. Those who had a taste of begging under the old regime and who abandoned it for demanding, know how fine and strong a thing it is to realize that you must take what is yours and not waste your energy proving that you are or will some day be worthy of a gift of power from your masters. On that glad day of discovery you have first freed yourself to fight for freedom. Alice Paul gave to thousands of women the essence of freedom.

And there was something so cleansing about the way in which she renovated ideas and processes, emotions and instincts. Her attack was so direct, so clear, so simple and unafraid. And her resistance had such a fine quality of strength.

Sometimes it was a roaring politician who was baffled by this non-resistant force. I have heard many an irate one come into her office in the early days to tell her how to run the woman's campaign, and struggle in vain to arouse her to combat. Having begun a tirade, honor would compel him to see it through even without help from a silent adversary. And so he would get more and more noisy until it would seem as if one lone shout from him might be enough to blow away the frail object of his attack. Ultimately he would be forced to retire, perhaps in the face of a serene smile, beaten and angered that he had been able to make so little impression. And many the delicious remark and delightful quip afterward at his expense!

Her gentle humor is of the highest quality. If only her opponents could have seen her amusement at their hysteria. At the very moment they were denouncing some plan of action and calling her "fanatical" and "hysterical" she would fairly beam with delight to see how well her plan had worked. Her intention had been to arouse them to just that state of mind, and how admirably they were living up to the plan. The hysteria was all on their side. She coolly sat back in her chair and watched their antics under pressure.

"But don't you know," would come another thundering one, "that this will make the Democratic leaders so hostile that . . ."

The looked-for note of surprise never came. She had counted ahead on all this and knew almost to the last shade the reaction that would follow from both majority and minority leaders. All this had been thoroughly gone over, first with herself, then with her colleagues. All the "alarms" had been rung. The male politician could not understand why his well-meaning and generously-offered advice caused not a ripple and not a change in plan. Such calm unconcern he could not endure. He was accustomed to emotional panics. He was not accustomed to a leader who had weighed every objection, every attack and counted the cost accurately.

Her ability to marshal arguments for keeping her own followers in line was equally marked. A superficial observer would rush into headquarters with, "Miss Paul, don't you think it was a great tactical mistake to force President Wilson at this time to state his position on the amendment? Will it not hurt our campaign to have it known that he is against us?"

"It is the best thing that could possibly happen to us. If he is against us, women should know it. They will be aroused to greater action if he is not allowed to remain silent upon something in which he does not believe. It will make it easier for us to campaign against him when the time comes."

And another time a friend of the cause would suggest, "Would it not have been better not to have tried for planks in party platforms, since we got such weak ones?"

"Not at all. We can draw the support of women with greater ease from a party which shows a weak hand on suffrage, than from one which hides its opposition behind silence."

She had always to combat the fear of the more timid ones who felt sure with each new wave of disapproval that we would be submerged. "Now, I have been a supporter of yours every step of the way," a "fearful" one would say, "but this is really going a little too far. I was in the Senate gallery to-day when two suffrage senators in speeches denounced the pickets and their suffrage banners. They said that we were setting suffrage back and that something ought to be done about it."

* * *

"Exactly so," would come the ready answer from Miss Paul. "And they will do something about it only if we continue to make them uncomfortable enough.

Of course even suffrage senators will object to our pickets and our banners because they do not want attention called to their failure to compel the Administration to act. They know that as friends of the measure their responsibility is greater." And the "fearful" one was usually convinced and made stronger.

I remember so well when the situation was approaching its final climax in Washington. Men and women, both, came to Miss Paul with, "This is terrible! Seven months' sentence is impossible. You must stop! You cannot keep this up!"

With an unmistakable note of triumph in her voice Miss Paul would answer, "Yes, it is terrible for us, but not nearly so terrible as for the government. The Administration has fired its heaviest gun. From now on we shall win and they will lose."

Stevens refers here to the imprisonment of suffragists in 1917 for picketing the White House.

Most of the doubters had by this time banished their fears and had come to believe with something akin to superstition that she could never be wrong, so swiftly and surely, did they see her policies and her predictions on every point vindicated before their eyes.

She has been a master at concentration, a master strategist—a great general. With passionate beliefs on all important social questions, she resolutely set herself against being seduced into other paths. Far from being naturally an ascetic, she has disciplined herself into denials and deprivations, cultural and recreational, to pursue her objective with the least possible waste of energy. Not that she did not want above all else to do this thing. She did. But doing it she had to abandon the easy life of a scholar and the aristocratic environment of a cultured, prosperous, Quaker family, of Moorestown, New Jersey, for the rigors of a ceaseless drudgery and frequent imprisonment. A flaming idealist, conducting the fight with the sternest kind of realism, a mind attracted by facts, not fancies, she has led fearlessly and with magnificent ruthlessness. Thinking, thinking day and night of her objective and never retarding her pace a moment until its accomplishment, I know no modern woman leader with whom to compare her. I think she must possess many of the same qualities that Lenin does, according to authentic portraits of him— cool, practical, rational, sitting quietly at a desk and counting the consequences, planning the next move before the first one is finished. And if she has demanded the ultimate of her followers, she has given it herself. Her ability to get women to work and never to let them stop is second only to her own unprecedented capacity for work.

Alice Paul came to leadership still in her twenties, but with a broad cultural equipment. Degrees from Swarthmore, the University of Pennsylvania, and special study abroad in English universities had given her a scholarly background in history, politics, and sociology. In these studies she had specialized, writing her doctor's thesis on the status of women. She also did factory work in English industries and there acquired first hand knowledge of the industrial position of women. In the midst of this work the English militant movement caught her imagination and she abandoned her studies temporarily to join that movement and go to prison with the English suffragists.

Convinced that the English women were fighting the battle for the women of the world, she returned to America fresh from their struggle, to arouse American women to action. She came bringing her gifts and concentration to this one struggle. She came with that inestimable asset, youth, and, born of youth, indomitable courage to carry her point in spite of scorn and misrepresentation.

Among the thousands of telegrams sent Miss Paul the day the amendment finally passed Congress was this interesting message from Walter Clark, Chief Justice of the Supreme Court of North Carolina, Southern Democrat, Confederate Veteran and distinguished jurist:

> "Will you permit me to congratulate you upon the great triumph in which you have been so important a factor? Your place in history is assured. Some years ago when I first met you I predicted that your name would be written 'on the dusty roll the ages keep.' There were politicians, and a large degree of public sentiment, which could only be won by the methods you adopted. . . . It is certain that, but for you, success would have been delayed for many years to come."

CRYSTAL EASTMAN

"Now We Can Begin," *The Liberator*, 1920

The House of Representatives passed the bill advocating the 19th Amendment (woman suffrage) on May 21, 1919. On June 4, the initiative went to the Senate, where it also passed. The next step was ratification by two-thirds of the states. Tennessee was the last of the needed 36 states to ratify the amendment.

Although Crystal Eastman is writing here after the suffrage amendment passed in 1920, her essay articulates the view of suffrage that many Villagers espoused throughout the 1910s: as a first step toward a larger movement for "women's freedom."

What is Eastman's feminist vision for the future? What does she call for that goes well beyond the demand of "votes for women?"

SOURCE: The Liberator. *Issue 33, December, 1920. 23–24.*

Most women will agree that August 23, the day when the Tennessee legislature finally enacted the Federal suffrage amendment, is a day to begin with, not a day to end with. Men are saying perhaps "Thank God, this everlasting woman's fight is over!" But women, if I know them, are saying, "Now at last we can begin." In fighting for the right to vote most women have tried to be either non-committal or thoroughly respectable on every other subject. Now they can say what they are really after; and what they are after, in common with all the rest of the struggling world, is freedom.

Freedom is a large word.

Many feminists are socialists, many are communists, not a few are active leaders in these movements. But the true feminist, no matter how far to the left she may be in the revolutionary movement, sees the woman's battle as distinct in its objects and different in its methods from the workers' battle for industrial freedom. She knows, of course, that the vast majority of women as well as men are without property, and are of necessity bread and butter slaves under a system of society which allows the very sources of life to be privately owned by a few, and she counts herself a loyal soldier in the working-class army that is marching to overthrow that system. But as a feminist she also knows that the whole of woman's slavery is not summed up in the profit system, nor her complete emancipation assured by the downfall of capitalism.

How does Eastman address the belief that economic social change will bring about women's freedom?

Woman's freedom, in the feminist sense, can be fought for and conceivably won before the gates open into industrial democracy. On the other hand, woman's freedom, in the feminist sense, is not inherent in the communist ideal. All feminists are familiar with the revolutionary leader who "can't see" the woman's movement. "What's the matter with the women? My wife's all right," he says. And his wife, one usually finds, is raising his children in a Bronx flat or a dreary suburb, to which he returns occasionally for food and sleep when all possible excitement and stimulus have been wrung from the fight. If we should graduate into communism tomorrow this man's attitude to his wife would not be changed. The proletarian dictatorship may or may not free women. We must begin now to enlighten the future dictators.

What, then, is "the matter with women"? What is the problem of women's freedom? It seems to me to be this: how to arrange the world so that women can be human beings, with a chance to exercise their infinitely varied gifts in infinitely varied ways, instead of being destined by the accident of their sex to one field of activity—housework and child-raising. And second, if and when they choose housework and child-raising, to have that occupation recognized by the world as work, requiring a definite economic reward and not merely entitling the performer to be dependent on some man.

Look at Eastman's understanding of feminism and the steps that she advocates to bring it to fruition.

This is not the whole of feminism, of course, but it is enough to begin with. "Oh, don't begin with economics," my friends often protest, "Woman does not live by bread alone. What she needs first of all is a free soul." And I can agree that women will never be great until they achieve a certain emotional freedom, a strong healthy egotism, and some un-personal sources of joy—that in this inner sense we cannot make woman free by changing her economic status. What we can do, however, is to create conditions of outward freedom in which a free woman's soul can be born and grow. It is these outward conditions with which an organized feminist movement must concern itself.

Freedom of choice in occupation and individual economic independence for women: How shall we approach this next feminist objective? First, by breaking down all remaining barriers, actual as well as legal, which make it difficult for women to enter or succeed in the various professions, to go into and get on in business, to learn trades and practice them, to join trades unions. Chief among these remaining barriers is inequality in pay. Here the ground is already broken. This is the easiest part of our program.

Second, we must institute a revolution in the early training and education of both boys and girls. It must be womanly as well as manly to earn your own living, to stand on your own feet. And it must be manly as well as womanly to know how to cook and sew and clean and take care of yourself in the ordinary exigencies of life. I need not add that the second part of this revolution will be more passionately resisted than the first. Men will not give up their privilege of helplessness without a struggle. The average man has a carefully cultivated ignorance about household matters—from what to do with the crumbs to the grocer's telephone number—a sort of cheerful inefficiency which protects him better than the reputation for having a violent temper. It was his mother's fault in the beginning, but even as a boy he was quick to see how a general reputation for being "no good around the house" would serve him throughout life, and half-consciously he began to cultivate that helplessness until today it is the despair of feminist wives.

A growing number of men admire the woman who has a job, and, especially since the cost of living doubled, rather like the idea of their own wives contributing to the family income by outside work. And of course for generations there have been whole towns full of wives who are forced by the bitterest necessity to spend the same hours at the factory that their husbands spend. But these bread-winning wives have not yet developed homemaking husbands. When the two come home from the factory the man sits down while his wife gets supper, and he does so with exactly the same sense of fore-ordained right as if he were "supporting her." Higher up in the economic scale the same thing is true. The business or professional woman who is married, perhaps engages a cook, but the responsibility is not shifted, it is still hers. She "hires and fires," she orders meals, she does the buying, she meets and resolves all domestic crises, she takes charge of moving, furnishing, settling. She may be, like her husband, a busy executive at her office all day, but unlike him, she is also an executive in a small way every night and morning at home. Her noon hour is spent in planning, and too often her Sundays and holidays are spent in "catching up."

Two business women can "make a home" together without either one being overburdened or over-bored. It is because they both know how and both feel responsible. But it is a rare man who can marry one of them and continue the homemaking partnership. Yet if there are no children, there is nothing essentially different in the combination. Two self-supporting adults decide to make a home together: if both are women it is a pleasant partnership, more fun than work; if one is a man, it is almost never a partnership—the woman simply adds running the home to her regular outside job. Unless she is very strong, it is too much for her, she gets tired and bitter over it, and finally perhaps gives up her outside work and condemns herself to the tiresome half-job of housekeeping for two.

Cooperative schemes and electrical devices will simplify the business of homemaking, but they will not get rid of it entirely. As far as we can see ahead people will always want homes, and a happy home cannot be had without a certain amount of rather monotonous work and responsibility. How can we change the nature of man so that he will honorably share that work and responsibility and thus make the homemaking enterprise a song instead of a burden? Most assuredly not by laws or revolutionary decrees. Perhaps we must cultivate or simulate a little of that highly prized helplessness ourselves. But fundamentally it is a problem of education, of early training—we must bring up feminist sons.

Sons? Daughters? They are born of women—how can women be free to choose their occupation, at all times cherishing their economic independence, unless they stop having children? This is a further question for feminism. If the feminist program goes to pieces on the arrival of the first baby, it is false and useless. For ninety-nine out of every hundred women want children, and seventy-five out of every hundred want to take care of their own children, or at any rate so closely superintend their care as to make any other full-time occupation impossible for at least ten or fifteen years. Is there any such thing then as freedom of choice in occupation for women? And is not the family the inevitable economic unit and woman's individual economic independence, at least during that period, out of the question?

The feminist must have an answer to these questions, and she has. The immediate feminist program must include voluntary motherhood. Freedom of any kind for women is hardly worth considering unless it is assumed that they will know how to control the size of their families. "Birth control" is just as elementary an essential in our propaganda as "equal pay." Women are to have children when they want them, that's the first thing. That ensures some freedom of occupational choice; those who do not wish to be mothers will not have an undesired occupation thrust upon them by accident, and those who do wish to be mothers may choose in a general way how many years of their lives they will devote to the occupation of child-raising.

But is there any way of insuring a woman's economic independence while child-raising is her chosen occupation? Or must she sink into that dependent state from which, as we all know, it is so hard to rise again? That brings us to the fourth feature of our program—motherhood endowment. It seems that the only way we can keep mothers free, at least in a capitalist society, is by the establishment of a principle that the occupation of raising children is peculiarly and directly a service to society, and that the mother upon whom the necessity and privilege of performing this service naturally falls is entitled to an adequate economic reward from the political government. It is idle to talk of real economic independence for women unless this principle is accepted. But with a generous endowment of motherhood provided by legislation, with all laws against voluntary motherhood and education in its methods repealed, with the feminist ideal of education accepted in home and school, and with all special barriers removed in every field of human activity, there is no reason why woman should not become almost a human thing.

It will be time enough then to consider whether she has a soul.

KARL MARX

"Bourgeois and Proletarians," *Manifesto of the Communist Party*, 1848

In this passage from the Manifesto, *Marx tells a story about the rise of new social groups: the bourgeoisie and the proletariat. According to Marx, these groups, like others before them, emerge out of the economic organization of society.*

Map the transformation of the West from feudalism, through the Age of Exploration and Discovery, to the Industrial Age. How does this economic organization change political systems and the social order?

Describe the proletariat. In what ways has this social group been dehumanized by industrialization, according to Marx? In what other ways does its very oppression offer the possibility of a new social system?

SOURCE: *Friedrich Engels, ed. "Manifesto of the Communist Party" (English edition, 1888). In* The Marx-Engels Reader *(2nd ed). New York: W. W. Norton & Co., 1978.*

*T*he history of all hitherto existing societies is the history of class struggles. Freeman and slave, patrician and plebeian, lord and serf, guild-master and journeyman, in a word, oppressor and oppressed, stood in constant opposition to one another, carried on an uninterrupted, now hidden, now open fight, a fight that each time ended, either in a revolutionary re-constitution of society at large, or in the common ruin of the contending classes.

In the earlier epochs of history, we find almost everywhere a complicated arrangement of society into various orders, a manifold gradation of social rank. In ancient Rome we have patricians, knights, plebeians, slaves; in the Middle Ages, feudal lords, vassals, guild masters, journeymen, apprentices, serfs; in almost all of these classes, again, subordinate gradations.

The modern bourgeois society that has sprouted from the ruins of feudal society has not done away with class antagonisms. It has but established new classes, new conditions of oppression, new forms of struggle in place of the old ones. Our epoch, the epoch of the bourgeoisie, possesses, however, this distinctive feature: it has simplified the class antagonisms. Society as a whole is more and more splitting up into two great hostile camps, into two great classes, directly facing each other: Bourgeoisie and Proletariat. From the serfs of the Middle Ages sprang the chartered burghers of the earliest towns. From these burgesses the first elements of the bourgeoisie were developed.

The discovery of America, the rounding of the Cape, opened up fresh ground for the rising bourgeoisie. The East Indian and Chinese markets, the colonisation of America, trade with the colonies, the increase in the means of exchange and in commodities generally, gave to commerce, to navigation, to industry, an impulse never before known, and thereby, to the revolutionary element in the tottering feudal society, a rapid development.

How do goods get produced and distributed in a society? Compare the medieval guild, the small manufacturing system of the fifteenth to seventeeth centuries, and the technology-driven industry of Marx's nineteenth century.

The feudal system of industry, under which industrial production was monopolised by closed guilds, now no longer sufficed for the growing wants of the new markets. The manufacturing system took its place. The guild-masters were pushed on one side by the manufacturing middle class; division of labour between the different corporate guilds vanished in the face of division of labour in each single workshop. Meantime the markets kept ever growing, the demand ever rising. Even manufacture no longer sufficed. Thereupon, steam and machinery revolutionised industrial production. The place of manufacture was taken by the giant, Modern Industry, the place of the industrial middle class, by industrial millionaires, the leaders of whole industrial armies, the modern bourgeois.

Modern industry has established the world-market, for which the discovery of America paved the way. This market has given an immense development to commerce, to navigation, to communication by land. This development has, in its time, reacted on the extension of industry; and in proportion as industry, commerce, navigation, railways extended, in the same proportion the bourgeoisie developed, increased its capital, and pushed into the background every class handed down from the Middle Ages.

We see, therefore, how the modern bourgeoisie is itself the product of a long course of development, of a series of revolutions in the modes of production and of exchange. Each step in the development of the bourgeoisie was accompanied by a corresponding political advance of that class. An oppressed class under the sway of the feudal nobility, an armed and self-governing association in the mediaeval commune; here independent urban republic (as in Italy and Germany), there taxable "third estate" of the monarchy (as in France), afterwards, in the period of manufacture proper, serving either the semi-feudal or the absolute monarchy as a counterpoise against the nobility, and, in fact, corner-stone of the great monarchies in general, the bourgeoisie has at last, since the establishment of Modern Industry and of the world-market, conquered for itself, in the modern representative State, exclusive political sway. The executive of the modern State is but a committee for managing the common affairs of the whole bourgeoisie.

Marx suggests that the new economic system has transformed the bourgeoisie through political power.

The bourgeoisie, historically, has played a most revolutionary part.

The bourgeoisie, wherever it has got the upper hand, has put an end to all feudal, patriarchal, idyllic relations. It has pitilessly torn asunder the motley feudal ties that bound man to his "natural superiors," and has left remaining no other nexus between man and man than naked self-interest, than callous "cash payment." It has drowned the most heavenly ecstasies of religious fervour, of chivalrous enthusiasm, of philistine sentimentalism, in the icy water of egotistical calculation. It has resolved personal worth into exchange value. And in place of the numberless and feasible chartered freedoms, has set up that single, unconscionable freedom—Free Trade. In one word, for exploitation, veiled by religious and political illusions, naked, shameless, direct, brutal exploitation. The bourgeoisie has stripped of its halo every occupation hitherto honoured and looked up to with reverent awe. It has converted the physician, the lawyer, the priest, the poet, the man of science, into its paid wage labourers.

The bourgeoisie, in turn, has overturned the values and virtues of many past centuries. What, according to Marx, has the bourgeoisie put in their place? What is the primary value of this social group?

The bourgeoisie has torn away from the family its sentimental veil, and has reduced the family relation to a mere money relation.

The bourgeoisie has disclosed how it came to pass that the brutal display of vigour in the Middle Ages, which Reactionists so much admire, found its fitting complement in the most slothful indolence. It has been the first to show what man's activity can bring about. It has accomplished wonders far surpassing Egyptian pyramids, Roman aqueducts, and Gothic cathedrals; it has conducted expeditions that put in the shade all former Exoduses of nations and crusades.

The bourgeoisie cannot exist without constantly revolutionising the instruments of production, and thereby the relations of production, and with them the whole relations of society. Conservation of the old modes of production in unaltered form, was, on the contrary, the first condition of existence for all earlier industrial classes. Constant revolutionising of production, uninterrupted disturbance of all social conditions, everlasting uncertainty and agitation distinguish the bourgeois epoch from all earlier

What must the bourgeoisie do to maintain itself in power?

ones. All fixed, fast-frozen relations, with their train of ancient and venerable prejudices and opinions, are swept away, all new-formed ones become antiquated before they can ossify. All that is solid melts into air, all that is holy is profaned, and man is at last compelled to face with sober senses, his real conditions of life, and his relations with his kind.

The need of a constantly expanding market for its products chases the bourgeoisie over the whole surface of the globe. It must nestle everywhere, settle everywhere, establish connexions everywhere.

The bourgeoisie has through its exploitation of the world-market given a cosmopolitan character to production and consumption in every country. To the great chagrin of Reactionists, it has drawn from under the feet of industry the national ground on which it stood. All old-established national industries have been destroyed or are daily being destroyed. They are dislodged by new industries, whose introduction becomes a life and death question for all civilised nations, by industries that no longer work up indigenous raw material, but raw material drawn from the remotest zones; industries whose products are consumed, not only at home, but in every quarter of the globe. In place of the old wants, satisfied by the productions of the country, we find new wants, requiring for their satisfaction the products of distant lands and climes. In place of the old local and national seclusion and self-sufficiency, we have intercourse in every direction, universal interdependence of nations. And as in material, so also in intellectual production. The intellectual creations of individual nations become common property. National one-sidedness and narrow-mindedness become more and more impossible, and from the numerous national and local literatures, there arises a world literature.

The bourgeoisie, by the rapid improvement of all instruments of production, by the immensely facilitated means of communication, draws all, even the most barbarian, nations into civilisation. The cheap prices of its commodities are the heavy artillery with which it batters down all Chinese walls, with which it forces the barbarians' intensely obstinate hatred of foreigners to capitulate. It compels all nations, on pain of extinction, to adopt the bourgeois mode of production; it compels them to introduce what it calls civilisation into their midst, i.e., to become bourgeois themselves. In one word, it creates a world after its own image.

In Marx's view, how has the bourgeoisie transformed everyday life in the nation? In the world?

The bourgeoisie has subjected the country to the rule of the towns. It has created enormous cities, has greatly increased the urban population as compared with the rural, and has thus rescued a considerable part of the population from the idiocy of rural life. Just as it has made the country dependent on the towns, so it has made barbarian and semi-barbarian countries dependent on the civilised ones, nations of peasants on nations of bourgeois, the East on the West.

The bourgeoisie keeps more and more doing away with the scattered state of the population, of the means of production, and of property. It has agglomerated production, and has concentrated property in a few hands. The necessary consequence of this was political centralisation. Independent, or but loosely connected provinces, with separate interests, laws, governments and systems of taxation, became lumped together into one nation, with one government, one code of laws, one national class-interest, one frontier and one customs-tariff. The bourgeoisie, during its rule of scarce one hundred years, has created more massive and more colossal productive forces than have all preceding generations together. Subjection of Nature's forces to man, machinery, application of chemistry to industry and agriculture, steam-navigation, railways, electric telegraphs, clearing of whole continents for cultivation, canalisation of rivers, whole populations conjured out of the ground—what earlier century had even a presentiment that such productive forces slumbered in the lap of social labour?

A summary of the rise of the bourgeoisie.

We see then: the means of production and of exchange, on whose foundation the bourgeoisie built itself up, were generated in feudal society. At a certain stage in the development of these means of production and of exchange, the conditions under which feudal society produced and exchanged, the feudal organisation of agriculture and manufacturing industry, in one word, the feudal relations of property became no longer compatible with the already developed productive forces; they became so many fetters. They had to be burst asunder; they were burst asunder. Into their place stepped free competition, accompanied by a social and political constitution adapted to it, and by the economical and political sway of the bourgeois class.

A similar movement is going on before our own eyes. Modern bourgeois society with its relations of production, of exchange and of property, a society that has conjured up such gigantic means of production and of exchange, is like the sorcerer, who is no longer able to control the powers of the nether world whom he has called up by his spells. For many a decade past the history of industry and commerce is but the history of the revolt of modern productive forces against modern conditions of production, against the property relations that are the conditions for the existence of the bourgeoisie and of its rule. It is enough to mention the commercial crises that by their periodical return put on its trial, each time more threateningly, the existence of the entire bourgeois society. In these crises a great part not only of the existing products, but also of the previously created productive forces, are periodically destroyed. In these crises there breaks out an epidemic that, in all earlier epochs, would have seemed an absurdity—the epidemic of overproduction. Society suddenly finds itself put back into a state of momentary barbarism; it appears as if a famine, a universal war of devastation had cut off the supply of every means of subsistence; industry and commerce seem to be destroyed; and why? Because there is too much civilisation, too much means of subsistence, too much industry, too much commerce. The productive forces at the disposal of society no longer tend to further the development of the conditions of bourgeois property; on the contrary, they have become too powerful for these conditions, by which they are fettered, and so soon as they overcome these fetters, they bring disorder into the whole of bourgeois society, endanger the existence of bourgeois property. The conditions of bourgeois society are too narrow to comprise the wealth created by them. And how does the bourgeoisie get over these crises? On the one hand enforced destruction of a mass of productive forces; on the other, by the conquest of new markets, and by the more thorough exploitation of the old ones. That is to say, by paving the way for more extensive and more destructive crises, and by diminishing the means whereby crises are prevented.

The bourgeoisie is so successful at stimulating productive forces that it finds itself in a crisis.

The weapons with which the bourgeoisie felled feudalism to the ground are now turned against the bourgeoisie itself. But not only has the bourgeoisie forged the weapons that bring death to itself; it has also called into existence the men who are to wield those weapons— the modern working class—the proletarians.

The bourgeoisie "calls into existence" its counterpart in industrial production: the proletariat.

In proportion as the bourgeoisie, i.e., capital, is developed, in the same proportion is the proletariat, the modern working class, developed—a class of labourers, who live only so long as they find work, and who find work only so long as their labour increases capital. These labourers, who must sell themselves piece-meal, are a commodity, like every other article of commerce, and are consequently exposed to all the vicissitudes of competition, to all the fluctuations of the market.

*In what ways is the proletariat,
the modern working class,
different from workers of
earlier ages?*

Owing to the extensive use of machinery and to division of labour, the work of the proletarians has lost all individual character, and consequently, all charm for the workman. He becomes an appendage of the machine, and it is only the most simple, most monotonous, and most easily acquired knack, that is required of him. Hence, the cost of production of a workman is restricted, almost entirely, to the means of subsistence that he requires for his maintenance, and for the propagation of his race. But the price of a commodity, and therefore also of labour, is equal to its cost of production. In proportion therefore, as the repulsiveness of the work increases, the wage decreases. Nay more, in proportion as the use of machinery and division of labour increases, in the same proportion the burden of toil also increases, whether by prolongation of the working hours, by increase of the work exacted in a given time or by increased speed of the machinery, etc.

Modern industry has converted the little workshop of the patriarchal master into the great factory of the industrial capitalist. Masses of labourers, crowded into the factory, are organised like soldiers. As privates of the industrial army they are placed under the command of a perfect hierarchy of officers and sergeants. Not only are they slaves of the bourgeois class, and of the bourgeois State; they are daily and hourly enslaved by the machine, by the over-looker, and, above all, by the individual bourgeois manufacturer himself. The more openly this despotism proclaims gain to be its end and aim, the more petty, the more hateful and the more embittering it is.

The less the skill and exertion of strength implied in manual labour, in other words, the more modern industry becomes developed, the more is the labour of men superseded by that of women. Differences of age and sex have no longer any distinctive social validity for the working class. All are instruments of labour, more or less expensive to use, according to their age and sex.

No sooner is the exploitation of the labourer by the manufacturer, so far, at an end, that he receives his wages in cash, than he is set upon by the other portions of the bourgeoisie, the landlord, the shopkeeper, the pawnbroker, etc.

The lower strata of the middle class—the small tradespeople, shopkeepers, retired tradesmen generally, the handicraftsmen and peasants—all these sink gradually into the proletariat, partly because their diminutive capital does not suffice for the scale on which Modern Industry is carried on, and is swamped in the competition with the large capitalists, partly because their specialized skill is rendered worthless by the new methods of production. Thus the proletariat is recruited from all classes of the population. The proletariat goes through various stages of development. With its birth begins its struggle with the bourgeoisie. At first the contest is carried on by individual labourers, then by the workpeople of a factory, then by the operatives of one trade, in one locality, against the individual bourgeois who directly exploits them. They direct their attacks not against the bourgeois conditions of production, but against the instruments of production themselves; they destroy imported wares that compete with their labour, they smash to pieces machinery, they set factories ablaze, they seek to restore by force the vanished status of the workman of the Middle Ages.

At this stage the labourers still form an incoherent mass scattered over the whole country, and broken up by their mutual competition. If anywhere they unite to form more compact bodies, this is not yet the consequence of their own active union, but of the union of the bourgeoisie, which class, in order to attain its own political ends, is compelled to set the whole proletariat in motion, and is moreover yet, for a time, able to do so. At this stage, therefore, the proletarians do not fight their enemies, but the enemies of their enemies, the remnants of absolute monarchy, the landowners, the non-industrial bourgeois, the petty bourgeoisie. Thus the whole historical movement is concentrated in the hands of the bourgeoisie; every victory so obtained is a victory for the bourgeoisie.

But with the development of industry the proletariat not only increases in number; it becomes concentrated in greater masses, its strength grows, and it feels that strength more. The various interests and conditions of life within the ranks of the proletariat are more and more equalised, in proportion as machinery obliterates all distinctions of labour, and nearly everywhere reduces wages to the same low level. The growing competition among the bourgeois, and the resulting commercial crises, make the wages of the workers ever more fluctuating. The unceasing improvement of machinery, ever more rapidly developing, makes their livelihood more and more precarious; the collisions between individual workmen and individual bourgeois take more and more the character of collisions between two classes. Thereupon the workers begin to form combinations (Trades Unions) against the bourgeois; they club together in order to keep up the rate of wages; they found permanent associations in order to make provision beforehand for these occasional revolts. Here and there the contest breaks out into riots.

Why does Marx think that the modern proletariat is a potential threat to the bourgeoisie?

Now and then the workers are victorious, but only for a time. The real fruit of their battles lies, not in the immediate result, but in the ever-expanding union of the workers. This union is helped on by the improved means of communication that are created by modern industry and that place the workers of different localities in contact with one another. It was just this contact that was needed to centralise the numerous local struggles, all of the same character, into one national struggle between classes. But every class struggle is a political struggle. And that union, to attain which the burghers of the Middle Ages, with their miserable highways, required centuries, the modern proletarians, thanks to railways, achieve in a few years.

This organisation of the proletarians into a class, and consequently into a political party, is continually being upset again by the competition between the workers themselves. But it ever rises up again, stronger, firmer, mightier. It compels legislative recognition of particular interests of the workers, by taking advantage of the divisions among the bourgeoisie itself. Thus the ten-hours' bill in England was carried.

Altogether collisions between the classes of the old society further, in many ways, the course of development of the proletariat. The bourgeoisie finds itself involved in a constant battle. At first with the aristocracy; later on, with those portions of the bourgeoisie itself, whose interests have become antagonistic to the progress of industry; at all times, with the bourgeoisie of foreign countries. In all these battles it sees itself compelled to appeal to the proletariat, to ask for its help, and thus, to drag it into the political arena. The bourgeoisie itself, therefore, supplies the proletariat with its own instruments of political and general education, in other words, it furnishes the proletariat with weapons for fighting the bourgeoisie.

Further, as we have already seen, entire sections of the ruling classes are, by the advance of industry, precipitated into the proletariat, or are at least threatened in their conditions of existence. These also supply the proletariat with fresh elements of enlightenment and progress.

Finally, in times when the class struggle nears the decisive hour, the process of dissolution going on within the ruling class, in fact within the whole range of society, assumes such a violent, glaring character, that a small section of the ruling class cuts itself adrift, and joins the revolutionary class, the class that holds the future in its hands. Just as, therefore, at an earlier period, a section of the nobility went over to the bourgeoisie, so now a portion of the bourgeoisie goes over to the proletariat, and in particular, a portion of the bourgeois ideologists, who have raised themselves to the level of comprehending theoretically the historical movement as a whole.

Of all the classes that stand face to face with the bourgeoisie today, the proletariat alone is a really revolutionary class. The other classes decay and finally disappear in the face of Modern Industry; the proletariat is its special and essential product. The lower middle class, the small manufacturer, the shopkeeper, the artisan, the peasant, all these fight against the bourgeoisie, to save from extinction their existence as fractions of the middle class. They are therefore not revolutionary, but conservative. Nay more, they are reactionary, for they try to roll back the wheel of history. If by chance they are revolutionary, they are so only in view of their impending transfer into the proletariat, they thus defend not their present, but their future interests, they desert their own standpoint to place themselves at that of the proletariat.

The "dangerous class," the social scum, that passively rotting mass thrown off by the lowest layers of old society, may, here and there, be swept into the movement by a proletarian revolution; its conditions of life, however, prepare it far more for the part of a bribed tool of reactionary intrigue.

In the conditions of the proletariat, those of old society at large are already virtually swamped. The proletarian is without property; his relation to his wife and children has no longer anything in common with the bourgeois family-relations; modern industrial labour, modern subjection to capital, the same in England as in France, in America as in Germany, has stripped him of every trace of national character. Law, morality, religion, are to him so many bourgeois prejudices, behind which lurk in ambush just as many bourgeois interests.

Why does Marx believe that the proletariat is a revolutionary class?

All the preceding classes that got the upper hand, sought to fortify their already acquired status by subjecting society at large to their conditions of appropriation. The proletarians cannot become masters of the productive forces of society, except by abolishing their own previous mode of appropriation, and thereby also every other previous mode of appropriation. They have nothing of their own to secure and to fortify; their mission is to destroy all previous securities for, and insurances of, individual property.

All previous historical movements were movements of minorities, or in the interests of minorities. The proletarian movement is the self-conscious, independent movement of the immense majority, in the interests of the immense majority. The proletariat, the lowest stratum of our present society, cannot stir, cannot raise itself up, without the whole superincumbent strata of official society being sprung into the air.

Though not in substance, yet in form, the struggle of the proletariat with the bourgeoisie is at first a national struggle. The proletariat of each country must, of course, first of all settle matters with its own bourgeoisie.

In depicting the most general phases of the development of the proletariat, we traced the more or less veiled civil war, raging within existing society, up to the point where that war breaks out into open revolution, and where the violent overthrow of the bourgeoisie lays the foundation for the sway of the proletariat.

Hitherto, every form of society has been based, as we have already seen, on the antagonism of oppressing and oppressed classes. But in order to oppress a class, certain conditions must be assured to it under which it can, at least, continue its slavish existence. The serf, in the period of serfdom, raised himself to membership in the commune, just as the petty bourgeois, under the yoke of feudal absolutism, managed to develop into a bourgeois. The modern laborer, on the contrary, instead of rising with the progress of industry, sinks deeper and deeper below the conditions of existence of his own class. He becomes a pauper, and pauperism develops more rapidly than population and wealth. And here it becomes evident, that the bourgeoisie is unfit any longer to be the ruling class in society, and to impose its conditions of existence upon society as an over-riding law. It is unfit to rule because it is incompetent to assure an existence to its slave within his slavery, because it cannot help letting him sink into such a state, that it has to feed him, instead of being fed by him. Society can no longer live under this bourgeoisie, in other words, its existence is no longer compatible with society.

The essential condition for the existence, and for the sway of the bourgeois class, is the formation and augmentation of capital; the condition for capital is wage-labour. Wage labour rests exclusively on competition between the labourers. The advance of industry, whose involuntary promoter is the bourgeoisie, replaces the isolation of the labourers, due to competition, by their revolutionary combination, due to association. The development of Modern Industry, therefore, cuts from under its feet the very foundation on which the bourgeoisie produces and appropriates products. What the bourgeoisie, therefore, produces, above all, is its own grave-diggers. Its fall and the victory of the proletariat are equally inevitable.

DANIEL DE LEON

"Anarchism Versus Socialism," 1901

In this speech given in Boston on October 13, Daniel De Leon (1852–1914), a prominent member of the Socialist Labor Party, addresses the issue of political violence. He is responding to the recent assassination of President William McKinley in September 1901, by the young anarchist Leon Czolgosz in Buffalo, New York. (Because Czolgosz had attended a speech by Emma Goldman in May and visited her briefly in July, Goldman was arrested for a short time for possible participation in the crime.)

Rather than decrying assassination as a political strategy, as did the more mainstream Socialist Party, De Leon wants to clarify that anarchist "direct action" emerges out of older, now declining, social realities. It is no longer effective in changing society. What is his argument?

De Leon co-founded the IWW in 1905 with Big Bill Haywood, but soon was expelled from the organization. As you read the speech, look for points of disagreement between De Leon and both Haywood and Goldman. What does De Leon offer the working class?

SOURCE: *"Socialism versus Anarchism: An Address." Brooklyn, NY: New York Labor News, 1980. Published without rights. First edition, 1901; unrecorded editions between 1901 and 1919; new edition with preface, 1919; reprinted, 1921; amplified edition, 1962 and 1970. https://archive.org/details /SocialismVersusAnarchismAnAddress*

*L*adies and Gentlemen:
. . . All those of you who remember the recent vulgar attacks upon Socialism on the part of the Republican press, which manufactured "Socialists" and put into their mouths cheers for the assassin of McKinley; all those of you who remember the equally obscene assaults by the Democratic press, which endeavored to connect Czolgosz directly with Socialism; all those of you who recollect the vulgar language hurled from the Protestant and Jewish pulpits, lumping Socialism and Anarchism in one; all those of you who remember the immoral attitude struck by the Princes of the Roman Catholic Hierarchy of this country, who, forgetful of their claim that they are "teachers of morality," have, on the occasion of the Buffalo tragedy, resorted to the immoral act of falsifying the tenets and principles of Socialism; all those of you who remember the language of the politicians, Democratic and Republican, on this subject, may possibly expect of me that I am going, this afternoon, to hit back. Nothing of the sort. The sun

hits not back against the dark clouds that may gather in its face; neither does the Socialist movement. . . .

I shall show you that these individualistic outbreaks have accomplished wonderful revolutions in their time, but in days gone by. I shall show you that, as humanity progresses, individual acts wane in strength, and I shall show you why, today, they are simply flashes in the pan; consequently, that this wholesale denunciation of individualistic revolutions, individualistic shots and individualistic assassinations, as acts incapable of accomplishing great results, shows that these gentlemen have no conception of what Anarchism really means, or where it has its roots. . . .

Anarchism does not imply homicide, however natural its development in that direction may seem. Anarchism is essentially a gubernatorial or governmental conception—a conception of government in social society.

A conception of government is a reflex of social conception; and that social conception in its turn is based upon not what we would like, or what we would fancy to be the desirous thing, but upon what material conditions dictate. You take your present raspingly-noisy and unseemly Elevated in Boston,[1] for instance; it is not what you would like; but it is a reflex of the conditions of things and capabilities of the time; and that reflex takes tangible form in the best way people know and are physically able to meet a certain condition of things.

Now, what is the social conception that lies at the root of Anarchism? I can hardly illustrate Socialism better than by drawing clear the essence of Anarchism. With that as a background, then Socialism, the reason therefore, what it means and the tactics to reach it, spring naturally to the eye.

What, then, is that governmental conception that manifests itself as Anarchism? What that social conception is the reflex of, I shall not start with stating. I shall mention some leading historic events, and thus enable you to answer the questions yourselves. Take one of the leading epochs in ancient history. We there come across a monumental being. His name has come down to our days; he has given names to cities; his sayings, his words, his conduct, have become proverbial.

That man was Alexander, named the Great. He built an empire that lapped over both sides of the Euxine; he conquered the formerly unconquerable Greeks; he spread eastward over the great empires of the Assyrians and Babylonians, or whatever names they had. His empire swamped Egypt, and raised the city of Alexandria, with all that it implied. That empire was the largest empire, properly speaking, using the word in a semi-technical sense, the largest the world had yet seen. Alexander was its head.

One day Alexander died. What became of his empire? Immediately upon his death, it shattered into a dozen different fragments. Without Alexander the empire of Alexander came to naught. The death of that man was not brought on by

---

1. The Elevated or "El" is the part of a subway system that goes over city streets. The footnote on page 211 gives additional information on the "El" in New York City.

homicide. His death is attributed to "a natural event in the course of nature." The fact that interests us most just now is what happened when that great Alexander died. What happened was the death of his empire. Leave that as one instance. . . .[2]

No need of multiplying examples. The mental kinship of all these instances is obvious. From them leaps to view the identical governmental conception together with the social conception that it is the reflex of. And what is that? It is obviously the social conception that the people do not count in society, except, at best, as food for cannon (laughter and applause); that government, accordingly, is something outside of, separate and apart from, and superimposed upon the people from above.

De Leon gives his description of an anarchist conception of society. It is the chessboard conception of society. One may have all his men on the board, but if his king is checkmated, the game is lost. Your opponent may have pawns, bishops, knights, rooks and queen, but if you have crowded his king to where he must surrender, then all his bishops, his pawns, his rooks, his knights, and even his queen, go for naught. And that conception is the essence of Anarchism. (Cheers and applause.) All else in Anarchism are but incidents and results that flow from this central principle. (Applause.) Now, then, as you may begin to perceive, this Anarchist conception of society and of government was natural enough, and in place, at a certain social stage. How much in place, and what sort of social stage, you may have an inkling from the illustration furnished by Alexander's empire, and from the effectiveness with which that conception of society was applied in the instances of Ehud and Judith, together with many other instances that these two readily suggest.

On the other hand, from the other instances cited, and the many more you can readily think of, together with the common experience of the declining effectiveness with which that Anarchist conception of society is applied, down to our own days, when its application regularly suffers shipwreck, as illustrated by the utter failure that attends and must inevitably attend all the "Purity Movements" that we have seen spring up periodically in the land—from all this it will be clear that, from the social conditions in Asia Minor and Palestine, many centuries before Christ, to those of the United States in the Twentieth Century; from the days of Ehud and Judith to those of Czolgosz and Seth Low (laughter and applause), a steady change

---

2. De Leon adds other examples of political leaders whose great nations and movements fail and disappear upon their deaths. De Leon hopes to show that in the past, political assassination of leaders was an effective strategy: Ehud smote the King Eglon of his Moabite oppressors; Judith beheaded Holofernes, general of an invading enemy army; in nearby Mexico revolutionary generals gained power by overtaking the capital city and its leader; even in present-day New York City a reform movement assumes it will purify government just by ousting the corrupt Tammany Hall leadership.

has been going on, until, today, the old Anarchist conception of government no longer fits with actual social conditions. (Applause.)[3]

Now, then, what is the reason the Ehuds and Judiths succeeded, while, today, the Czolgoszes and Lows have failed, and will continue to fail? Before going to the bottom of the matter, and detailing the fundamental and remote, it is well to first point out the immediate reason.

The immediate reason is a sociological development pregnant with significance. It is this: For reasons that I shall presently take up more fully, the masses are stepping more and more upon the stage of history, and not as "supes" or scene-shifters, but as stars in the performance. (Applause.) . . .

De Leon argues that contemporary industrial society is based on the masses.

Under the modern industrial order, the masses have grown into society—and not a few of the epileptic fits that capitalist society is being continually thrown into are the result of the attempt on the part of the capitalist class to ignore, while seeking to profit by, the change; of the efforts of that class to brace itself against the Niagara–like torrent of evolution that has removed government down and away from the skies and planted it on earth, and that marks it flesh of the people's flesh, and bone of their bone—part and parcel of, inseparable from, society. (Applause.)

The further back one traces the race, the fewer are concerned in the government; the fewer are so concerned, the more natural, because the easiest, is the system of effecting changes—aye, improvements—by "despatching" the government. The further we move forward, the more intimate becomes the blending of "government" with the rest of society; in even step the system of "despatching" a government, whether by assassination or some newer method, grows more barren in results: To the Red Terror ever succeeds the White; the individually benign McKinley is succeeded by the Spiked Police-Club Roosevelt. (Applause.) . . .[4]

Now, if you have followed me so far, looking from one end to the other end of the gamut—from the basso profundo of the Democratic party and the Republican party up to the Catholic Hierarchy and the Jewish and Protestant pulpits—you find written over all their faces, as clear as it is possible for a man to see who has eyes to see—ANARCHISM. (Loud applause.) Anarchism backward; Anarchism forward.

The difference between these [political parties and religious pulpits] and the outspoken Anarchists—in that the former imagine conditions can be changed by the mere capturing of governments, while the latter hold that conditions can be changed by the mere decapitations of governments[3]—is a difference, not of kind, but of variety. They both belong to the same species, the mark of which is that

---

3. Seth Low was the mayor of New York City (1901–1902) who championed Progressive reforms.

4. Vice-president Theodore Roosevelt assumed the presidency after McKinley's death. He was famous for attempting to rid New York City of corruption and vice during his time as its police commissioner (1895–1897). He introduced the large club as the police weapon of the era.

conception of government—correct at one time, rendered less so from social cycle to social cycle, until today it is preposterous that consists in holding that government is something outside, separate and apart from, the people. (Applause.) Now, against that conception the Socialist movement stands out alone in the United States. It says today, at the present stage of civilization, there is no reform worth speaking possible by simply monkeying with the government. You must educate the masses first. (Applause.) You cannot move faster than the masses move with you in this Twentieth Century. . . .

De Leon explains how the modes of production influence political organization. In the past the individual was "the architect of his own fortune."

Under the social system where the tool of production is so small that every single man can operate it himself, he, under that social system, owns his tool, and, along with that, owns the product of his toil. If he started without implements of labor, he could easily acquire them. He was the architect of his own fortune.

Production at that stage had not a few satisfactory features; it had, however, a very unsatisfactory one. The individual producer could not produce enough to free him from that animal condition of having to grub for his material sustenance all his life. Man aspires to freedom from the necessity of worrying as to how he will live, or whether he will enjoy shelter. Man's ambition is to be free from that; and the potentiality of his freedom in that direction increases in even step with the perfection of the implements of labor.

In the present period of industrialization, people must work together.

Hand in hand with this development goes another. The more perfect the tool of production becomes, the more are men compelled to cooperate in production. . . . Cooperation brings about a multiplication of the fruitfulness of labor many times more than the amount the individual could raise. If ten men produce a certain quantity individually, under the cooperative labor superinduced by the modern perfected machine they would produce, not ten times as much, but a hundred times more. . . .

The individualistic farmer was self-supporting, and consequently was exposed to all the evils that beset the beasts of the jungle. Those farmers alternated between a feast and a fast; in cases of drought or a failure in the crops, they had to suffer prolonged hunger. The work of these people was arduous and continuous. There was little time for educational development. . . .

That changed by degrees with the introduction of the perfected machine, together with the increased productivity of cooperative labor that the improved system of production forced upon the people. The final aspect which the change brought on is that, today, no one man in the United States is any longer independent of all others. Today, no one city, county, or state is any longer independent of any other city, county, or state. The Massachusetts weavers could not work if the miners in Pennsylvania, Ohio, Indiana, and as far west as Kansas, did not dig for coal; and the miners of Pennsylvania, Indiana, Ohio, and Kansas, could not work if the farmers did not produce grain; and the farmers could not do their work if the shoemakers of Massachusetts and other industrial centers did not furnish them with shoes; and none of them could exist if the great railroads of the country did not transport their products. Today there is absolute cooperation.

Now, under such a system of production there must be a central directing authority, a government. As Marx puts it, a single violinist can be his own director. He raps himself to order, he puts his violin to his shoulder and sets his music to suit himself; he plays fast or slow, loud or otherwise, and stops whenever it suits him; but if you want an orchestra, if you want have that combination of tones that comes from cooperation and an even assortment of musical instruments; if you want the blending of the bass drum, the cornet, the cymbal, and the flute with those of the violincello, then you must have an orchestra director. . . .

Likewise in this productive system of today. It is a large orchestra of production. In order to conduct this productive orchestra there must be a central directing authority. Under such social conditions, the central directing authority, the government, is like the skin on a man's body. . . .

People who have the Anarchist conception of government have not yet learned the lesson that every boy has learned who has climbed up a tree, and watched the eggs hatch in the bird's nest, and see the wings and the feathers of the wings sprout out of the body itself, until the bird takes flight. That boy knows that wings could never stead the bird to fly with it fastened on from the outside. They must grow from within. They must be a structural limb of the body. So, at all points, with "government." (Applause.) Consequently, today, arrayed against the whole clerical and lay Anarchistic conception of government, which, logically enough, produces such assassinations as the recent one in Buffalo, and to which such idiotic campaigns as the municipal campaign now on in New York are closely akin—arrayed against the whole pack stands the Socialist movement. (Applause.) It says to the workingman: True enough, you must seek to capture the government, but not as either a finality or a starter. The overthrow of the government you must aim at must be to the end of using the governmental power to perfect the revolution that must have preceded your conquest of the public powers. (Applause.) The initial revolution must be accomplished in your minds. You must have divorced yourselves from the habits of thought that have been used to your enslavement; you must have come to an understanding that you are the sole producers of all wealth. (Applause.) You must have been able to draw the logical conclusion that the capitalist class is a parasite on your backs. (Applause.) You must have raised yourselves to appreciate your high mission in the evolution of society, in that only the economic program of your class is able to abolish the slavery of the race. (Loud applause.) You must, in consequence, have first learned what use to make of the government, when gotten, to wit, to use it as a social lever with which to establish the Socialist Republic and install the government that our needs require and that civilization needs.

De Leon notes the individualist political organizations of past centuries and asks what kind of political organization is necessary in an era of economic cooperation.

De Leon presents his vision of the socialist movement.

Accordingly, the Socialist movement, says not to the workingmen: Vote the Socialist ticket. It explains to them why they should vote that ticket, and it adds: If you do not yet understand why, then, for heaven's sake, cast not your votes with us, because, when elected, the Socialists, the government you shall have chosen, must, in order to be effective, be something, not outside, not separate and apart from you; it must be flesh of your flesh and bone of your bone; it must have men at its back. (Prolonged applause.) There is a providential dispensation in what is going on. The question is often put in these days, whether perhaps this Czolgosz affair might not cause the vote of the Socialists to go down. What of it? What would be the meaning of the vote's going down? It would simply mean that the men who leave the party at this election, voted for it at the last election when they were not fit for the ranks of the Socialists. (Applause.) It would mean that in that part of the structure for the emancipation of our people which the Socialist movement is rearing, the ground had sagged. It would mean that the ground would have to be pounded harder to make a more solid foundation. . . .

One thing, however, the whole gamut of the Anarchist organizations—clerical and lay—in the land cannot do, and that is to cause the banner of the Socialist movement to be lowered one inch. (Loud and prolonged applause and cheers.) The party will carry on its work of education despite anything that may happen. It carries on that work encouraged by the knowledge that it is making progress. It carries it on encouraged by the knowledge that the Revolution is being perfected in the minds of hundreds and of thousands of men in the nation.

The party carries on its work of education encouraged by the knowledge that some day, somehow, something is bound to rip. And then, at that crisis, when the people, who have allowed themselves to be misled from Mumbo Jumbo to Jumbo Mumbo, will be running around like chickens without a head, there will be one beacon light in the land burning as clear in that darkness as it is burning 'midst the clouds today; one beacon, whose steady light will serve as guide; whose tried firmness will inspire confidence; and whose rock-ribbed sides will serve as a natural point of rally from which to save civilization. (Prolonged cheers.)

JANE ADDAMS

"Industrial Amelioration," *Democracy and Social Ethics*, 1902

Jane Addams responds in this essay to the Pullman Strike of 1894, the first national strike in U.S. history, finally including some 150,000 strikes in 27 states. It was also the first labor dispute in which the president of the United States called on federal troops to quell the strike by force. *The strike against the Pullman Palace Car Company, which made train cars, paralyzed the railway system, the primary means of transportation of goods and people at the end of the nineteenth century.*

While Addams calls for changes in the relationship between industrial labor and management, she turns to "social ethics" as a solution. What does she mean by "social ethics"?

How does she describe the benevolent businessman and his notion of the common good? Why is he in error? How does Addams describe industrial workers and their ideas of the common good? Why are they commonly misunderstood? What does Addams propose for the future?

SOURCE: Democracy and Social Ethics, *reprint edition. New York: MacMillan, 1907 (originally published 1902). 137–177.*

*T*here is no doubt that the great difficulty we experience in reducing to action our imperfect code of social ethics arises from the fact that we have not yet learned to act together, and find it far from easy even to fuse our principles and aims into a satisfactory statement. We have all been at times entertained by the futile efforts of half a dozen highly individualized people gathered together as a committee. Their aimless attempts to find a common method of action have recalled the wavering motion of a baby's arm before he has learned to coordinate his muscles.

Addams contrasts the efficient, often apparently successful, effort of individual action with the messy attempts of groups to bring about change. And yet she asserts that associated action is more valuable today. Why?

If, as is many times stated, we are passing from an age of individualism to one of association, there is no doubt that for decisive and effective action the individual still has the best of it. He will secure efficient results while committees are still deliberating upon the best method of making a beginning. And yet, if the need of the times demand associated effort, it may easily be true that the action which appears ineffective, and yet is carried out upon the more highly developed line of associated effort, may represent a finer social quality and have a greater social value than the more effective individual action. It is possible that an individual may be successful, largely because he conserves all his powers for individual achievement and does not put any of his energy into the training which will give him the ability to act with others. The individual acts promptly, and we are dazzled by his success while only dimly conscious of the inadequacy of his code. Nowhere is this illustrated more clearly than in industrial relations, as existing between the owner of a large factory and his employees.

A growing conflict may be detected between the democratic ideal, which urges the workmen to demand representation in the administration of industry, and the accepted position, that the man who owns the capital and takes the risks has the exclusive right of management. It is in reality a clash between individual or aristocratic management, and corporate or democratic management. A large and highly developed factory presents a sharp contrast between its socialized form and individualistic ends.

The man who disassociates his ambition, however disinterested, from the cooperation of his fellows, always takes this risk of ultimate failure. He does not take advantage of the great conserver and guarantee of his own permanent success which associated efforts afford. Genuine experiments toward higher social conditions must have a more democratic faith and practice than those which underlie private venture. Public parks and improvements, intended for the common use, are after all only safe in the hands of the public itself; and associated effort toward social progress, although much more awkward and stumbling than that same effort managed by a capable individual, does yet enlist deeper forces and evoke higher social capacities.

Addams refers to the case of a factory owner who provided a model town and housing for his workers, demanding that the workers adhere to his moral values. This philanthropist was shocked at the workers' ingratitude.

The successful business man who is also the philanthropist is in more than the usual danger of getting widely separated from his employees. The men already have the American veneration for wealth and successful business capacity, and, added to this, they are dazzled by his good works. The workmen have the same kindly impulses as he, but while they organize their charity into mutual benefit associations and distribute their money in small amounts in relief for the widows and insurance for the injured, the employer may build model towns, erect college buildings, which are tangible and enduring, and thereby display his goodness in concentrated form.

By the very exigencies of business demands, the employer is too often cut off from the social ethics developing in regard to our larger social relationships, and from the great moral life springing from our common experiences. This is sure to happen when he is good "to" people rather than "with" them, when he allows himself to decide what is best for them instead of consulting them. He thus misses the rectifying influence of that fellowship which is so big that it leaves no room for sensitiveness or gratitude. Without this fellowship we may never know how great the divergence between ourselves and others may become, nor how cruel the misunderstandings. . . .

Addams defends the value of labor organizations even when they blunder or appear chaotic.

But we judge labor organizations as we do other living institutions, not by their declaration of principles, which we seldom read, but by their blundering efforts to apply their principles to actual conditions, and by the oft-time failure of their representatives, when the individual finds himself too weak to become the organ of corporate action.

The very blunders and lack of organization too often characterizing a union, in marked contrast to the orderly management of a factory, often confuse us as to the real issues involved, and we find it hard to trust uncouth and unruly manifestations of social effort. The situation is made even more complicated by the fact that those who are formulating a code of associated action so often break through the established code of law and order. As society has a right to demand of the reforming individual that he be sternly held to his personal and domestic claims, so it has a right to insist that labor organizations shall keep to the hardly won standards of public law and order; and the community performs but its plain duty when it registers its protest every time law and order are subverted, even in the interest of the so-called social effort. Yet in moments of industrial stress and strain the community is confronted by a moral perplexity which may arise from the mere fact that the good of yesterday is opposed to the good of today, and that which may appear as a choice between virtue and vice is really but a choice between virtue and virtue. In the disorder and confusion sometimes incident to growth and progress, the community may be unable to see anything but the unlovely struggle itself. . . .

At times of social disturbance the law-abiding citizen is naturally so anxious for peace and order, his sympathies are so justly and inevitably on the side making for the restoration of law, that it is difficult for him to see the situation fairly. He becomes insensible to the unselfish impulse which may prompt a sympathetic strike in behalf of the workers in a non-union shop, because he allows his mind to dwell exclusively on the disorder which has become associated with the strike. He is completely side-tracked by the ugly phases of a great moral movement. It is always a temptation to assume that the side which has respectability, authority, and superior intelligence, has therefore righteousness as well, especially when the same side presents concrete results of individual effort as over against the less tangible results of associated effort.

It is as yet most difficult for us to free ourselves from the individualistic point of view sufficiently to group events in their social relations and to judge fairly those who are endeavoring to produce a social result through all the difficulties of associated action. The philanthropist still finds his path much easier than do those who are attempting a social morality. In the first place, the public, anxious to praise what it recognizes as an undoubted moral effort often attended with real personal sacrifice, joyfully seizes upon this manifestation and overpraises it, recognizing the philanthropist as an old friend in the paths of righteousness, whereas the others are strangers and possibly to be distrusted as aliens. It is easy to confuse the response to an abnormal number of individual claims with the response to the social claim. An exaggerated personal morality is often mistaken for a social morality, and until it attempts to minister to a social situation its total inadequacy is not discovered. To attempt to attain a social

Addams proposes social morality as hope for the nation.

morality without a basis of democratic experience results in the loss of the only possible corrective and guide, and ends in an exaggerated individual morality but not in social morality at all. We see this from time to time in the care-worn and overworked philanthropist, who has taxed his individual will beyond the normal limits and has lost his clew to the situation among a bewildering number of cases. A man who takes the betterment of humanity for his aim and end must also take the daily experiences of humanity for the constant correction of his process. He must not only test and guide his achievement by human experience, but he must succeed or fail in proportion as he has incorporated that experience with his own. Otherwise his own achievements become his stumbling-block, and he comes to believe in his own goodness as something outside of himself. He makes an exception of himself, and thinks that he is different from the rank and file of his fellows.

He forgets that it is necessary to know of the lives of our contemporaries, not only in order to believe in their integrity, which is after all but the first beginnings of social morality, but in order to attain to any mental or moral integrity for ourselves or any such hope for society.

Seal, Women's Trade Union League, C. 1908

Describe the WTUL emblem. How does it present itself as an organization and its mission? How does it present the woman worker and her social role? What does the seal suggest about the WTUL's view of industrial capitalism and social class?

SOURCE: *Women's Trade Union League Seal by Julia Bracken Wendt,* Proceedings of the Second Biennial Convention of the National Women's Trade Union League of America, *September 27– October 1, 1909.*

JOE HILL

"Ta-ra-ra-boom-de-ay," *The Little Red Songbook,* 1909

The Swedish-born IWW songwriter Joe Hill, born Joel Hagglund but known for the name he Americanized and then reduced to seem more proletarian, was executed in Colorado in 1915 after a controversial trial for murder. He celebrates labor's resistance to exploitation in this joyful call to sabotage.

SOURCE: The Little Red Song Book. *Spokane, Washington, 1909. 22–23.*

I had a job once threshing wheat, worked sixteen hours
　　with hands and feet.
And when the moon was shining bright, they kept me
　　working all the night.
One moonlight night, I hate to tell, I "accidentally" slipped
　　and fell.
My pitchfork went right in between some cog wheels of
　　that thresh-machine.

CHORUS
Ta-ra-ra-boom-de-ay!
It made a noise that way,
And wheels and bolts and hay,
Went flying every way.
That stingy rube said, "Well!
A thousand gone to hell."
But I did sleep that night,
I needed it all right.

Next day that stingy rube did say, I'll bring my eggs to
　　town today;
You grease my wagon up, you mutt, and don't forget to
　　screw the nut.
I greased his wagon all right, but I plumb forgot to
　　screw the nut,
And when he started on that trip, the wheel slipped off
　　and broke his hip.

SECOND CHORUS

Ta-ra-ra-boom-de-ay!

It made a noise that way,

That rube was sure a sight,

And mad enough to fight;

His whiskers and his legs

Were full of scrambled eggs;

I told him, That's too bad—

I'm feeling very sad.

And then that farmer said, You turk! I bet you are an
        I-Won't-Work.

He paid me off right there, By Gum! So I went home and
        told my chum.

Next day when threshing did commence, My chum was
        Johnny on the fence;

And 'pon my word, that awkward kid, he dropped his
        pitchfork, like I did.

THIRD CHORUS

Ta-ra-ra-boom-de-ay!

It made a noise that way,

And part of that machine

Hit Reuben on the bean.

He cried, Oh me, oh my;

I nearly lost my eye.

My partner said, You're right—

It's bedtime now, good night.

But still that rube was pretty wise, these things did open
        up his eyes.

He said, There must be something wrong; I think I work
        my men too long.

He cut the hours and raised the pay, gave ham and eggs
        for every day,

Now gets his men from union hall, and has no "accidents"
        at all.

FOURTH CHORUS

Ta-ra-ra-boom-de-ay!

That rube is feeling gay;

He learned his lesson quick,

Just through a simple trick.

For fixing rotten jobs

And fixing greedy slobs
This is the only way,
Ta-ra-ra-boom-de-ay!

EMMA GOLDMAN

"Anarchism: What It Really Stands For," *Anarchism and Other Essays*, 1910

Although communists and anarchists may want to join forces in bringing down an Old Order, they do not agree on the social structures that would replace it. Contrast Goldman's view of the ideal future with that of Marx. Where are their points of agreement? Where do they clash?

SOURCE: *Emma Goldman, Hippolyte Havel*. Anarchism and Other Essays with a Biographic Sketch by Hippolyte Havel. *New York: Mother Earth Publishing Association, 1910. 53–74.*

*T*HE history of human growth and development is at the same time the history of the terrible struggle of every new idea heralding the approach of a brighter dawn. In its tenacious hold on tradition, the Old has never hesitated to make use of the foulest and cruelest means to stay the advent of the New, in whatever form or period the latter may have asserted itself. Nor need we retrace our steps into the distant past to realize the enormity of opposition, difficulties, and hardships placed in the path of every progressive idea. The rack, the thumbscrew, and the knout are still with us; so are the convict's garb and the social wrath, all conspiring against the spirit that is serenely marching on.

Anarchism could not hope to escape the fate of all other ideas of innovation. Indeed, as the most revolutionary and uncompromising innovator, Anarchism must needs meet with the combined ignorance and venom of the world it aims to reconstruct. . . .

Anarchism urges man to think, to investigate, to analyze every proposition; but that the brain capacity of the average reader be not taxed too much, I also shall begin with a definition, and then elaborate on the latter.

Goldman's definition of anarchism.

ANARCHISM:—The philosophy of a new social order based on liberty unrestricted by man-made law; the theory that all forms of government rest on violence, and are therefore wrong and harmful, as well as unnecessary.

The new social order rests, of course, on the materialistic basis of life; but while all Anarchists agree that the main evil today is an economic one, they maintain that the solution of that evil can be brought about only through the consideration of *every phase* of life,—individual, as well as the collective; the internal, as well as the external phases.

A thorough perusal of the history of human development will disclose two elements in bitter conflict with each other; elements that are only now beginning to be understood, not as foreign to each other, but as closely related and truly harmonious, if only placed in proper environment: the individual and social instincts. The individual and society have waged a relentless and bloody battle for ages, each striving for supremacy, because each was blind to the value and importance of the other. The individual and social instincts, the one a most potent factor for individual endeavor, for growth, aspiration, self realization; the other an equally potent factor for mutual helpfulness and social wellbeing.

The explanation of the storm raging within the individual, and between him and his surroundings, is not far to seek. The primitive man, unable to understand his being, much less the unity of all life, felt himself absolutely dependent on blind, hidden forces ever ready to mock and taunt him. Out of that attitude grew the religious concepts of man as a mere speck of dust dependent on superior powers on high, who can only be appeased by complete surrender. All the early sagas rest on that idea, which continues to be the *Leitmotiv* of the biblical tales dealing with the relation of man to God, to the State, to society. Again and again the same motif, *man is nothing, the powers are everything.* Thus Jehovah would only endure man on condition of complete surrender. Man can have all the glories of the earth, but he must not become conscious of himself. The State, society, and moral laws all sing the same refrain: Man can have all the glories of the earth, but he must not become conscious of himself.

What does Goldman mean by "man becoming conscious of himself"? What is the ideal that she envisions?

Anarchism is the only philosophy which brings to man the consciousness of himself; which maintains that God, the State, and society are non-existent, that their promises are null and void, since they can be fulfilled only through man's subordination. Anarchism is therefore the teacher of the unity of life; not merely in nature, but in man. There is no conflict between the individual and the social instincts, any more than there is between the heart and the lungs: the one the receptacle of a precious life essence, the other the repository of the element that keeps the essence pure and strong. The individual is the heart of society, conserving the essence of social life; society is the lungs which are distributing the element to keep the life essence—that is, the individual—pure and strong.

"The one thing of value in the world," says Emerson, "is the active soul; this every man contains within him. The soul active sees absolute truth and utters truth and creates." In other words, the individual instinct is the thing of value in the world. It is the true soul that sees and creates the truth alive, out of which is to come a still greater truth, the reborn social soul.

Anarchism is the great liberator of man from the phantoms that have held him captive; it is the arbiter and pacifier of the two forces for individual and social harmony. To accomplish that unity, Anarchism has declared war on the pernicious influences which have so far prevented the harmonious blending of individual and social instincts, the individual and society.

What are the "phantoms" that have kept men from the anarchist ideal proposed by Goldman?

Religion, the dominion of the human mind; Property, the dominion of human needs; and Government, the dominion of human conduct, represent the stronghold of man's enslavement and all the horrors it entails. Religion! How it dominates man's mind, how it humiliates and degrades his soul. God is everything, man is nothing, says religion. But out of that nothing God has created a kingdom so despotic, so tyrannical, so cruel, so terribly exacting that naught but gloom and tears and blood have ruled the world since gods began. Anarchism rouses man to rebellion against this black monster. Break your mental fetters, says Anarchism to man, for not until you think and judge for yourself will you get rid of the dominion of darkness, the greatest obstacle to all progress.

Property, the dominion of man's needs, the denial of the right to satisfy his needs. Time was when property claimed a divine right, when it came to man with the same refrain, even as religion, "Sacrifice! Abnegate! Submit!" The spirit of Anarchism has lifted man from his prostrate position. He now stands erect, with his face toward the light. He has learned to see the insatiable, devouring, devastating nature of property, and he is preparing to strike the monster dead.[1]

"Property is robbery," said the great French Anarchist Proudhon. Yes, but without risk and danger to the robber. Monopolizing the accumulated efforts of man, property has robbed him of his birthright, and has turned him loose a pauper and an outcast. Property has not even the time-worn excuse that man does not create enough to satisfy all needs. The A B C student of economics knows that the productivity of labor within the last few decades far exceeds normal demand. But what are normal demands to an abnormal institution? The only demand that property recognizes is its own gluttonous appetite for greater wealth, because wealth means power; the power to subdue, to crush, to exploit, the power to enslave, to outrage, to degrade. America is particularly boastful of her great power, her enormous national wealth. Poor America, of what avail is all her wealth, if the individuals comprising the nation are wretchedly poor? If they live in squalor, in filth, in crime, with hope and joy gone, a homeless, soilless army of human prey.

It is generally conceded that unless the returns of any business venture exceed the cost, bankruptcy is inevitable. But those engaged in the business of producing wealth have not yet learned even this simple lesson. Every year the cost of production in human life is growing larger (50,000 killed, 100,000 wounded in America last year); the returns to the masses, who help to create wealth, are ever getting smaller. Yet America continues to be blind to the inevitable bankruptcy of our business of production. Nor is this the only crime of the latter. Still more fatal is the crime of turning the producer into a mere particle of a machine, with less will and decision than his master of steel and iron. Man is being robbed not merely of the products of his labor, but of the power of free initiative, of originality, and the interest in, or desire for, the things he is making.

---

1. Pierre-Joseph Proudhon (1809–1865).

Real wealth consists in things of utility and beauty, in things that help to create strong, beautiful bodies and surroundings inspiring to live in. But if man is doomed to wind cotton around a spool, or dig coal, or build roads for thirty years of his life, there can be no talk of wealth. What he gives to the world is only gray and hideous things, reflecting a dull and hideous existence,—too weak to live, too cowardly to die. Strange to say, there are people who extol this deadening method of centralized production as the proudest achievement of our age. They fail utterly to realize that if we are to continue in machine subserviency, our slavery is more complete than was our bondage to the King. They do not want to know that centralization is not only the death-knell of liberty, but also of health and beauty, of art and science, all these being impossible in a clock-like, mechanical atmosphere.

Anarchism cannot but repudiate such a method of production: its goal is the freest possible expression of all the latent powers of the individual. Oscar Wilde defines a perfect personality as "one who develops under perfect conditions, who is not wounded, maimed, or in danger." A perfect personality, then, is only possible in a state of society where man is free to choose the mode of work, the conditions of work, and the freedom to work. One to whom the making of a table, the building of a house, or the tilling of the soil, is what the painting is to the artist and the discovery to the scientist,—the result of inspiration, of intense longing, and deep interest in work as a creative force. That being the ideal of Anarchism, its economic arrangements must consist of voluntary productive and distributive associations, gradually developing into free communism, as the best means of producing with the least waste of human energy. Anarchism, however, also recognizes the right of the individual, or numbers of individuals, to arrange at all times for other forms of work, in harmony with their tastes and desires.

Goldman explains an anarchist ideal of work.

Such free display of human energy being possible only under complete individual and social freedom, Anarchism directs its forces against the third and greatest foe of all social equality; namely, the State, organized authority, or statutory law,—the dominion of human conduct.

Just as religion has fettered the human mind, and as property, or the monopoly of things, has subdued and stifled man's needs, so has the State enslaved his spirit, dictating every phase of conduct. "All government in essence," says Emerson, "is tyranny." It matters not whether it is government by divine right or majority rule. In every instance its aim is the absolute subordination of the individual.

Referring to the American government, the greatest American Anarchist, David Thoreau, said: "Government, what is it but a tradition, though a recent one, endeavoring to transmit itself unimpaired to posterity, but each instance losing its integrity; it has not the vitality and force of a single living man. Law never made man a whit more just; and by means of their respect for it, even the well disposed are daily made agents of injustice."

Indeed, the keynote of government is injustice. With the arrogance and self-sufficiency of the King who could do no wrong, governments ordain, judge, condemn, and punish the most insignificant offenses, while maintaining themselves by the greatest of all offenses, the annihilation of individual liberty. Thus Ouida[2] is right when she maintains that "the State only aims at instilling those qualities in its public by which its demands are obeyed, and its exchequer is filled. Its highest attainment is the reduction of mankind to clockwork. In its atmosphere all those finer and more delicate liberties, which require treatment and spacious expansion, inevitably dry up and perish. The State requires a taxpaying machine in which there is no hitch, an exchequer in which there is never a deficit, and a public, monotonous, obedient, colorless, spiritless, moving humbly like a flock of sheep along a straight high road between two walls."

Yet even a flock of sheep would resist the chicanery of the State, if it were not for the corruptive, tyrannical, and oppressive methods it employs to serve its purposes. Therefore Bakunin[3] repudiates the State as synonymous with the surrender of the liberty of the individual or small minorities,—the destruction of social relationship, the curtailment, or complete denial even, of life itself, for its own aggrandizement. The State is the altar of political freedom and, like the religious altar, it is maintained for the purpose of human sacrifice. . . .

| *Why is Goldman optimistic?*

Will it [Anarchism] not lead to a revolution? Indeed, it will. No real social change has ever come about without a revolution. People are either not familiar with their history, or they have not yet learned that revolution is but thought carried into action.

Anarchism, the great leaven of thought, is today permeating every phase of human endeavor. Science, art, literature, the drama, the effort for economic betterment, in fact every individual and social opposition to the existing disorder of things, is illumined by the spiritual light of Anarchism. It is the philosophy of the sovereignty of the individual. It is the theory of social harmony. It is the great, surging, living truth that is reconstructing the world, and that will usher in the Dawn.

---

2. Ouida, pen name of Marie Louise Ramé (1839–1908), a popular English novelist.

3. Mikhail Bakunin (1814–1876), one of the first anarchist theorists.

JAMES OPPENHEIM

"Bread And Roses," *The American Magazine,* 1911

Soon set to music, Oppenheim's poem became an anthem for women in labor movements. What does he mean by "the rising of the women means the rising of the race"? How might women's contribution to a labor movement change it?

SOURCE: The American Magazine, *V. 73, December, 1911. http://babel.hathitrust.org/cgi/pt?id=mdp .39015012106988;view=1up;seq=230*

As we go marching, marching, in the beauty of the day,
A million darkened kitchens, a thousand mill lofts gray,
Are touched with all the radiance that a sudden sun discloses,
For the people hear us singing: Bread and Roses! Bread and Roses!

As we go marching, marching, we battle too for men,
For they are women's children, and we mother them again.
Our lives shall not be sweated from birth until life closes;
Hearts starve as well as bodies; give us bread, but give us roses.

As we go marching, marching, unnumbered women dead
Go crying through our singing their ancient call for bread.
Small art and love and beauty their drudging spirits knew.
Yes, it is bread we fight for, but we fight for roses too.

As we go marching, marching, we bring the greater days,
The rising of the women means the rising of the race.
No more the drudge and idler, ten that toil where one reposes,
But a sharing of life's glories: Bread and roses, bread and roses.

Our lives shall not be sweated from birth until life closes;
hearts starve as well as bodies; bread and roses, bread and roses.

WILLIAM HAYWOOD

"The General Strike," March 16, 1911

"Big Bill" Haywood gave this speech at a benefit for the Buccafori Defense, a support for the IWW shoemaker Vincent S. Buccafori, at the time jailed and accused of killing his foreman. Here Haywood takes the opportunity to explain the importance and goals of the general strike, one of the IWW's most important strategies.

In what ways does his general strike differ from a factory strike? Consider the following: how the strikes begin, how they are conducted, and their short and long-term goals.

SOURCE: The General Strike. *(Pamphlet.) Chicago: n.d. Published by the Industrial Workers of the World. http://www.iww.org/history/library/Haywood/GeneralStrike*

. . . We never had any trouble about closing the mines down, and could keep them closed down for an indefinite period. It was always the craft unions that caused us to lose our fights when we did lose. I recall the first general strike in the Coeur d'Alenes, when all the mines in that district were closed down to prevent a reduction of wages. The mine owners brought in thugs the first thing. They attempted to man the mines with men carrying six shooters and

Here Haywood explains why a strike of a single craft does not suffice.

rifles. There was a pitched battle between miners and thugs. A few were killed on each side. And then the mine owners asked for the soldiers, and the soldiers came. Who brought the soldiers? Railroads manned by union men; engines fired with coal mined by union men. That is the division of labor that might have lost us the strike in the Coeur d'Alenes. It didn't lose it, however. We were successful in that issue. But in Leadville we lost the strike there because they were able to bring in scab labor from other communities where they had the force of the government behind them, and the force of the troops. In 1899 we were compelled to fight the battle over in a great general strike in the Coeur d'Alenes again. Then came the general strike in Cripple Creek, the strike that has become a household word in labor circles throughout the world. In Cripple Creek 5,000 men were on strike in sympathy with 45 men belonging to the Millmen's Union in Colorado City; 45 men who had been discharged simply because they were trying to improve their standard of living. By using the state troops and the influence of the Federal Government they were able to man the mills in Colorado City with scab millmen; and after months of hardship, after 1,600 of our men had been arrested and placed in the Victor Armory in one single room that they called the "bullpen," after 400 of them had been loaded aboard special trains guarded by soldiers, shipped away from their homes, dumped out on the prairies down in New Mexico and Kansas; after the women who had taken up the work of distributing strike relief had been placed under arrest—we find then that they were able to man the mines with scabs, the mills running with scabs, the railroads conveying the ore from Cripple Creek to Colorado City run by union men—the connecting link of a proposition that was scabby at both ends! We were not thoroughly organized. There has been no time when there has been a general strike in this country.

There are three phases of a general strike. They are:

A general strike in an industry

A general strike in a community; or

A general national strike.

Haywood's definition of a general strike.

The conditions for any of the three have never existed. So how any one can take the position that a general strike would not be effective and not be a good thing for the working class is more than I can understand. We know that the capitalist uses the general strike to good advantage. There is the position that we find the working class and the capitalists in. The capitalists have wealth; they have money. They invest the money in machinery, in the resources of the earth. They operate a factory, a mine, a railroad, a mill. They will keep that factory running just as long as there are profits coming in. When anything happens to disturb the profits, what do the capitalists do? They go on strike; don't they? They withdraw their finances from that particular mill. They close it down because there are no profits to be made there. They don't care what becomes of the working class. But the working class, on the other hand, has always been taught to take care of the capitalist's interest in the property. You don't look after your own interest, your labor power, realizing that without a certain amount of provision you can't reproduce it. You are always looking after the interest of the capitalist, while a general strike would displace his interest and would put you in possession of it.

That is what I want to urge upon the working class; to become so organized on the economic field that they can take and hold the industries in which they are employed. Can you conceive of such a thing? Is it possible? What are the forces that prevent you from doing so? You have all the industries in your own hands at the present time. There is this justification for political action; and that is, to control the forces of the capitalists that they use against us; to be in a position to control the power of government so as to make the work of the army ineffective, so as to abolish totally the secret service and the force of detectives. That is the reason that you want the power of government. That is the reason that you should fully understand the power of the ballot. Now, there isn't any one, Socialist, S. L. P.,[1] Industrial Worker or any other workingman or woman, no matter what society you belong to, but what believes in the ballot. There are those—and I am one of them—who refuse to have the ballot interpreted for them. I know, or think I know, the power of it, and I know that the industrial organization, as I stated in the beginning, is its broadest interpretation. I know, too, that when the workers are brought together in a great organization they are not going to cease to vote. That is when the workers will *begin* to vote, to vote for directors to operate the industries in which they are all employed. So the general strike is a fighting weapon as well as a constructive force. It can be used, and should be used, equally as forcefully by the Socialist as by the Industrial Worker. The Socialists believe in the general strike. They also believe in the organization of industrial forces after the general strike is successful. So, on this great force of the working class I believe we can agree that we should unite into one great organization—big enough to take in the children that are now working; big enough to take in the black man; the white man; big enough to take in all nationalities—an organization that will be strong enough to obliterate state boundaries, to obliterate national boundaries, and one that will become the great industrial force of the working class of the world. (Applause.)

Why does Haywood believe that a general strike would be effective as both a "fighting weapon" and a "constructive force"?

Questions from the audience
1.
Q.—Don't you think there is a lot of waste involved in the general strike in that the sufferers would be the workers in larger portion than the capitalists? The capitalist

---

1. S.L.P. is the Socialist Labor Party.

class always has money and can buy food, while the workers will just have to starve and wait. I was a strong believer in the general strike myself until I read some articles in *The Call* a while ago on this particular phase.[2]

A.—The working class haven't got anything. They can't lose anything. While the capitalist class have got all the money and all the credit, still if the working class laid off the capitalists couldn't get food at any price. This is the power of the working class. If the workers are organized (remember now, I say "if they are organized"—by that I don't mean 100 per cent, but a good strong minority), all they have to do is to put their hands in their pockets and they have got the capitalist class whipped. The working class can stand it a week without anything to eat—I have gone pretty nearly that long myself, and I wasn't on strike. In the meantime I hadn't lost any meals I just postponed them. (Laughter.) I didn't do it voluntarily, I tell you that. But all the workers have to do is to organize so that they can put their hands in their pockets; when they have got *their* hands there, the capitalists can't get theirs in. If the workers can organize so that they can stand idle they will then be strong enough so that they can take the factories. Now, I hope to see the day when the man who goes *out* of the factory will be the one who will be called a scab; when the good union man will stay in the factory, whether the capitalists like it or not; when we lock the bosses out and run the factories to suit ourselves. That is our program. We will do it.

2.

Q.—Doesn't the trend of your talk lead to direct action or what we call revolution? For instance, we try to throw the bosses out; don't you think the bosses will strike back? Another thing: Of course, the working class can starve eight days, but they can't starve nine. You don't have to teach the workingman how to starve, because there were teachers before you. There is no way out but fight, as I understand it. Do you think you will get your industrialism through peace or through revolution?

A.—Well, comrade, you have no peace now. The capitalist system, as peaceable as it is, is killing off hundreds of thousands of workers every year. That isn't peace. One hundred thousand workers were injured in this state last year. I do not care whether it's peaceable or not; I want to see it come.

As for starving the workers eight days, I made no such program. I said that they could, but I don't want to see them do it. The fact that I was compelled to postpone a few meals was because I wasn't in the vicinity of any grub. I suggest that you break down that idea that you must protect the boss's property. That is all we are fighting for—what the boss calls his "private property," what he calls his private interest in the things that the people must have as a whole, to live. Those are the things we are after.

---

2. *The Call* was a New York socialist newspaper.

3.

Q.—Do the Industrial Unionists believe in political action? Have they got any special platforms that they support?

A.—The Industrial Workers of the World is not a political organization.

Q.—Just like the A. F. of L.?

A.—No.

Q.—*They* don't believe in any political action, either, so far as that is concerned.

A.—Yes, the A. F. of L. does believe in political action. It is a political organization. The Industrial Workers of the World is an economic organization without affiliation with any political party or any non-political sect. I as an Industrialist say that industrial unionism is the broadest possible political interpretation of the working-class political power, because by organizing the workers industrially you at once enfranchise the women in the shops, you at once give the black men who are disfran-

Haywood reveals his position on the vote.

chised politically a voice in the operation of the industries; and the same would extend to every worker. That to my mind is the kind of political action that the working class wants. You must not be content to come to the ballot box on the first Tuesday after the first Monday in November, the ballot box erected by the capitalist class, guarded by capitalist henchmen, and deposit your ballot to be counted by black-handed thugs, and say, "That is political action." You must protect your ballot with an organization that will enforce the mandates of your class. I want political action that counts. I want a working class that can hold an election every day if they want to.

4.

Q. (By a woman comrade)—Isn't a strike, theoretically, a situation where the workingmen lay down their tools and the capitalist class sits and waits, and they both say, "Well, what are you going to do about it"; And if they go beyond that, and go outside the law, is it any longer a strike? Isn't it a revolution?

A.—A strike is an incipient revolution. Many large revolutions have grown out of a small strike.

Q.—Well, I heartily believe in the general strike if it is a first step toward the revolution, and I believe in what you intimate—that the workers are damn fools if they don't *take* what they want, when they can't get it any other way. (Applause.)

A.—That is a better speech than I can make. If I didn't think that the general strike was leading on to the great revolution which will emancipate the working class I wouldn't be here. I am with you because I believe that in this little meeting there is a nucleus here that will carry on the work and propagate the seed that will grow into the great revolution that will overthrow the capitalist class.

SOCIALIST PARTY PLATFORM OF 1912

Indianapolis, Indiana, May 12, 1912

In 1912, the Socialist Party of America put up Eugene V. Debs as its candidate for president of the United States. A native of Indiana, Debs could demonstrate that socialism was not a foreign theory, but rather a vibrant movement seeped in American values.

In the campaign against Republican incumbent William Howard Taft, Democrat Woodrow Wilson, and the newly formed Progressive Party's Theodore Roosevelt, Debs gained 5.99 percent of the popular vote. (Wilson won and was inaugurated in 1913.)

To whom would the Socialist Party appeal?

SOURCE: Iowa Official Register. *Vol. 25. 1913. 362–364.*

*T*he Socialist party declares that the capitalist system has outgrown its historical function, and has become utterly incapable of meeting the problems now confronting society. We denounce this outgrown system as incompetent and corrupt and the source of unspeakable misery and suffering to the whole working class.

Under this system the industrial equipment of the nation has passed into the absolute control of a plutocracy which exacts an annual tribute of hundreds of millions of dollars from the producers. Unafraid of any organized resistance, it stretches out its greedy hands over the still undeveloped resources of the nation—the land, the mines, the forests and the water powers of every State of the Union.

> *The Party describes the nation as a plutocracy, the rule by the wealthy for the wealthy.*

In spite of the multiplication of labor-saving machines and improved methods in industry which cheapen the cost of production, the share of the producers grows ever less, and the prices of all the necessities of life steadily increase. The boasted prosperity of this nation is for the owning class alone. To the rest it means only greater hardship and misery. The high cost of living is felt in every home. Millions of wage-workers have seen the purchasing power of their wages decrease until life has become a desperate battle for mere existence.

Multitudes of unemployed walk the streets of our cities or trudge from State to State awaiting the will of the masters to move the wheels of industry. The farmers in every state are plundered by the increasing prices exacted for tools and machinery and by extortionate rents, freight rates and storage charges.

Capitalist concentration is mercilessly crushing the class of small business men and driving its members into the ranks of property-less wage-workers. The overwhelming majority of the people of America are being forced under a yoke of bondage by this soulless industrial despotism.

It is this capitalist system that is responsible for the increasing burden of armaments, the poverty, slums, child labor, most of the insanity, crime and prostitution, and much of the disease that afflicts mankind.

Under this system the working class is exposed to poisonous conditions, to frightful and needless perils to life and limb, is walled around with court decisions, injunctions and unjust laws, and is preyed upon incessantly for the benefit of the controlling oligarchy of wealth. Under it also, the children of the working class are doomed to ignorance, drudging toil and darkened lives.

In the face of these evils, so manifest that all thoughtful observers are appalled at them, the legislative representatives of the Republican and Democratic parties remain the faithful servants of the oppressors. . . .

Nor has this plutocracy been seriously restrained or even threatened by any Republican or Democratic executive. It has continued to grow in power and insolence alike under the administration of Cleveland, McKinley, Roosevelt and Taft.

We declare, therefore, that the longer sufferance of these conditions is impossible, and we purpose to end them all. We declare them to be the product of the present system in which industry is carried on for private greed, instead of for the welfare of society. We declare, furthermore, that for these evils there will be and can be no remedy and no substantial relief except through Socialism under which industry will be carried on for the common good and every worker receive the full social value of the wealth he creates. Society is divided into warring groups and classes, based upon material interests. Fundamentally, this struggle is a conflict between the two main classes, one of which, the capitalist class, owns the means of production, and the other, the working class, must use these means of production, on terms dictated by the owners.

The capitalist class, though few in numbers, absolutely controls the government, legislative, executive and judicial. This class owns the machinery of gathering and disseminating news through its organized press. It subsidizes seats of learning—the colleges and schools—and even religious and moral agencies. It has also the added prestige which established customs give to any order of society, right or wrong.

The working class, which includes all those who are forced to work for a living whether by hand or brain, in shop, mine or on the soil, vastly outnumbers the capitalist class. Lacking effective organization and class solidarity, this class is unable to enforce its will. Given such a class solidarity and effective organization, the workers will have the power to make all laws and control all industry in their own interest. All political parties are the expression of economic class interests. All other parties than the Socialist party represent one or another group of the ruling capitalist class. Their political conflicts reflect merely superficial rivalries between competing capitalist groups. However they result, these conflicts have no issue of real value to the workers. Whether the Democrats or Republicans win politically, it is the capitalist class that is victorious economically. The Socialist party is the political expression of the economic interests of the workers. Its defeats have been their defeats and its victories their victories. It is a party founded on the science and laws of social development. It proposes that, since all social necessities today are socially produced, the means of their production and distribution shall be socially owned and democratically controlled.

How does the Socialist Party differ from the Republicans, Democrats, and Progressives, all of whom espouse change in this campaign?

In the face of the economic and political aggressions of the capitalist class the only reliance left the workers is that of their economic organizations and their political power. By the intelligent and class conscious use of these, they may resist successfully the capitalist class, break the fetters of wage slavery, and fit themselves for the future society, which is to displace the capitalist system. The Socialist party appreciates the full significance of class organization and urges the wage-earners, the working farmers and all other useful workers to organize for economic and political action, and we pledge ourselves to support the toilers of the fields as well as those in the shops, factories and mines of the nation in their struggles for economic justice. In the defeat or victory of the working class party in this new struggle for freedom lies the defeat or triumph of the common people of all economic groups, as well as the failure or triumph of popular government. Thus the Socialist party is the party of the present day revolution which makes the transition from economic individualism to socialism, from wage slavery to free co-operation, from capitalist oligarchy to industrial democracy.

What does the Socialist Party propose? What would happen if the Party wins the election?

ART YOUNG

"Uncle Sam Ruled Out," *Solidarity*, June 7, 1913

Young, a cartoonist who published in The Masses *as well as the* IWW's *magazine* Solidarity, *takes on corporate capitalism in "Uncle Sam Ruled Out." What is he saying about the United States, its values, and its reforms in this cartoon? What is he saying about the Paterson strike?*

SOURCE: *Art Young, "Uncle Sam Ruled Out,"* Solidarity, *June 7, 1913. Original image courtesy of the Industrial Workers of the World (www.iww.org).*

ELIZABETH GURLEY FLYNN

"The I.W.W. Call to Women," *Solidarity*, July 31, 1915

The firebrand Flynn, aka "Gurley," asserts that women should not organize on the basis of gender, but rather on the basis of social class. What are the "women's issues" that she addresses here and how, in her opinion, will the IWW address them?

SOURCE: Solidarity, *July 31, 1915. 9.*

*I*n the tremendous process of merging all groups of labor into a unified whole; of infusing their humblest daily struggle with the urge of a great ideal—industrial freedom—women are as vitally concerned as men. But the I.W.W., the instrument through which "the world for the workers" is taking concrete form, makes no special appeal to women as such. To us society moves in grooves of class, not sex. Sex distinctions affect us insignificantly and would less, but for economic differences. It is to those women who are wage earners, or wives of workers, that the I.W.W. appeals. We see no basis in fact for feminist mutual interest, no evidence of natural "sex conflict," nor any possibility—nor present desirability—of solidarity among women alone. The success of our program will benefit workers, regardless of sex, and injure all who, without effort, draw profits for a livelihood.

How does Gurley respond to the idea that women have common interests based on their biological sex?

I have seen prosperous, polite, daintily-gowned ladies become indignant over police brutality in the Spokane free speech fight of 1909, and lose all interest—even refuse to put up bail for pregnant women when they realized that the I.W.W. intended to organize the lumber, mining, and farming industries, whence the golden stream flowed to pay for their comfort and leisure.

Yet more horrible a glimpse into the chasm that divides woman and woman is afforded by the bloodthirsty approval of the Ludlow massacre by the "good women" of Trinidad, Colo[rado]. Mrs. Northcutt, wife of the lawyer, said: "There has been a lot of maudlin sentiment about those women and children. There were only two women and they make such a fuss!" Mrs. Rose, wife of the superintendent of the coal railroad, said: "They're nothing but cattle! They ought to be shot!" Mrs. Chandler, wife of the Presbyterian minister, said "The miners probably killed the women and children themselves, because they were a drain on the union!" and, "They ought to have shot Tikas to start with!" This of the Greek leader who had over thirty bullets in his body and his head laid open with the butt of a gun.

The solution of labor troubles agreed upon by a dozen representative women was, "Shoot them down."

The "queen of the parlor" has no interest in common with the "maid in the kitchen"; the wife of the department store owner shows no sisterly concern for the seventeen-year-old girl who finds prostitution the only door to a $5 a week clerk. The sisterhood of women, like the brotherhood of man, is a hollow sham to labor. Behind all its smug hypocrisy and sickly sentimentality loom the sinister outlines of the class war.

ECONOMIC INDEPENDENCE

Gurley addresses arguments about women's special concerns: work, the home, and prostitution.

Fifty years ago earnest advocates of woman's rights were demanding "economic independence." Today Olive Schreiner, in her book, "Woman and Labor," expresses woman's need "for our share of honored and socially useful human toil—labor and the training that fits us for labor." This may be applicable to an insignificant group of white-handed idlers, whose life consists of pleasure-seeking to counteract ennui; but it is meaningless to eight million women wage earners and the innumerable housekeepers.

Women have been engaged in useful human toil since the dawn of time. True enough, much that was once "woman's work"—spinning, weaving, churning, etc.—has been absorbed by the factory system. The old division—men doing the outdoor and women the indoor tasks—ended with the advent of power-operated machinery. But woman was not left idle-handed. Rather it was now possible and inevitable that she should follow her work and take her place with man, at the factory gate; 21 per cent of the total employees in the U.S. are women, 45 per cent of the total in England.

The private ownership of industry and the property-less status of labor become a common problem. But entering the industrial arena later than her brother, she is under the disadvantage in common with the immigrant, of being compelled to work cheaper to secure the job. Hunger, want, scarcity of work, drives all workers to accept an ever lower standard, and the women the lowest. . . .

Whatever superficial semblance of sex hatred appears is due, like "race hatred," to the struggle for the pay-envelope. The woman worker is no freer from "masculine domination," even though self-supporting, while mercilessly exploited by an employer; and the fundamental unity of interest between her and her brother is to organize as a class. STANDARDIZE WAGES, AND REDISTRIBUTE EMPLOYMENT, THROUGH THE SHORTER WORKDAY.

THE SACRED HOME

Ancient illusions die hard, and one of the most hoary is "the sanctity of the home." But a visit to Lawrence, Mass., would bring rapid disillusionment. The golden dream of youth, that marriage brings release from irksome toil, is rudely shattered by the capitalist system. Whole families toil for a living wage. The heaviest burden is on the tired frame of the woman. Child-bearing and housework remain. Pregnant women stand at the looms until the labor pains commence. A few weeks after, the puny babe is left at a day nursery with amateur "nurses"—with the result that 300 babies out of every thousand born die in the first month. The gutter is the baby's playground, and amid the deafening clatter of the looms the mother's heart is torn with anxiety about her children. Miscarriage from overstrain is common, and unscrupulous doctors secure exorbitant sums to perform abortions, that the women may keep at work. But to tell these women toilers how to control birth is a state prison offense in the United States; and so they die, 25,000 yearly from operations. The burden of family, added to the day's mill work, means that while father smokes his pipe and takes his ease, mother has the innumerable household tasks still to do.

As soon as her children's tiny hands can handle machinery, and their tender forms pass for legal age, they too, are fed to the insatiable looms. Tragic indeed is the lot of the woman toiler! Her youth, her love, her home, her babies are "ground into dollars for parasites' pleasure."

PROSTITUTION

Hardly more attractive is the lot of the young girl toiler, who sells beautiful articles she is denied, who weaves delicate fabrics she never wears, who makes fine garments and shivers home in winter's snows with barely enough to cover her nakedness. Full of life and spirit, craving enjoyment, good clothes and youthful pleasures—is it any wonder that when resistance is weakened by hunger, many in despair sell their sex to secure what honest effort denies them; 350,000 prostitutes in the U.S.; 20,000 added every year, five per cent of the total working group (although all do not come from that source)—is a staggering condemnation of our present society. "Starvation or prostitution?"—how many girls last winter, with three million unemployed in the land, were compelled to face that question?

The I.W.W. relies upon the organized power of labor to sweep away such nauseous conditions. White slaves, investigation, rescue houses, etc., help a hundred, but the juggernaut of industry crushes a thousand. The department store owner is the largest procurer today, and the fresh, youthful faces of our daughters and sisters should spur us on to break his power. POVERTY, The root of all crime and vice, must be destroyed and labor be free to enjoy the plentitude it creates. Carefree childhood, flowering youth, happy homes, are denied to countless girls who work in the textile towns of the East, and the boys driven into the migratory life of the West, and will be until industry is owned by labor and adjusted to the happiness of the toiler.

THE I.W.W. APPEAL

The I.W.W. appeals to women to organize side by side with their men folks, in the union that shall increasingly determine its own rules of work and wages—until its solidarity and power shall the world command. It points out to the young girl that marriage is no escape from the labor problem, and to the mother, that the interest of herself and her children are woven in with the interests of the class, and to both that this industrial ENFRANCHISEMENT is possible for all, women and children, citizens and immigrants, every nation and color.

WOMEN AND THE CRAFT UNIONS

Where a secluded home environment has produced a psychological attitude of "me and mine"—how is the I.W.W. to overcome conservatism and selfishness? By driving women into an active participation in union affairs, especially strikes, where the mass meetings, mass picketing, women's meetings, and children's gatherings are a tremendous emotional stimulant. The old unions never have considered the women as part of the strike. They were expected to stay home and worry about the empty larder, the hungry kiddies, and the growling landlord, easy prey to the agents of the company. But the strike was "a man's business." The men had the joy of the fight, the women not even an intelligent explanation of it.

Never does a bricklayers' or street carmens' union[1] have a woman's meeting. So the women worry and wait, and weaken the spirit of the men by tears and complaining.

WOMEN AND THE I.W.W. STRIKES

Women can be the most militant or most conservative element in a strike, in proportion to their comprehension of its purpose. The I.W.W. has been accused of putting the women in the front. The truth is, the I.W.W. does not keep them in the back, and they go to the front. Mothers nursing their babes stood in the snow at the Lawrence common meetings. Young girls, Josephine Liss, Hannah Silverman, were flaming spirits in Lawrence and Paterson. Hundreds went to jail, with a religious devotion to the cause. . . .

WOMAN'S PLACE THE HOME?

Note Gurley's famous quote about the IWW's position on women.

A familiar query is, "What effect would the democratization of industry have on the family?" The I.W.W. is at war with the ruthless invasion of family life by capitalism, with the unnatural and shameful condition of a half million able-bodied unemployed men in New York City alone, last winter, yet there are 27,000 children under 16 years of age in cotton mills in the South. We are determined that industry shall be so organized that all adults, men and women, may work and receive in return a sufficiency to make

---

1. Street carmen are street car men, those who run the trolleys, subways, and other public transportation services.

child labor a relic of barbarism. This does not imply that mothers must work, or that women must stay at home, if they prefer otherwise. Either extreme is equally absurd. House work will probably be reduced to a minimum through the application of machinery, now more costly than the labor of women but the care of children will remain an absorbing interest with the vast majority of women. The free choice of work is the IWW ideal—which does not mean to put women forcibly back into the home, but certainly does mean to end capitalism's forcibly taking her out of the home.

GLIMMERINGS INTO THE FUTURE

Exact details of the readjustment of human relations after an economic revolution cannot be mapped out. The historical destiny of our times is to establish industrial freedom. What mighty superstructure our progeny will rear upon our work, we can only vaguely prophesy. . . .

CHARLOTTE PERKINS STETSON (GILMAN)

FROM *Women and Economics: A Study Of The Economic Relation Between Men And Women,* 1898

Here Gilman describes the benefits that will occur when women step out of the "family relation" to assert their identities as individuals. But what changes must be made in society for this to be even imaginable?

A note: Charlotte Perkins was married twice. When she wrote Women and Economics, *she used her first married name, Stetson. Some years after this marriage ended in divorce, she married again and took the name Gilman. Charlotte Perkins Gilman is the name she is known by today.*

SOURCE: *Chapter XIV,* Women and Economics: A Study of the Economic Relation Between Men and Women. *Boston: Small, Maynard & Company, 1898. 295–317.*

The changes in our conception and expression of home life, so rapidly and steadily going on about us, involve many far-reaching effects, all helpful to human advancement. Not the least of these is the improvement in our machinery of social intercourse.

This necessity of civilization was unknown in those primitive ages when family intercourse was sufficient for all, and when any further contact between individuals meant war. Trade and its travel, the specialization of labor and the distribution of its products, with their ensuing development, have produced a wider, freer, and more frequent movement and interchange among the innumerable individuals whose interaction makes society. Only recently, and as yet but partially, have women as individuals come to their share of this fluent social intercourse which is the essential condition of civilization. It is not merely a pleasure or an indulgence: it is the human necessity.

For women as individuals to meet men and other women as individuals, with no regard whatever to the family relation, is a growing demand of our time. As a social necessity, it is perforce being met in some fashion; but its right development is greatly impeded by the clinging folds of domestic and social customs derived from the sexuo-economic relation. The demand for a wider and freer social intercourse between the sexes rests, primarily, on the needs of their respective natures, but is developed in modern life to a far subtler and higher range of emotion than existed in the primitive state, where they had

Marriage as a "sexo-economic relation."

but one need and but one way of meeting it; and this demand, too, calls for a better arrangement of our machinery of living.

Always in social evolution, as in other evolution, the external form suited to earlier needs is but slowly outgrown; and the period of transition, while the new functions are fumbling through the old organs, and slowly forcing mechanical expression for themselves, is necessarily painful. So far in our development, acting on a deep-seated conviction that the world consisted only of families and the necessary business arrangements involved in providing for those families, we have conscientiously striven to build and plan for family advantage, and either unconsciously or grudgingly have been forced to make transient provision for individuals. Whatever did not tend to promote family life, and did tend to provide for the needs of individuals not at the time in family relation, we have deprecated in principle, though reluctantly forced to admit it in practice.

To this day articles are written, seriously and humorously, protesting against the increasing luxury and comfort of bachelor apartments for men, as well as against the pecuniary independence of women, on the ground that these conditions militate against marriage and family life. Most men, even now, pass through a period of perhaps ten years, when they are individuals, business calling them away from their parental family, and business not allowing them to start new families of their own. Women, also, more and more each year, are entering upon a similar period of individual life. And there is a certain permanent percentage of individuals, "odd numbers" and "broken sets," who fall short of family life or who are left over from it; and these need to live.

> Men and women as individuals: a temporary experience or essential characteristic?

The residence hotel, the boarding-house, club, lodging-house, and restaurant are our present provision for this large and constantly increasing class. It is not a traveling class. These are people who want to live somewhere for years at a time, but who are not married or otherwise provided with a family. Home life being in our minds inextricably connected with married life, a home being held to imply a family, and a family implying a head, these detached persons are unable to achieve any home life, and are thereby subjected to the inconvenience, deprivation, and expense, the often inhygienic, and sometimes immoral influences, of our makeshift substitutes.

What the human race requires is permanent provision for the needs of individuals, disconnected from the sex-relation. Our assumption that only married people and their immediate relatives have any right to live in comfort and health is erroneous. Every human being needs a home,—bachelor, husband, or widower, girl, wife, or widow, young or old. They need it from the cradle to the grave, and without regard to sex-connections. We should so build and arrange for the shelter and comfort of humanity as not to interfere with marriage, and yet not to make that comfort dependent upon marriage. With the industries of home life managed professionally, with rooms and suites of rooms and houses obtainable by any person or persons desiring them, we could live singly without losing home comfort and general companionship, we could meet bereavement without being robbed of the common conveniences of living as well as of the heart's love, and we could marry in ease and freedom without involving any change in the economic base of either party concerned.

Married people will always prefer a home together, and can have it; but groups of women or groups of men can also have a home together if they like, or contiguous rooms. And individuals even could have a house to themselves, without having, also, the business of a home upon their shoulders.

Take the kitchens out of the houses, and you leave rooms which are open to any form of arrangement and extension; and the occupancy of them does not mean "housekeeping." In such living, personal character and taste would flower as never before; the home of each individual would be at last a true personal expression; and the union of individuals in marriage would not compel the jumbling together of all the external machinery of their lives,—a process in which much of the delicacy and freshness of love, to say nothing of the power of mutual rest and refreshment, is constantly lost. The sense of lifelong freedom and self-respect and of the peace and permanence of one's own home will do much to purify and uplift the personal relations of life, and more to strengthen and extend the social relations. The individual will learn to feel himself an integral part of the social structure, in close, direct, permanent connection with the needs and uses of society.

This is especially needed for women, who are generally considered, and who consider themselves, mere fractions of families, and incapable of any wholesome life of their own. The knowledge that peace and comfort may be theirs for life, even if they do not marry,—and may be still theirs for life, even if they do,—will develop a serenity and strength in women most beneficial to them and to the world. It is a glaring proof of the insufficient and irritating character of our existing form of marriage that women must be forced to it by the need of food and clothes, and men by the need of cooks and housekeepers. We are absurdly afraid that, if men or women can meet these needs of life by other means, they will cheerfully renounce the marriage relation. And yet we sing adoringly of the power of love!

How does Gilman view contemporary marriage? What does she imagine that it could be?

In reality, we may hope that the most valuable effect of this change in the basis of living will be the cleansing of love and marriage from this base admixture of pecuniary interest and creature comfort, and that men and women, eternally drawn together by the deepest force in nature, will be able at last to meet on a plane of pure and perfect love. We shame our own ideals, our deepest instincts, our highest knowledge, by this gross assumption that the noblest race on earth will not mate, or, at least, not mate monogamously, unless bought and bribed through the common animal necessities of food and shelter, and chained by law and custom.

The depth and purity and permanence of the marriage relation rest on the necessity for the prolonged care of children by both parents,—a law of racial development which we can never escape. When parents are less occupied in getting food and cooking it, in getting furniture and dusting it, they may find time to give new thought and new effort to the care of their children. The necessities of the child are far deeper than for bread and bed; those are his mere racial needs, held in common with all his kind. What he needs far more and receives far less is the companionship, the association, the personal touch, of his father and mother. When the common labors of life are removed from the home, we shall have the time, and perhaps the inclination, to make the personal acquaintance of our children. They will seem to us not so much creatures to be waited on as people to be understood. As the civil and military protection of society has long since superseded the tooth-and-claw defence of the fierce parent, without in the least endangering the truth and intensity of the family relation, so the economic provision of society will in time supersede the bringing home of prey by the parent, without evil effects to the love or prosperity of the family. These primitive needs and primitive methods of meeting them are unquestionably at the base of the family relation; but we have long passed them by, and the ties between parent and child are not weakened, but strengthened, by the change.

The more we grow away from these basic conditions, the more fully we realize the deeper and higher forms of relation which are the strength and the delight of human life. Full and permanent provision for individual life and comfort will not cut off the forces that draw men and women together or hold children to their parents; but it will purify and intensify these relations to a degree which we can somewhat foretell by observing the effect of such changes as are already accomplished in this direction. And, in freeing the individual, old and young, from enforced association on family lines, and allowing this emergence into free association on social lines, we shall healthfully assist the development of true social intercourse.

The present economic basis of family life holds our friendly and familiar intercourse in narrow grooves. Such visiting and mingling as is possible to us is between families rather than between individuals; and the growing specialization of individuals renders it increasingly unlikely that all the members of a given family shall please a given visitor or he please them. This, on our present basis, either checks the intercourse or painfully strains the family relation. The change of economic relation in families from a sex-basis to a social basis will make possible wide individual intercourse without this accompanying strain on the family ties.

Gilman explains the need for social intercourse beyond the family relations.

This outgoing impulse among members of families, their growing desire for general and personal social intercourse, has been considered as a mere thirst for amusement, and deprecated by the moralist. He has so far maintained that the highest form of association was association with one's own family, and that a desire for a wider and more fluent relationship was distinctly unworthy. "He is a good family man," we say admiringly of him who asks only for his newspaper and slippers in the evening; and for the woman who dares admit that she wishes further society than that of her husband we have but one name. With the children, too, our constant effort is to "keep the boys at home," to "make home attractive," so that our ancient ideal, the patriarchal ideal, of a world of families and nothing else, may be maintained.

But this is a world of persons as well as of families. We are persons as soon as we are born, though born into families. We are persons when we step out of families, and persons still, even when we step into new families of our own. As persons, we need more and more, in each generation, to associate with other persons. It is most interesting to watch this need making itself felt, and getting itself supplied, by fair means or foul, through all these stupid centuries. In our besotted exaggeration of the sex-relation, we have crudely supposed that a wish for wider human relationship was a wish for wider sex-relationship, and was therefore to be discouraged, as in Spain it was held unwise to teach women to write, lest they become better able to communicate with their lovers, and so shake the foundations of society.

But, when our sex-relation is made pure and orderly by the economic independence of women, when sex-attraction is no longer a consuming fever, forever convulsing the social surface, under all its bars and chains, we shall not be content to sit down forever with half a dozen blood relations for our whole social arena. We shall need each other more, not less, and shall recognize that social need of one another as the highest faculty of this the highest race on earth.

The force which draws friends together is a higher one than that which draws the sexes together, higher in the sense of belonging to a later race-development. "Passing the love of women" is no unmeaning phrase. Children need one another: young people need one another. Middle-aged people need one another: old people need one another. We all need one another, much and often. Just as every human creature needs a place to be alone in, a sacred, private "home" of his own, so all human creatures need a place to be together in, from the two who can show each other their souls uninterruptedly, to the largest throng that can throb and stir in unison.

Humanity means being together, and our unutterably outgrown way of living keeps us apart. How many people, if they dare face the fact, have often hopelessly longed for some better way of seeing their friends, their own true friends, relatives by soul, if not by body! . . .

Gilman explains that women, especially, need more social interaction with peers.

There is a constant thirst among us for fuller and truer social intercourse; but our social machinery provides no means for quenching it.

Men have satisfied this desire in large measure; but between women, or between men and women, it is yet far from accomplishment. Men meet one another freely in their work, while women work alone. But the difference is sharpest in their play. "Girls don't have any fun!" say boys, scornfully; and they don't have very much. What they do have must come, like their bread and butter, on lines of sex. Some man must give them what amusement they have, as he must give them everything else. Men have filled the world with games and sports, from the noble contests of the Olympic plain to the brain and body training sports of to-day, good, bad, and indifferent. Through all the ages the men have played; and the women have looked on, when they were asked. Even the amusing occupation of seeing other people do things was denied them, unless they were invited by the real participants. The "queen of the ball-room" is but a wall-flower, unless she is asked to dance by the real king.

Even to-day, when athletics are fast opening to women, when tennis and golf and all the rest are possible to them, the two sexes are far from even in chances to play. To want a good time is not the same thing as to want the society of the other sex, and to make a girl's desire for a good time hang so largely on her power of sex-attraction is another of the grievous strains we put upon that faculty. That people want to see each other is construed by us to mean that "he" wants to see "her," and "she" wants to see "him." The fun and pleasure of the world are so interwound with the sex-dependence of women upon men that women are forced to court "attentions," when not really desirous of anything but amusement; and, as we force the association of the sexes on this plane, so we restrict it on a more wholesome one. . . .

The economic independence of woman will change all these conditions as naturally and inevitably as her dependence has introduced them. In her specialization in industry, she will develop more personality and less sexuality; and this will lower the pressure on this one relation in both women and men. And, in our social intercourse, the new character and new method of living will allow of broad and beautiful developments in human association. As the private home becomes a private home indeed, and no longer the woman's social and industrial horizon; as the workshops of the world—woman's sphere as well as man's—become homelike and beautiful under her influence; and as men and woman move freely together in the exercise of common racial functions, we shall have new channels for the flow of human life. . . .

> *Gilman's hope for the future.*

ELSIE CLEWS PARSONS

"Ethical Considerations," *The Family: An Ethnographical and Historical Outline with Descriptive Notes, Planned as a Text-Book for the Use of College Lecturers and Directors of Home Reading Clubs,* 1906

Parsons shocked academia with her textbook on the family. A lecturer in sociology at Barnard College (1899–1905), Parsons took care to rely on serious scientific study of "what is"—the kinds of family structures throughout the world—to undermine common notions of a universal kind of human family. The last chapter, "Ethical Considerations," examines the modern nuclear family and presents "what ought to be" regarding the emancipation of women, sex education, prostitution, eugenics, divorce law, and "trial marriages."

Which of her ideas were to become the most explosive topics of the next decades?

SOURCE: The Family: An Ethnographical and Historical Outline with Descriptive Notes, Planned as a Text-Book for the Use of College Lecturers and Directors of Home Reading Clubs. *New York: G.P. Putnam's Sons, 1906. 340–355.*

. . . *A*lthough we have not explicitly discussed the ethical side of any topic in our account of the family, yet it was not difficult to surmise at the very beginning the form that such a discussion would take. Here, at any rate, biology and ethics do not conflict. The highest type of family is the one which is so organised that infancy may be prolonged and that the advantages possible through its prolongation may be secured to offspring. In other words, immature offspring must be supported, protected, and educated throughout the period of immaturity in such a way that they will be perfectly adapted to their total environment, and will also be able to avail themselves of whatever opportunities for progressive individual variations may spring from their own natures and *be tolerated in their environment.* All questions of the ethical fitness of given traits of family structure must be referred to this standard for judgment. The character of parental care should depend, then, on the nature of the child and on that of his actual and *potential* surroundings. . . .

Parsons asserts that the family is organized to raise children for their specific societies.

Parental duty begins, paradoxically speaking, long before parenthood. Individuals influence the lot of their unborn children (1a) through their own education in general, (1b) through their special preparation as educators, (2) through their choice of a husband or wife who is to share with them responsibilities of inheritance and education.

1a. We have been led to believe that character, finely developed womanhood or manhood, is the goal of our education. We have also been taught that we owe services to our community. In the ideas that through the making of our own character we are making that of our children, and that successful child-rearing is one of the most, if not the most, important service we can render society the two aims of our education combine. . . .

1b. Herbert Spencer, in his treatise on education, gave as one of his five divisions of education training in the education of others, i.e, the education of the potential parent. As yet we have paid little or no attention to this view, but the time will undoubtedly come when a child-study course will be part of everybody's education. . . .

2. There are signs already of the spread of the idea that the individual is bound to consider the effects upon society of his or her marriage.

Individuals tainted by epilepsy, insanity, inebriacy, deaf-mutism, venereal disease: etc., are thought by many to be morally guilty if they marry. There is a growing realisation of the cost to the state of reproduction by its diseased or vicious subjects, and at the same time a growing inclination to prevent these classes from reproducing themselves by segregation, castration, etc. . . .[1]

According to our view of the family's function, the relation between married persons should be that best fitting them for their task of parenthood. It should be one allowing for or rather encouraging a full development of their natures, for all their capabilities should be taxed in their role of parenthood. Polygyny, including concubinage, prostitution, etc., have tended to distribute womanly functions in different classes of women. Generally speaking, the concubine, prostitute, or mistress serve for sexual sympathy and gratification, the chief or legal wife for reproduction. Economic activities are also apt to fall unequally upon these different classes of women. Monogamy is therefore from the point of view of parenthood a superior form of sexual intercourse, for it allows of a combination of womanly functions in one woman. The resulting type of woman is a better educator and her children fall heir to a richer inheritance of personality than is the case where women are differentiated into child-bearing and non-child-bearing or productive and non-productive classes.

Parsons argues that monogamy is a superior relationship for child-rearing. Note that she does not use a moral or religious justification for her view.

Again reciprocity of conjugal rights and duties is desirable for parenthood. If marriage have a proprietary character, neither the owner nor the owned is entirely fit to develop free personalities in his or her children. Moreover the idea of marital ownership more or less involves that of parental ownership, and the latter, as we have seen, is incompatible with a high type of parenthood. The custom of proprietary marriage inevitably leads, for example, to restrictions upon female education. Now just in so far as a woman's education is limited is she handicapped as an educator of her children. It is unfortunate that in the *emancipation of woman* agitation of the past half-century the reformers failed to emphasise the social as adequately as the individualistic need of change. If women are to be fit wives and mothers they must have all, perhaps more, of the opportunities for personal development that men have. All the activities hitherto reserved to men must at least be open to them, and many of these activities, certain functions of citizenship, for example, must be expected of them. Moreover, whatever the lines may be along which the fitness of women to labour will be experimentally determined, the underlying position must be established that for the sake of individual and race character she is to be a producer as well as a consumer of social values. As soon as this ethical necessity is

---

1. Parsons alludes to eugenics, a popular movement in the early twentieth century that hoped to improve society by selective breeding of the "fit" as well as sterilization/birth control to impede reproduction of those deemed unfit.

generally recognised the conditions of modern industry will become much better adapted to the needs of women workers than they are now, the hygiene of workshop, factory, and office will improve, and child bearing and rearing will no longer seem incompatible with productive activity.

In view of the necessity of conjugal reciprocity of rights and duties for personal development and of mutual affection and respect for enduring monogamy, sexual choice becomes a very important matter, a matter needing mature judgment and therefore preclusive of very early marriage. . . .

Here we are face to face with what is perhaps the most difficult task and what promises to become one of the most puzzling problems of current morality. Hitherto in almost all societies late marriage has either been accompanied by a lack of chastity before marriage on the part of the youth of both sexes or, where female chastity is valued, by the lack of chastity on the part of males with the growth of a prostitute class. Now it is unnecessary to more than point out that modern democracy is as incompatible with prostitution as with slavery. Our toleration of prostitution is a survival of clan morality, and taboo upon discussion of the subject is largely responsible for our failure to realise its clash with modern points of view. The argument is brief. If we desire monogamy we must condemn prostitution, but we must necessarily condemn male as well as female prostitutes. If, on the other hand, we do not condemn promiscuity in men, it must be on the ground that their nature is radically unadapted to monogamy and that monogamy is undesirable. In this case we should not discriminate against the women necessary to the gratification of men's polygynous instincts. If the social stigma were taken off the prostitute, if she were no longer a segregated person, prostitution might then become, in the sense of a division of labour, more consistent with a democratic point of view. It would nevertheless be untrue to democracy in its large meaning, *i.e.,* equal opportunities for the total development of man or woman. We have therefore, given late marriage and the passing of prostitution, two alternatives, the requiring of absolute chastity of both sexes until marriage or the toleration of freedom of sexual intercourse on the part of the unmarried of both sexes before marriage, *i.e.,* before the birth of offspring. In this event condemnation of sex license would have a different emphasis from that at present. Sexual intercourse would not be of itself disparaged or condemned, it would be disapproved of only if indulged in at the expense of health or of emotional or intellectual activities in oneself or in others. As a matter of fact, truly monogamous relations seem to be those most conducive to emotional or intellectual development and to health, so that, quite apart from the question of prostitution promiscuity is not desirable or even tolerable. It would therefore, seem well from this point of view, to encourage early *trial* marriage, the relation to be entered into with a view to permanency, but with the privilege of breaking it if proved unsuccessful and in the *absence of offspring* without suffering any great degree of public condemnation. . . .

Parsons explains the dilemma: late marriage and the problem of celibacy.

Parsons offers a solution: trial marriage.

Voluntarily childless marriage, or the restriction of child-bearing to the birth of one or two children, a much more general occurrence, is no doubt a very serious condition, and one, too, that seems to be on the increase. Unfortunately it seems to affect the classes who, for the sake of the cultural progress of the race, would do well to have a more numerous offspring, The classes, on the other hand, who from economic and cultural points of view, can least afford child-bearing are those who are most prone to it. This state is, of course, inevitably characteristic of the classes which are the least culturally developed, and therefore the least self controlled. If, however, the educational agencies which reach these classes would frankly teach them that reproduction irrespective of circumstances was criminal instead of righteous, at least one of the bars to right conduct in this matter would fall away.

As it is, a high infant mortality rate is, as we have seen already, the accompaniment of this high birth rate. The *laissez faire* argument that the one rate offsets the other, and that through the survival of the fittest here as elsewhere the species prospers is, in the case of urban populations at any rate, fallacious. The survivors themselves, in the wretched environment of the average city labourer's family, are only too commonly maimed, diseased, and undeveloped creatures, fit only to be a source of disaster to the community.

As soon as we fully realize the solidarity of interests of all parts of a society, and the contagious nature of social evil in whatever part of a group it may exist for the whole group, our present *laissez faire* policy in regard to the welfare of childhood is bound to change. The history of child-labour, age-of-consent, and compulsory education laws points to a developing public opinion in this connection. The care of children during the first five or six years of life, the most important years, from an educational standpoint, is still almost wholly left however, to parents irrespective of their qualifications as parents. The training of girls of all economic classes in the care of young children, and a system of state supervision of the home education of actual and potential public school children are suggested as initial methods in this social reform. In this connection it may also be suggested that gradual legal restrictions upon the right of parents to the earnings of their children would serve a double purpose in being a check upon the birth-rate, and in facilitating the operation of child-labour and compulsory education laws.

What would Parsons teach young people of the laboring classes? Of the well to-do classes?

As for our over-prudential, well-to-do classes, mere exhortations to the married persons among them to enlarge their families would seem to be of little avail. The education of young people of both sexes on questions of sex and reproduction on the one hand, and on the ethics of economic production and consumption on the other, would be more to the point. Through ignorance of one another's natures and of sex hygiene in general, husbands and wives create conditions very unfavourable both to enduring monogamy and to reproduction. Franker and more intelligent teaching of girls in particular would make them realise the handicap of an undue postponement of marriage and child-bearing, and the necessity for their own development of substituting child-bearing for the meretricious kind of self-cultivation too often at present in vogue. Discussion of the question of the teaching of certain standards of production and consumption to boys and girls would take us too far afield; it is enough to suggest that if both boys and girls were educated to be productively efficient and were inspired to work irrespective of any economic necessity to work, a long step would be taken to the solution of "race-suicide," not to speak of many other current "problems." Were it the "fashion" for every able-bodied adult person to be a producer as well as a consumer, of social values, much of our present wasteful and unrewarding kind of consumption would disappear, and other wants, among them the desire for offspring, would have a chance to become more effectual.

The general economic and cultural advances of the nineteenth century succeeded in sidetracking most of the survivals of the patriarchal family of our ancestors. The general division of labour more or less necessitated the carrying on of production outside of the family. Freedom of migration tended to disintegrate kinship ties. Advances in science weakened the religious sanction of custom in general and of family custom in particular. Finally, the spirit of freedom for individual development and initiative undermined marital and paternal privilege. This disintegration of the proprietary family has seemed to some people to bode that of every form of the family. They argue that any type of family organization is inconsistent with our rampant individualism. Many facts seem to justify this argument; nevertheless are there not more optimistic signs in view? Is there not a growing realisation that individualism and altruism are mutually dependent, that the state must develop through the individual, but that the individual must also develop through the state? And is not the conception that child-rearing is a social as well as an individualistic function, a natural corollary of such a political philosophy? Through the working out of this conception the family may regain its lost prestige.

Parsons describes the decline of the "proprietary family," family ownership over its members, and suggests that a new kind of family may be emerging.

EMMA GOLDMAN

"The Tragedy of Woman's Emancipation," *Anarchism and Other Essays*, 1910

Goldman sees no intrinsic value in the vote for women nor in work as an opportunity for self-development. To the contrary, the emancipated woman seems to her to be an "artificially grown plant" and an "empty vessel."

What does Goldman consider to be woman's true nature? How does a woman fulfill this "true nature?"

SOURCE: *Emma Goldman, Hippolyte Havel*. Anarchism and Other Essays with a Biographic Sketch by Hippolyte Havel. *New York: Mother Earth Publishing Association, 1910. 219–232.*

J begin with an admission: Regardless of all political and economic theories, treating of the fundamental differences between various groups within the human race, regardless of class and race distinctions, regardless of all artificial boundary lines between woman's rights and man's rights, I hold that there is a point where these differentiations may meet and grow into one perfect whole.

With this I do not mean to propose a peace treaty. The general social antagonism which has taken hold of our entire public life today, brought about through the force of opposing and contradictory interests, will crumble to pieces when the reorganization of our social life, based upon the principles of economic justice, shall have become a reality.

> What does Goldman think about "equality" of the sexes?

Peace or harmony between the sexes and individuals does not necessarily depend on a superficial equalization of human beings; nor does it call for the elimination of individual traits and peculiarities. The problem that confronts us today, and which the nearest future is to solve, is how to be one's self and yet in oneness with others, to feel deeply with all human beings and still retain one's own characteristic qualities. This seems to me to be the basis upon which the mass and the individual, the true democrat and the true individuality, man and woman, can meet without antagonism and opposition. The motto should not be: Forgive one another; rather, Understand one another. The oft-quoted sentence of Madame de Staël: "To understand everything means to forgive everything,"[1] has never particularly appealed to me; it has the odor of the confessional; to forgive one's fellow-being conveys the idea of pharisaical superiority. To understand one's fellow being suffices. The admission partly represents the fundamental aspect of my views on the emancipation of woman and its effect upon the entire sex.

Emancipation should make it possible for woman to be human in the truest sense. Everything within her that craves assertion and activity should reach its fullest expression; all artificial barriers should be broken, and the road towards greater freedom cleared of every trace of centuries of submission and slavery.

This was the original aim of the movement for woman's emancipation. But the results so far achieved have isolated woman and have robbed her of the fountain springs of that happiness which is so essential to her. Merely external emancipation has made of the modern woman an artificial being, who reminds one of the products of French arboriculture with its arabesque trees and shrubs, pyramids,

---

1. Madame Germaine de Stael (1766–1817), a French-Swiss woman of letters.

wheels, and wreaths; anything, except the forms which would be reached by the expression of her own inner qualities. Such artificially grown plants of the female sex are to be found in large numbers, especially in the so-called intellectual sphere of our life.

Liberty and equality for woman! What hopes and aspirations these words awakened when they were first uttered by some of the noblest and bravest souls of those days. The sun in all his light and glory was to rise upon a new world; in this world woman was to be free to direct her own destiny—an aim certainly worthy of the great enthusiasm, courage, perseverance, and ceaseless effort of the tremendous host of pioneer men and women, who staked everything against a world of prejudice and ignorance.

What has gone wrong in the emancipation of women?

My hopes also move towards that goal, but I hold that the emancipation of woman, as interpreted and practically applied today, has failed to reach that great end. Now, woman is confronted with the necessity of emancipating herself from emancipation, if she really desires to be free. This may sound paradoxical, but is, nevertheless, only too true.

What has she achieved through her emancipation? Equal suffrage in a few States. Has that purified our political life, as many well-meaning advocates predicted? Certainly not. Incidentally, it is really time that persons with plain, sound judgment should cease to talk about corruption in politics in a boarding school tone. Corruption of politics has nothing to do with the morals, or the laxity of morals, of various political personalities. Its cause is altogether a material one. Politics is the reflex of the business and industrial world, the mottos of which are: "To take is more blessed than to give"; "buy cheap and sell dear"; "one soiled hand washes the other." There is no hope even that woman, with her right to vote, will ever purify politics.

Emancipation has brought woman economic equality with man; that is, she can choose her own profession and trade; but as her past and present physical training has not equipped her with the necessary strength to compete with man, she is often compelled to exhaust all her energy, use up her vitality, and strain every nerve in order to reach the market value. Very few ever succeed, for it is a fact that women teachers, doctors, lawyers, architects, and engineers are neither met with the same confidence as their male colleagues, nor receive equal remuneration. And those that do reach that enticing equality, generally do so at the expense of their physical and psychical well-being. As to the great mass of working girls and women, how much independence is gained if the narrowness and lack of freedom of the home is exchanged for the narrowness and lack of freedom of the factory, sweat-shop, department store, or office? In addition is the burden which is laid on many women of looking after a "home, sweet home"—cold, dreary, disorderly, uninviting—after a day's hard work. Glorious independence! No wonder that hundreds of girls are so willing to accept the first offer of marriage, sick and tired of their "independence" behind the counter, at the sewing or typewriting machine.

They are just as ready to marry as girls of the middle class, who long to throw off the yoke of parental supremacy. A so-called independence which leads only to earning the merest subsistence is not so enticing, not so ideal, that one could expect woman to sacrifice everything for it. Our highly praised independence is, after all, but a slow process of dulling and stifling woman's nature, her love instinct, and her mother instinct.

Nevertheless, the position of the working girl is far more natural and human than that of her seemingly more fortunate sister in the more cultured professional walks of life, teachers, physicians, lawyers, engineers, etc., who have to make a dignified, proper appearance, while the inner life is growing empty and dead.

The narrowness of the existing conception of woman's independence and emancipation; the dread of love for a man who is not her social equal; the fear that love will rob her of her freedom and independence; the horror that love or the joy of motherhood will only hinder her in the full exercise of her profession—all these together make of the emancipated modern woman a compulsory vestal, before whom life, with its great clarifying sorrows and its deep, entrancing joys, rolls on without touching or gripping her soul.

Emancipation, as understood by the majority of its adherents and exponents, is of too narrow a scope to permit the boundless love and ecstasy contained in the deep emotion of the true woman, sweetheart, mother, in freedom.

The tragedy of the self-supporting or economically free woman does not lie in too many, but in too few experiences. True, she surpasses her sister of past generations in knowledge of the world and human nature; it is just because of this that she feels deeply the lack of life's essence, which alone can enrich the human soul, and without which the majority of women have become mere professional automatons.

That such a state of affairs was bound to come was foreseen by those who realized that, in the domain of ethics, there still remained many decaying ruins of the time of the undisputed superiority of man; ruins that are still considered useful. And, what is more important, a goodly number of the emancipated are unable to get along without them. Every movement that aims at the destruction of existing institutions and the replacement thereof with something more advanced, more perfect, has followers who in theory stand for the most radical ideas, but who, nevertheless, in their every-day practice, are like the average Philistine, feigning respectability and clamoring for the good opinion of their opponents. There are, for example, Socialists, and even Anarchists, who stand for the idea that property is robbery, yet who will grow indignant if anyone owe them the value of a half-dozen pins.

The same Philistine can be found in the movement for woman's emancipation. Yellow journalists and milk-and-water litterateurs have painted pictures of the emancipated woman that make the hair of the good citizen and his dull companion stand up on end. Every member of the woman's rights movement was pictured as a George Sand in her absolute disregard of morality.[2] Nothing was sacred to her. She had no respect for the ideal relation between man and woman. In short, emancipation stood only for a reckless life of lust and sin; regardless of society, religion, and morality. The exponents of woman's rights were highly indignant at such misrepresentation, and, lacking humor, they exerted all their energy to prove that they were not at all as bad as they were painted, but the very reverse.

According to Goldman, where did the woman's emancipation movement go wrong?

Of course, as long as woman was the slave of man, she could not be good and pure, but now that she was free and independent she would prove how good she could be and that her influence would have a purifying effect on all institutions in society. True, the movement for woman's rights has broken many old fetters, but it has also forged new ones. The great movement of *true* emancipation has not met with a great race of women who could look liberty in the face. Their narrow, Puritanical vision banished man, as a disturber and doubtful character, out of their emotional life. Man was not to be tolerated at any price, except perhaps as the father of a child, since a child could not very well come to life without a father. Fortunately, the most rigid Puritans never will be strong enough to kill the innate craving for motherhood. But woman's freedom is closely allied with man's freedom, and many of my so-called emancipated sisters seem to overlook the fact that a child born in freedom needs the love and devotion of each human being about him, man as well as woman. Unfortunately, it is this narrow conception of human relations that has brought about a great tragedy in the lives of the modern man and woman. . . .

A rich intellect and a fine soul are usually considered necessary attributes of a deep and beautiful personality. In the case of the modern woman, these attributes serve as a hindrance to the complete assertion of her being. For over a hundred years the old form of marriage, based on the Bible, "till death doth part," has been denounced as an institution that stands for the sovereignty of the man over the woman, of her complete submission to his whims and commands, and absolute dependence on his name and support. Time and again it has been conclusively proved that the old matrimonial relation restricted woman to the function of man's servant and the bearer of his children. And yet we find many emancipated women who prefer marriage, with all its deficiencies, to the narrowness of an unmarried life: narrow and unendurable because of the chains of moral and social prejudice that cramp and bind her nature.

The explanation of such inconsistency on the part of many advanced women is to be found in the fact that they never truly understood the meaning of emancipation. They thought that all that was needed was independence from external tyrannies; the internal tyrants, far more harmful to life and growth—ethical and social conventions—were left to take care of themselves; and they have taken care of themselves. They seem to get along as beautifully in the heads and hearts of the most active exponents of woman's emancipation, as in the heads and hearts of our grandmothers.

---

2. George Sand was the pen name of Amantine-Lucile-Aurore Dupin (1804–1876), a French novelist who was infamous for her many love affairs with well-known artists and writers.

These internal tyrants, whether they be in the form of public opinion or what will mother say, or brother, father, aunt, or relative of any sort; what will Mrs. Grundy[3], Mr. Comstock[4], the employer, the Board of Education say? All these busybodies, moral detectives, jailers of the human spirit, what will they say? Until woman has learned to defy them all, to stand firmly on her own ground and to insist upon her own unrestricted freedom, to listen to the voice of her nature, whether it call for life's greatest treasure, love for a man, or her most glorious privilege, the right to give birth to a child, she cannot call herself emancipated. How many emancipated women are brave enough to acknowledge that the voice of love is calling, wildly beating against their breasts, demanding to be heard, to be satisfied. . . .

The greatest shortcoming of the emancipation of the present day lies in its artificial stiffness and its narrow respectabilities, which produce an emptiness in woman's soul that will not let her drink from the fountain of life. I once remarked that there seemed to be a deeper relationship between the old-fashioned mother and hostess, ever on the alert for the happiness of her little ones and the comfort of those she loved, and the truly new woman, than between the latter and her average emancipated sister. The disciples of emancipation pure and simple declared me a heathen, fit only for the stake. Their blind zeal did not let them see that my comparison between the old and the new was merely to prove that a goodly number of our grandmothers had more blood in their veins, far more humor and wit, and certainly a greater amount of naturalness, kind-heartedness, and simplicity, than the majority of our emancipated professional women who fill the colleges, halls of learning, and various offices. This does not mean a wish to return to the past, nor does it condemn woman to her old sphere, the kitchen and the nursery.

Salvation lies in an energetic march onward towards a brighter and clearer future. We are in need of unhampered growth out of old traditions and habits. The movement for woman's emancipation has so far made but the first step in that direction. It is to be hoped that it will gather strength to make another. The right to vote, or equal civil rights, may be good demands, but true emancipation begins neither at the polls nor in courts. It begins in woman's soul. History tells us that every oppressed class gained true liberation from its masters through its own efforts. It is necessary that woman learn that lesson, that she realize that her freedom will reach as far as her power to achieve her freedom reaches. It is, therefore, far more important for her to begin with her inner regeneration, to cut loose from the weight of prejudices, traditions, and customs. The demand for equal rights in every vocation of life is just and fair; but, after all, the most vital right is the right to love and be loved. Indeed, if partial emancipation

What does Goldman propose?

---

3. Mrs. Grundy was a fictional name for a prude.

4. Anthony Comstock was a Post Office official and author of the Act for the Suppression of Trade in, and Circulation of, Obscene Literature and Articles for Immoral Use (1873). The Act confiscated and destroyed pornography as well as information on birth control and abortion. Purveyors faced jail sentences.

is to become a complete and true emancipation of woman, it will have to do away with the ridiculous notion that to be loved, to be sweetheart and mother, is synonymous with being slave or subordinate. It will have to do away with the absurd notion of the dualism of the sexes, or that man and woman represent two antagonistic worlds.

Pettiness separates; breadth unites. Let us be broad and big. Let us not overlook vital things because of the bulk of trifles confronting us. A true conception of the relation of the sexes will not admit of conqueror and conquered; it knows of but one great thing: to give of one's self boundlessly, in order to find one's self richer, deeper, better. That alone can fill the emptiness, and transform the tragedy of woman's emancipation into joy, limitless joy.

HUTCHINS HAPGOOD

"The Bohemian, the American and the Foreigner," *Types From City Streets*, 1910

Hapgood was well known as a flâneur, *or a "man about town," who strolled through city streets looking for the vital life force of New York. His* Spirit of the Ghetto *looked at the Jewish Lower East Side. In* Types from City Streets, *he continues his search through the "low life" with a look at grafters (con men), rounders (drunks), "Tenderloin" girls (prostitutes who worked in the Tenderloin district), and Bowery hobos.*

A Harvard-educated writer, he also reflects on the bohemian life that he has adopted. What are the qualities that describe the American bohemian? Why does Hapgood think that the American bohemian could bring around a renewal of intellectual and social life?

SOURCE: Types from City Streets. *New York: Funk & Wagnalls Company, 1910. 113–124.*

The Bohemian is interesting primarily because of his temperament, because of his gaiety and his joy in life. He differs essentially from the tough on the one hand and the Rounder on the other; altho some toughs are Bohemians. The tough is interesting because of the simplicity with which he reposes on the bottom, and his resulting and significant eloquence; the characteristic of the Rounder is the hardness of his nature and his lack of expressiveness. The Bohemian is best portrayed in Murger's *"Vie de Bohème."*[1] There his qualities

---

1. The French Henri Murger wrote the stories collected in his *La Vie de Bohème* (Bohemian Life) in 1851. He later turned it into a popular play that was then adapted by the Italian Giacomo Puccini for his famous opera La Bohème (1896).

are felt to be youth, joy, and freedom—qualities temperamental rather than intellectual or critical. Charles Lamb said that a man can never have too much time, nor too little to do. That was a temperamental, a delightfully Bohemian remark. Bohemianism, generally associated with poverty, is in reality independent of it; poverty, indeed, helps to throw a man on simple pleasures and to test his youthful appreciation of them. If a man can be gay and poor, he is indeed a Bohemian, tho he does not necessarily cease to be such when he becomes rich.

There is very little Bohemian atmosphere in New York, for it is a very "swift" town. Even the rapid man from Chicago notices that there is a peculiarly strident character to the nervous haste of the metropolis. The rumbling "L," the shrieking trolley, overflowing with people all having an expression of wild eagerness on their faces, these are the most fitting external expressions of the jumping unrest at the heart of our city.[2] We are palpitant, eager in the functions of life. We hurry our business in order to get at our pleasure, and hurry our pleasure in order to get at our business. We all have occasional backaches and headaches, and anything slow, from a thoughtful play to a provincial, brings to our nerves the shock of the unfamiliar. Contemplation is the one thing completely shut out of the life of a New Yorker who is thoroughly saturated with the most American spirit of the town. Thought with him is a nervous impulse, quickly over, having no genial, philosophic fringe, looking not before nor after, but pinned to the exciting moment. To use a rather undignified figure, the man who is "in it" in New York is like the nervous system of the frog of the psychological laboratory which the operator, by the application of acid, galvanizes into vivid but unmeaning activity.

When a man is entirely addicted either to practical affairs or to personal amusement, there is only one line of things which are in their nature fitted to lead him away from them. In some way or other a man who is interested only in events, in the temporal, superficial flux of things, can be changed as to his nature only by learning to see things *sub specie aternitatis,* from the point of view of eternity. From this eternal, unvarying view-point there are two and only two forms in which the world is mirrored; either in what we call art or in what we call philosophy. Either of these molds extracts the thing in itself from the eddy of accident and gives it a comparatively immortal shape.

One way in which philosophy and art are found is in books, but the nervous New Yorker is too busy to read. Through books, therefore, he comes only very incompletely into contact with the contemplative, the eternal, the artistic. The only practicable means of subjecting the typical city American to the contemplative is therefore through some influence which is connected with his daily, practical life

---

2. The "L" or "El" stands for the Elevated train, part of the New York City subway system that went over the streets and buildings. John Sloan paints the Sixth Avenue El as it rumbles through Greenwich Village in "Daybreak Express," "Sixth Avenue El," "Six O'Clock, Winter," and "The City from Greenwich Village."

and amusements. Now, this element is partly found in what is contributed to our metropolitan existence by the foreigners.

Almost everything, indeed, which has to do with the contemplative in New York—that is to say, the artistic—is traceable in one way or another to foreign influence. Take, to begin with, our plastic art, our painting. Most of our painters are influenced either by the French or the Japanese school. Then, too, our galleries are filled with foreign works of art. Our painting vocabulary is taken straight from the ateliers of Paris, and our city is full of French, German, and Italian artists who command high prices because of the widely spread opinion, which is after all in essentials correct, that for the art atmosphere we must hark back to Europe.

Again, take our drama. Broadway, to be sure, is full of plays both foreign and domestic, in which there is no art, in which there are no characters and no literature which has any of the permanent quality in art or philosophy; few that have any meaning. Those of the modern plays which have value are preponderatingly foreign. This, too, is so well recognized that our business managers say they won't have any "art" and tend to reject just those plays which do introduce the element of the contemplative, the philosophic, the artistic.

The best company in New York is a German company. At this theater and at the Yiddish theaters more serious drama is given or attempted (for the production at the Yiddish theater lags frequently behind the intention) in one season than at all the Broadway houses taken together in several seasons. The dominant note at the Broadway houses is amusement. A play must not be too thoughtful, and it must have a large amount of claptrap in it. Then, of course, our music is almost entirely foreign in origin and inspiration.

The presence of this foreign art in our American life has already, no doubt, begun to have its effect. Genuine Americans begin to have more respect for "art" than they used to have. To be sure, as yet they do not largely enjoy it, but they tolerate it and recommend it to others and to their children. They even "do" it, when it assumes a "swell garb," tho it is far from being such a fad in New York as it has been in Boston and Chicago.

Another way in which the foreigners in New York tend to make the Americans more contemplative and less exclusively active is that they have introduced, to a large extent, *Gemüthlichkeit;* and the spirit of gentle loafing and amusement. The fearful Anglo-Saxon habit of standing at a bar and draining off whisky, as an indication of good-fellowship, has been much modified by the foreign cafe, and particularly by the German type of family beer-hall. At these places a couple of friends, or a man, his wife, and family, sit down comfortably, drink light beer or wine moderately, and talk in a rational and pleasant way, sometimes for hours. It is in this mood of gently sensuous loafing that the contemplative point of view is induced; philosophy and the artistic habit of mind are fostered by a certain amount of unnervous ease and agreeable companionship. Ideas as well as friends are discussed, and one naturally gets to see the relations of things and to put the practical object of the moment in its proper light, attribute to it only its proper value. Americans, when they begin to come in contact with this spirit, feel its eloquence to a certain extent, and thus with growing culture they begin to see the charm of the contemplative, the artistic, to care to look at things *sub specie aternitatis*. The esthetic habit of mind grows. One learns to love the graceful phrase, the melancholy pleasing reflection, the philosophic saw; the picture of life on the stage whose underlying interest is truth, whatever its superficial excitement may be; and one gradually leaves off calling the Italian a "dago" and the German a "Dutchman," and awakens to a subtler joy in things than he has felt before.

What do we learn when we "loaf intelligently"?

As yet, however, American Bohemians are very few, for when a man is not busy in America, he is generally a "bum" or a foreigner. The man who desires to loaf intelligently and temperamentally; to do only enough work to express himself, is a rare bird in this country. The genuine Bohemian charm is almost unknown. A truth which quite escapes the ordinary nervous, moral, and busy American is that when men sit together around a table, or wander through the town together, the second hour brings a quality that the first hour can not have; that up to the tenth or even the twentieth hour there is a gradual attuning of the senses and intelligence to a state where certain truths are attained that can be derived in no other way. The busy man who can spend only an hour for sociability believes that men who sit around for ten hours are "bums," that they merely like animal pleasantness and drink.

But the busy man sees only a part of the truth. He does not understand that there is such a thing as the summation of stimuli; and that the whole is often other and greater than the sum of its parts. He does not know that some moods have to be "cooked" as carefully as some dishes; and that much time is necessary for the process. He does not know that art, temperament, beauty, all result not from intelligence alone, not from the senses alone, but from a mixture of the two. When the mind plays freely about the facts of sense, about the fundamental and original interests of sensual man, then we have art and literature and everything that is beautiful. Mix flesh and intellect and we have spirit and imagination. But it takes some time for harassed man to arrive at that stage of comfort where his mind does consent to take an interest in his senses—much time helped by drink and good fellowship. The few intelligent Americans who, without being "bums," can "sit around" all day and all night, attain glimpses into some aspects of human nature that are forever shut out from the "unco" proper, the over-busy, and the intensely practical.

The American, even when he is a Bohemian, is seldom the "real thing": he always retains an element of strenuousness. He not only occasionally works hard, but it is his common practise to "talk hard." He even talks extremely; a real Bohemian, however, does nothing in excess; he avoids stress of any kind. Then again the American Bohemian is not entirely careless and disreputable, and the foreign Bohemian generally is. Of those foreign nations who are represented in New York the Italians and the Germans are the most important. There are, to be sure, very interesting Jews who lead, in New York's Ghetto, an artistic, intellectual, poverty-stricken existence. They are, however, intellectual debauchees rather than

Bohemians; for they are full of passion, of storm, and stress: expelled from Russia, and belligerent with ideas about politics, literature, and life, they lack the repose and balance which is an essential of the true Bohemian.

An intelligent, but busy American reproached me one day for my constant use of the word "gemüthlich." "It is not English," he said. " 'Pleasant' means the same thing, and it is mere laziness or ostentation to use the foreign word. Moreover," he proceeded, "I dislike the whole thing, anyway. There is no interest to me in these beer-guzzling Germans who sit stupidly all day long and call their stupidity by the magic word 'gemüthlichkeit.' "

Mere ignorance in others does not, as a rule, arouse me to anger, but I have a few idols which I do not care to have shattered. I lived in Germany for two years; and although there is a great deal that to me is disagreeable about the German character, yet I know that the best of the Teutonic race is expressed in the word "Gemüthlichkeit," so I answered, with some heat, altho it was at dinner, and gave the following discourse on the famous German word:

Plato divides the soul into three parts, the first representing that which is purely intellectual, the third that which is purely physical; and the second, or middle part of the soul, that which partakes of both the physical and the intellectual. The Greek word for this second division of the soul the Germans translate by 'das Gemüth.' To this division of the soul are due all human beauty and all human art. The pure intellect—the first division of the soul—perceives only the Things-In-Themselves; while the third division of the soul perceives only the facts of the gross senses. Poetry and beauty come in when the intellect plays about the facts of sense, when the first and third divisions of the soul are brought into relationship.

Now the Germans are an intellectual race. Their science and philosophy show that. Also they are very physical. You, yourself, have perceived that, as your strictures show. They like their beer and their gross meats and cheeses, and they like to walk in the woods and mountains. They like to think and they like to feel, but they like particularly to think and feel at the same time; for, then, they are 'gemüthlich'; then they are enjoying themselves, and their enjoyment is heightened because of the intellectual element involved.

Take the typical German University student. He works hard all the week with pure science. On Saturday night he goes to the 'Kneipe' to enjoy himself. He drinks a great deal of beer and the healthy waitress is an attractive object to him; he sings the good old German songs and he talks with his fellows and enjoys himself to the uttermost. He is very 'gemüthlich': why? Not primarily because of the beer and the girl, but because by means of the beer and the girl his intellect, which has been held rigid all through the week, is relaxed. His mind occupies itself with physical things. He is neither a beast on the one hand, nor a mere intelligence on the other. It is in this mood that poetry, music, and philosophy which is not abstract are conceived. The students talk together freely, harmoniously. Their trained intellects give point to the interests of their healthy senses. They are not coarse; for, no matter how free their talk, there is always in it the intellectual element. The more learned the man the longer it takes him to relax, the more beer he needs to drink. The time comes when he is delightful, when his knowledge and learning and acumen are expressed with charming urbanity, tolerance, and richness of imagination and fancy. Then, indeed, he is 'gemüthlich.' A man can be 'pleasant,' as you say, without being intellectual; but he can't be 'gemüthlich' unless he has brains.

In one sense, indeed, the best that is German is "low." There is something of the peasant in every German. In another sense it is very high. Low Living and High Thinking apply peculiarly to the Teuton. Beer and pretzels and philosophy go together. If it were not for the careless element in Bohemianism—an element the Teuton lacks—the German would be the most perfect of Bohemians. As it is, he possesses the best of what is bohemian; and much more besides. For much more than Bohemianism is implied in "Gemüthlichkeit." This is true at the present time, however, only of the South German. The Prussian has been spoiled, has been stripped of his true German quality by commercial and military success. The old German virtues of simplicity, poetry, and humility have given place in the modern Prussian to arrogance, stiffness, and the quality of the "parvenu." One day I crossed an Alpine pass in the same coach with an old German with white hair. I told how I had met in Strasburg two or three young Germans. who, in their enthusiasm, their high ideals, the simplicity of their lives, reminded me of Schiller and his time. *"Ach, mein Herr,"* said the old German, *"so haben Sie ein grosses Glück gehabt."* (Ah, Sir, then you were lucky.) That was the kind of German whom in his youth my old friend knew, but who is rare now that Germany has become a world Power.

FLOYD DELL

"The Feminist Movement," *Women as World Builders*, 1913

Dell, a self-proclaimed male supporter of feminism, wrote a series of book reviews on women writers for the literary supplement of the Chicago Evening Post. *The following year, he collected these essays into his book,* Women as World Builders. *What do you think he means by this title?*

Why does Dell think that men should support the women's movement? How does he explain men's hostility to feminism?

SOURCE: *Originally published in* Friday Literary Review, *1912*. Women as World Builders: Studies in Modern Feminism. *Chicago: Forbes and Company, 1913. 19–21.*

... $\mathcal{B}$ut first the explanation of why I, a man, write these articles on feminism. It involves the betrayal of a secret: the secret, that is, of the apparent indifference or even hostility of men toward the woman's movement. The fact is, as has been bitterly recited by the rebellious leaders of their sex, that women have always been what men wanted them to be—have changed to suit his changing ideals. The fact is, furthermore, that the woman's movement of today is but another example of that readiness of women to adapt themselves to a masculine demand.

Men are tired of subservient women; or, to speak more exactly, of the seemingly subservient woman who effects her will by stealth—the pretty slave with all the slave's subtlety and cleverness. So long as it was possible for men to imagine themselves masters, they were satisfied. But when they found out that they were dupes, they wanted a change. If only for self-protection, they desired to find in woman a comrade and an equal. In reality they desired it because it promised to be more fun.

So that we have as the motive behind the rebellion of women an obscure rebellion of men. Why, then, have men appeared hostile to the woman's rebellion? Because what men desire are real individuals who have achieved their own freedom. It will not do to pluck freedom like a flower and give it to the lady with a polite bow. She must fight for it.

We are, to tell the truth, a little afraid that unless the struggle is one which will call upon all her powers, which will try her to the utmost, she will fall short of becoming that self-sufficient, able, broadly imaginative and healthy minded creature upon whom we have set our masculine desire.

It is, then, as a phase of great human renaissance inaugurated by men that the woman's movement deserves to be considered. And what more fitting than that a man should sit in judgment upon the contemporary aspects of that movement, weighing out approval or disapproval! Such criticism is not a masculine impertinence, but a masculine right, a right properly pertaining to those who are responsible for the movement and whose demands it must ultimately fulfill.

FLOYD DELL

"Charlotte Perkins Gilman," *Women as World Builders*, 1913

Dell begins his book with the essay "Charlotte Perkins Gilman." The other "world-builders" who interest him include: Emmeline Pankhurst, Jane Addams, Olive Schreiner, Isadora Duncan, Beatrice Webb, Emma Goldman, Margaret Dreier Robins, Ellen Key, and Dora Maraden.

What does Dell see as Charlotte Perkins Gilman's major contributions to feminism? According to Dell, how does Gilman view the woman "content with Hendom"? What would Gilman change? How does Dell think Gilman's New Woman would improve men's lives?

SOURCE: *Originally published in* Friday Literary Review, *1912.* Women as World Builders: Studies in Modern Feminism. *Chicago: Forbes and Company, 1913. 22–29.*

O f the women who represent and carry on this many-sided movement today, the first to be considered from this masculine viewpoint should, I think, be Charlotte Perkins Gilman. For she is, to a superficial view, the most intransigent feminist of them all, the one most exclusively concerned with the improvement of the lot of woman, the least likely to compromise at the instance of man, child, church, state or devil.

Mrs. Gilman is the author of "Women and Economics" and several other books of theory, "What Diantha Did," and several other books of fiction; she is the editor and publisher of a remarkable journal, the *Forerunner*, the whole varied contents of which is written by herself; she has a couple of plays to her credit, and she has published a book of poems. If in spite of all this publicity it is still possible to misunderstand the attitude of Mrs. Gilman, I can only suppose it to be because her poetry is less well known than her prose. For in this book of verse, "In This Our World," Mrs. Gilman has so completely justified herself that no man need ever be afraid of her—nor any woman who, having a lingering tenderness for the other sex, would object to living in a beehive world, full of raging, efficient women, with the men relegated to the position of the drone.

Of course, I do but jest when I speak of this fear; but there is, to the ordinary male, something curiously objectionable at the first glance in Mrs. Gilman's arguments, whether they are for co-operative kitchens or for the labor of women outside the home. And the reason for that objection lies precisely in the fact that her plans seem to be made in a complete forgetfulness of him and his interests. It all has the air of a feminine plot. The co-operative kitchens, and the labor by which women's economic independence is to be achieved, seem the means to an end.

And so they are. But the end, as revealed in Mrs. Gilman's poems, is that one which all intelligent men must desire. I do not know whether or not the more elaborate co-operative schemes of Mrs. Gilman are practical; and I fancy that she rather exaggerates the possibilities of independent work for women who have or intend to have children. But the spirit behind these plans is one which cannot but be in the greatest degree stimulating and beneficent in its effect upon her sex.

For Mrs. Gilman is, first of all, a poet, an idealist. She is a lover of life. She rejoices in beauty and daring and achievement, in all the fine and splendid things of the world. She does not merely disapprove of the contemporary "home" as

The Home? ▍ wasteful and inefficient—she hates it because it vulgarizes life. In this "home," this private food-preparing and baby-rearing establishment, she sees a machine which breaks down all that is good and noble in women, which degrades and pettifies them. The contrast between the instinctive ideals of young women and the sordid realities into which housekeeping plunges them is to her intolerable. And in the best satirical verse of modern times she ridicules these unnecessary shams. In one spirited piece she points out that the soap-vat, the pickle-tub, even the loom and wheel, have lost their sanctity, have been banished to shops and factories:

> But bow ye down to the Holy Stove,
> The Altar of the Home!

The real feeling of Mrs. Gilman is revealed in these lines which voice, indeed, the angry mood of many an outraged housewife, who finds herself the serf of a contraption of cast iron:

> We toil to keep the altar crowned
> With dishes new and nice,
> And Art and Love, and Time and Truth,
> We offer up, with Health and Youth
> In daily sacrifice.[1]

Mrs. Gilman is not under the illusion that the conditions of work outside the home are perfect; she is, indeed, a socialist, and as such is engaged in the great task of revolutionizing the basis of modern industry. But she has looked into women's souls, and turned away in disgust at the likeness of a dirty kitchen which those souls present.

Into these lives, corrupted by the influences of the "home," nothing can come unspoiled, nothing can enter in its original stature and beauty, she says;

> Birth comes. Birth—
> The breathing re-creation of the earth!
> All earth, all sky, all God, life's sweet deep whole,
> Newborn again to each new soul!
> "Oh, are you? What a shame! Too bad, my dear!
> How well you stand it, too! It's very queer

---

1. Note on the cast-iron coal stove: In 1899 the Boston School of Housekeeping conducted an experiment on the work needed to keep a stove working over a six-day period: 292 pounds of coal and 14 pounds of kindling to be put in and 27 pounds of ashes to be taken out. Each day's chores included: sift ashes, lay fires, tend fires, empty ashes, bring in new coal, and blacken the stove to keep it from rusting.

The dreadful trials women have to carry;
But you can't always help it when you marry.
Oh, what a sweet layette! What lovely socks!
What an exquisite puff and powder box!
Who is your doctor? Yes, his skill's immense—
But it's a dreadful danger and expense!"

And so with love, and death, and work—all are smutted and debased. And her revolt is a revolt against that which smuts and debases them—against those artificial channels which break up the strong, pure stream of woman's energy into a thousand little, stagnant canals, covered with spiritual pond scum.

It is a part of her idealism to conceive life in terms of war. So it is that she scorns compromise, for in war compromise is treason. And so it is that she has heart for the long, slow marshaling of forces, and the dingy details of the commissariat—for these things are necessary if the cry of victory is ever to ring out over the battlefield. Some of her phrases have so militant an air that they seem to have been born among the captains and the shouting. They make us ashamed of our vicious civilian comfort. . . .

Mrs. Gilman's attitude toward the bearing and rearing of children is easy to misunderstand. She does seem to relegate these things to the background of women's lives. She does deny to these things a tremendous impor- *Children?* tance. Why, she asks, is it so important that women should bear and rear children to live lives as empty and poor as their own? Surely, she says, it is more important to make life something worth giving to children! No, she insists, it is not sufficient to be a mother: an oyster can be a mother. It is necessary that a woman should be a person as well as a mother. She must know and do.

And as for the ideal of love which is founded on masculine privilege, she satirizes it very effectively in some verses entitled "Wedded Bliss": *Marriage?*

"O come and be my mate!" said the Eagle to the Hen;
"I love to soar, but then
I want my mate to rest
Forever in the nest!"
Said the Hen, "I cannot fly,
I have no wish to try,
But I joy to see my mate careening through the sky!"
They wed, and cried, "Ah, this is Love, my own!"
And the Hen sat, the Eagle soared, alone.

Woman, in Mrs. Gilman's view, must not be content with Hendom: the sky is her province, too. Of all base domesticity, all degrading love, she is the enemy. She gives her approval only to that work which has in it something high and free, and that love which is the dalliance of the eagles.

RANDOLPH BOURNE

"Youth," *The Atlantic Monthly,* April 1912

To overthrow established authorities and to change the world through a scientific method of experimentation is Bourne's prescription for progress. As you read this essay, put together a description of the ideal society that Bourne is advocating. What would his "youthful" society be like?

SOURCE: *Originally published in* The Atlantic Monthly. *CIX. March, 1913. 433–41. Youth and Life. Boston: Houghton Mifflin Company. 1913.*

*I*n this conflict between youth and its elders, youth is the incarnation of reason pitted against the rigidity of tradition. Youth puts the remorseless questions to everything that is old and established—Why: What is this thing good for? And when it gets the mumbled, evasive answers of the defenders, it applies its own fresh, clean spirit of reason to institutions, customs, and ideas, and finding them stupid, inane, or poisonous, turns instinctively to overthrow them and build in their place the things with which its visions teem.

This constant return to purely logical activity with each generation keeps the world supplied with visionaries and reformers, that is to say, with saviors and leaders. New movements are born in young minds, and lack of experience enables youth eternally to recall civilization to sound bases. The passing generation smiles and cracks its weatherworn jokes about youthful effusions; but this new, ever-hopeful, ever-daring, ever doing, youthful enthusiasm, ever returning to the logical bases of religion, ethics, politics, business, art, and social life—this is the salvation of the world.

This was the youthful radicalism of Jesus, and his words sound across the ages "calling civilization ever back to sound bases." With him, youth eternally reproaches the ruling generation—"O ye of little faith?" There is so much to be done in the world; so much could be done if you would only dare. You seem to be doing so little to cure the waste and the muddle and the lethargy all around you. Don't you really care, or are you only fainthearted? If you do not care, it must be because you do not know; let us point out to you the shockingness of exploitation, and the crass waste of human personality all around you in this modern world. And if you are fainthearted, we will supply the needed daring and courage, and lead you straight to the attack.

These are the questions and challenges that the youth puts to his elders, and it is their shifty evasions and quibblings that confound and dishearten him. He becomes intolerant, and can see all classes in no other light than that of accomplices in a great crime. If they only knew! Swept along himself in an irrationality of energy, he does not see the small part that reason plays in the intricate social life, and only gradually does he come to view life as a "various and splendid disorder of forces," and exonerate weak human nature from some of its heavy responsibility. But this insight brings him to appreciate and almost to reverence the forces of science and conscious social progress that are grappling with that disorder, and seeking to tame it.

Youth is the leaven that keeps all these questioning, testing attitudes fermenting in the world. If it were not for this troublesome activity of youth, with its hatred of sophisms and glosses, its insistence on things as they are, society would die from sheer decay. It is the policy of the older generation as it gets adjusted to the world to hide away the unpleasant things where it can, or preserve a conspiracy of silence and an elaborate pretense that they do not exist. But meanwhile the sores go on festering just the same. Youth is the drastic antiseptic. It will not let its elders cry peace, where there is no peace. By its fierce sarcasms it keeps issues alive in the world until they are settled right. It drags skeletons from closets and insists that they be explained. No wonder the older generation fears and distrusts the younger. Youth is the avenging Nemesis on its trail. "It is young men who provided the logic, decision, and enthusiasm necessary to relieve society of the crushing burden that each generation seeks to roll upon the shoulders of the next." Our elders are always optimistic in their views of the present, pessimistic in their views of the future; youth is pessimistic toward the present and gloriously hopeful for the future. And it is this hope which is the lever of progress—one might say, the only lever of progress. The lack of confidence which the ruling generation feels in the future leads to that distrust of machinery, or the use of means for ends, which is so characteristic of it today. Youth is disgusted with such sentimentality. It can never understand that curious paralysis which seizes upon the elders in the face of urgent social innovations; that refusal to make use of a perfectly definite program or administrative scheme which has worked elsewhere. Youth concludes that its elders discountenance the machinery, the means, because they do not really believe in the end, and adds another count to the indictment. Youth's attitude is really the scientific attitude. Do not be afraid to make experiments, it says. You cannot tell how anything will work until you have tried it. Suppose "science confined its interests to those things that have been tried and tested in the world," how far should we get? It is possible that your experiments may produce by accident a social explosion, but we do not give up chemistry because occasionally a wrong mixture of chemicals blows up a scientist in a laboratory, or medical research because an investigator contracts the disease he is fighting. The whole philosophy of youth is summed up in the word Dare! Take chances and you will attain! The world has nothing to lose but its chains—and its own soul to gain!

WALTER LIPPMANN

"Introduction," *Drift and Mastery: An Attempt to Diagnose the Current Unrest*, 1914

In this introduction, Lippmann challenges readers to articulate a vision for a new, invigorated democracy. How does he propose that this should be done? How does his proposal differ from the ideals of the Suffrage faction? How does his proposal differ from the dreams of Labor?

SOURCE: Drift and Mastery: An Attempt to Diagnose the Current Unrest. *New York: Mitchell Kennerly, 1914. xv–xxvi.*

*I*n the early months of 1914 widespread unemployment gave the anarchists in New York City an unusual opportunity for agitation. The newspapers and the police became hysterical, men were clubbed and arrested on the slightest provocation, meetings were dispersed. The issue was shifted, of course, from unemployment to the elementary rights of free speech and assemblage. Then suddenly, the city administration, acting through a new police commissioner, took the matter in hand, suppressed official lawlessness, and guaranteed the men who were conducting the agitation their full rights. This had a most disconcerting effect on the anarchists. They were suddenly stripped of all the dramatic effect that belongs to a clash with the police. They had to go back to the real issue of unemployment, and give some message to the men who had been following them. But they had no message to give: they knew what they were against but not what they were for, and their intellectual situation was as uncomfortable as one of those bad dreams in which you find yourself half-clothed in a public place.

Without a tyrant to attack an immature democracy is always somewhat bewildered. Yet we have to face the fact in America that what thwarts the growth of our civilization is not the uncanny, malicious contrivance of the plutocracy, but the faltering method, the distracted soul, and the murky vision of what we call grandiloquently the will of the people. If we flounder, it is not because the old order is strong, but because the new one is weak. Democracy is more than the absence of czars, more than freedom, more than equal opportunity. It is a way of life, a use of freedom, an embrace of opportunity. For republics do not come in when kings go out, the defeat of a propertied class is not followed by a cooperative commonwealth, the emancipation of woman is more than a struggle for rights. A servile community will have a master, if not a monarch, then a landlord or a boss, and no legal device will save it. A nation of uncritical drifters can change only the form of tyranny, for like Christian's sword, democracy is a weapon in the hands of those who have the courage and the skill to wield it; in all others it is a rusty piece of junk.

The issues that we face are very different from those of the last century and a half. The difference, I think, might be summed up roughly this way: those who went before inherited a conservatism and overthrew it; we inherit freedom, and have to use it. The sanctity of property, the patriarchal family, hereditary caste, the dogma of sin, obedience to authority, the rock of ages, in brief, has been blasted for *us*. Those who are young today are born into a world in which the foundations of the older order survive only as habits or by default. So Americans can carry through their purposes when they have them. If the standpatter is still powerful amongst us it is because we have not learned to use our power, and direct it to fruitful ends. The American conservative, it seems to me, fills the vacuum where democratic purpose should be.

So far as we are concerned, then, the case is made out against absolutism, commercial oligarchy, and unquestioned creeds. *The rebel program is stated.* Scientific invention and blind social currents have made the old authority impossible in fact, the artillery fire of the iconoclasts has shattered its prestige. We inherit a rebel tradition. The dominant forces in our world are not the sacredness of property, nor the intellectual leadership of the priest; they are not the divinity of the constitution, the glory of industrial push, Victorian sentiment, New England respectability, the Republican Party, or John D. Rockefeller. Our time, of course, believes in change. The adjective "progressive" is what we like, and the word "new," be it the New Nationalism of Roosevelt, the New Freedom of Wilson, or the New Socialism of the syndicalists. The conservatives are more lonely than the pioneers, for almost any prophet to-day can have disciples. The leading thought of our world has ceased to regard commercialism either as permanent or desirable, and the only real question among intelligent people is how business methods are to be altered, not whether they are to be altered. For no one, unafflicted with invincible ignorance, desires to preserve our economic system in its existing form.

The business man has stepped down from his shrine; he is no longer an oracle whose opinion on religion, science, and education is listened to dumbly as the valuable byproduct of a paying business. We have scotched the romance of success. In the emerging morality the husband is not regarded as the proprietor of his wife, nor the parents as autocrats over the children. We are met by women who are "emancipated"; for what we hardly know. We are not stifled by a classical tradition in art: in fact artists to-day are somewhat stunned by the rarefied atmosphere of their freedom. There is a wide agreement among thinking people that the body is not a filthy thing, and that to implant in a child the sense of sin is a poor preparation for a temperate life.

The battle for us, in short, does not lie against crusted prejudice, but against the chaos of a new freedom.

This chaos is our real problem. So if the younger critics are to meet the issues of their generation they must give their attention, not so much to the evils of authority, as to the weaknesses of democracy. But how is a man to go about doing such a task? He faces an enormously complicated world, full of stirring and confusion and ferment. He hears of movements and agitations, criticisms and reforms, knows people who are devoted to "causes," feels angry or hopeful at different times, goes to meetings, reads radical books, and accumulates a sense of uneasiness and pending change.

He can't, however, live with any meaning unless he formulates for himself a vision of what is to come out of the unrest. I have tried in this book to sketch such a vision for myself. At first thought it must seem an absurdly presumptuous task. But it is a task that everyone has to attempt if he is to take part in the work of his time. For in so far as we can direct the future at all, we shall do it by laying what we see against what other people see.

Lippmann asks us to create a vision to guide the future. What does he mean by a vision that "is made out of latent promise in the actual world"?

This doesn't mean the constructing of utopias. The kind of vision which will be fruitful to democratic life is one that is made out of latent promise in the actual world. There is a future contained in the trust and the union, the new status of women, and the moral texture of democracy. It is a future that can in a measure be foreseen and bent somewhat nearer to our hopes. A knowledge of it gives a sanction to our efforts, a part in a larger career, and an invaluable sense of our direction. We make our vision, and hold it ready for any amendment that experience suggests. It is not a fixed picture, a row of shiny ideals which we can exhibit to mankind, and say: Achieve these or be damned. All we can do is to search the world as we find it, extricate the forces that seem to move it, and surround them with criticism and suggestion. Such a vision will inevitably reveal the bias of its author; that is to say it will be a human hypothesis, not an oracular revelation. But if the hypothesis is honest and alive it should cast a little light upon our chaos. It should help us to cease revolving in the mere routine of the present or floating in a private utopia. For a vision of latent hope would be woven of vigorous strands; it would be concentrated on the crucial points of contemporary life, on that living zone where the present is passing into the future. It is the region where thought and action count. Too far ahead there is nothing but your dream; just behind, there is nothing but your memory. But in the unfolding present, man can be creative if his vision is gathered from the promise of actual things.

The day is past, I believe, when anybody can pretend to have laid down an inclusive or a final analysis of the democratic problem. Everyone is compelled to omit infinitely more than he can deal with; everyone is compelled to meet the fact that a democratic vision must be made by the progressive collaboration of many people. Thus I have touched upon the industrial problem at certain points that seem to me of outstanding importance, but there are vast sections and phases of industrial enterprise that pass unnoticed. The points I have raised are big in the world I happen to live in, but obviously they are not the whole world. . . .

This book, then, is an attempt to diagnose the current unrest and to arrive at some sense of what democracy implies. It begins with the obvious drift of our time and gropes for the conditions of mastery. I have tried in the essays that follow to enter the American problem at a few significant points in order to trace a little of the immense suggestion that radiates from them. I hope the book will leave the reader, as it does me, with a sense of the varied talents and opportunities, powers and organizations that may contribute to a conscious revolution. I have not been able to convince myself that one policy, one party, one class, one set of tactics, is as fertile as human need.

It would be very easy if such a belief were possible. It would save time and energy and no end of grubbing: just to keep on repeating what you've learnt, eloquent, supremely confident, with the issues clean, a good fight and an inevitable triumph: Marx, or Lincoln, or Jefferson with you always as guide, counselor and friend. All the thinking done by troubled dead men for the cocksure living; no class to consider but your own; no work that counts but yours; every party but your party composed of fools and rascals; only a formula to accept and a specific fight to win,—it would be easy. It might work on the moon.

WALTER LIPPMANN

"A Note On The Woman's Movement," *Drift and Mastery: An Attempt to Diagnose the Current Unrest,* 1914

In this essay, Lippmann makes the case that social and economic changes have already transformed women's lives and asks what will women do with the new freedoms.

How does he understand feminism? How would his version of feminism change the family and the education of children?

SOURCE: Drift and Mastery: An Attempt to Diagnose the Current Unrest. *New York: Mitchell Kennerly, 1914. 213–239.*

Liberty may be an uncomfortable blessing unless you know what to do with it. That is why so many freed slaves returned to their masters, why so many emancipated women are only too glad to give up the racket and settle down. For between announcing that you will live your own life, and the living of it lie the real difficulties of any awakening.

If all that women needed were "rights,"—the right to work, the right to vote, and freedom from the authority of father and husband, then feminism would be the easiest human question on the calendar. For while there will be a continuing opposition, no one supposes that these elementary freedoms can be withheld from women. In fact, they will be forced upon millions of women who never troubled to ask for any of these rights. And that isn't because Ibsen wrote the *Doll's House*, or because Bernard Shaw writes prefaces.[1] The mere withdrawal of industries from the home has drawn millions of women out of the home, and left millions idle within it. There are many other forces, all of which have blasted the rock of ages where woman's life was centered. The self-conscious modern woman may insist that she has a life of her own to lead, which neither father, nor priest, nor husband, nor Mrs. Grundy is fit to prescribe for her. But when she begins to prescribe life for herself, her real problems begin.

Lippmann explains that there is no precedent for women beyond the role of wife and mother.

Every step in the woman's movement is creative. There are no precedents whatever, not even bad ones. Now the invention of new ways of living is rare enough among men, but among women it has been almost unknown. Housekeeping and baby-rearing are the two most primitive arts in the whole world. They are almost the last occupations in which rule of thumb and old wives' tales have resisted the application of scientific method. They are so immemorially backward, that nine people out of ten hardly conceive the possibility of improving upon them. They are so backward that we have developed a maudlin sentimentality about them, have associated family life and the joy in childhood with all the stupidity and wasted labor of the inefficient home. The idea of making the home efficient will cause the average person to shudder, as if you were uttering some blasphemy against monogamy. "Let science into the home, where on earth will Cupid go to?" Almost in vain do women like Mrs. Gilman insist that the institution of the family is not dependent upon keeping woman a drudge amidst housekeeping arrangements inherited from the early Egyptians.[2] Women have invented almost nothing to lighten their labor. They have made practically no attempt to specialize, to cooperate. They have been the great routineers.

So people have said that woman was made to be the natural conservative, the guardian of tradition. She would probably still be guarding the tradition of weaving her own clothes in the parlor if an invention hadn't thwarted her. She still guards the tradition of buying food retail, of going alone and unorganized

---

1. Norwegian Henrik Ibsen's (1828–1906) play, *A Doll's House* (1879) shocked audiences when the married woman protagonist abandoned her husband and home. Irish playwright George Bernard Shaw (1856–1950), noted for the literary and social criticism in his "prefaces" to literary works, brought progressive issues to the contemporary stage.

2. Mrs. Gilman is Charlotte Perkins Stetson Gilman, whose vision of the family appears in *Women and Economics* on page 194.

to market. And she has been, of course, a faithful conservator of superstition, the most docile and credulous of believers. In all this, I am saying nothing that awakened women themselves aren't saying, nor am I trying to take a hand in that most stupid of all debates as to whether men are superior to women. Nor am I trying to make up my mind whether the higher education of women and their political enfranchisement will produce in the next generation several Darwins and a few Michaelangelos. The question is not even whether women can be as good doctors and lawyers and business organizers as men.

It is much more immediate, and far less academic than that. The feminists could almost afford to admit the worst that Schopenhauer, Weininger. and Sir Almoth Wright can think of,[3] and then go on pointing to the fact that competent or incompetent they have got to adjust themselves to a new world. The day of the definitely marked "sphere" is passing under the action of forces greater than any that an irritated medical man can control. It is no longer possible to hedge the life of women in a set ritual, where their education, their work, their opinion, their love, and their motherhood, are fixed in the structure of custom. To insist that women need to be moulded by authority is a shirking of the issue. For the authority that has moulded them is passing. And if woman is fit only to live in a harem, it will have to be a different kind of harem from any that has existed.

The more you pile up the case against woman in the past the more significant does feminism become. For one fact is written across the whole horizon, the prime element in any discussion. That fact is the absolute necessity for a readjusting of woman's position. And so, every time you insist that women are backward you are adding to the revolutionary meaning of their awakening. But what these anti-feminists have in mind, of course, is that women are by nature incapable of any readjustment. However, the test of that pudding is in the eating. What women will do with the freedom that is being forced upon them is something, that no person can foresee by thinking of women in the past.

Women to-day are embarked upon a career for which their tradition is no guide. The first result, of course is a vast amount of trouble. The emancipated woman has to fight something worse than the crusted prejudices of her uncles; she has to fight the bewilderment in her own soul. She who always took what was given to her has to find for herself. She who passed without a break from the dominance of her father to the dominance of her husband is suddenly compelled to govern herself. Almost at one stroke she has lost the authority of a little world and has been thrust into a very big one, which nobody, man or woman, understands very well. I have tried to suggest

What will women do with their new freedoms from domestic roles?

---

3. German philosopher Arthur Schopenhauer (1788–1860), young Austrian philosopher Otto Weininger (1880–1903), and English biologist Almoth Wright (1861–1947) were well known for their anti-feminist views. In 1913 Wright published his *The Unexpurgated Case Against Woman Suffrage.*

what this change from a world of villages has meant for politicians, clergymen and social thinkers. Well, for women, the whole problem is aggravated by the fact that they come from a still smaller world and from a much more rigid authority.

It is no great wonder if there is chaos among the awakening women. Take a cry like that for a "single standard" of morality. It means two utterly contradictory things. For the Pankhursts it is assumed that men should adopt women's standards, but in the minds of thousands it means just the reverse.[4] For some people feminism is a movement of women to make men chaste, for others the enforced chastity of women is a sign of their slavery. Feminism is attacked both for being too "moral" and too "immoral." And these contradictions represent a real conflict, not a theoretical debate. There is in the movement an uprising of women who rebel against marriage which means to a husband the ultimate haven of a sexual career. There is also a rebellion of women who want for themselves the larger experience that most men have always taken. Christabel Pankhurst uses the new freedom of expression to drive home an Old Testament morality with Old Testament fervor. She finds her book suppressed by Mr. Anthony Comstock, who differs from her far less than he imagines. And she rouses the scorn of great numbers of people who feel that she is out, not to free women, but to enslave men. There is an immense vacillation between a more rigid Puritanism and the idolatry of freedom. Women are discovering what reformers of all kinds are learning, that there is a great gap between the overthrow of authority and the creation of a substitute. That gap is called liberalism: a period of drift and doubt. We are in it to-day.

WOMEN AND WORK

Lippmann addresses women and paid labor. | The first impulse of emancipation seems to be in the main that woman should model her career on man's. But she cannot do that for the simple reason that she is a woman. Towards love and children her attitude is not man's, as everyone but a doctrinaire knows. She cannot taboo her own character in order to become suddenly an amateur male. And if she could, it would be the sheerest folly, for there are plenty of men on this earth.

Yet at the very time when enlightened people are crying out against the horrors of capitalism, you will find many feminists urging women to enter capitalism as a solution of their problems. Of course, millions have been drawn in against their will, but there is still a good number who go in voluntarily, because they feel that their self-respect demands it.

---

4. In 1903 the British Emmeline Pankhurst (1858–1928) established the pro-suffrage Women's Social and Political Union. She was joined by her daughter Christabel (1880–1958). Other daughters Sylvia and Adela distanced themselves from the WSPU, especially from its militant tactics.

They go in response to the desire for economic independence. And they find almost no real independence in the industrial world. What has happened, it seems to me, is this: the women who argue for the necessity of making one's own living are almost without exception upper class women, either because they have special talents or because they have special opportunities. Some time ago I attended a feminist meeting where a brilliant woman was presented to the audience as an example of how it was possible to earn a living and have twins at the same time. But it happened that the woman was a lecturer who could earn a very comfortable sum by speaking a few hours a week. Another woman at the same meeting was an actress, another had been a minister, another was a popular novelist; the only woman present who was concerned with factory work said not one word about the pleasure of earning your own living.

Now, only a very small percentage of men or women can enter the professions. For the great mass, economic independence means going to work. And the theorists of feminism have yet to make up their minds whether they can seriously urge women to go into industry as it is to-day or is likely to be in the near future. I, for one, should say that the presence of women in the labor market is an evil to be combatted by every means at our command. The army of women in industry to-day is not a blessing but the curse of a badly organized society. Their position there is not the outpost of an advance toward a fuller life but an outrage upon the race, and I believe that the future will regard it as a passing phase of human servitude.

WOMEN'S WORK IN THE NEW CENTURY

For the great mass, women's work in the future will, I believe, be in the application of the arts and sciences to a deepened and more extensively organized home. There is nothing narrowing about that, no thrusting of women back into the chimney corner. There is opportunity for every kind of talent, and for the sharing of every kind of interest. It does not mean that women need not concern themselves with industry. Far from it. For any decent kind of home women will have to develop beyond anything we have today an intelligent and powerful consumers' control. They must go into politics, of course, for no home exists that doesn't touch in a hundred ways upon the government of cities, states and the nation. They have the whole educational system to deal with, not only from the public school up, but also, what is beginning to be recognized as most important of all, from infancy to school age. Nor does it mean that every women must be an incompetent amateur of all the arts, as she is today, a cook, a purchaser, a housekeeper, a trained nurse and a kindergarten teacher. Woman's work can and will be specialized, as Mrs. Gilman has pointed out, so that a woman will have a very wide choice in a host of new careers that are going to be created. A great many things which are done in each house will be done by the collective action of a group of houses. The idea of having forty kitchens, forty furnaces, forty laundries, and forty useless backyards in one square block, managed by forty separate overworked women, each going helplessly to market, each bringing up children by rule of thumb,—all that is a kind of individualism which the world will get away from.

To get away from it is an effort that will provide ample careers for most women. The elementary facts of cooperation and division of labor are being forced upon women by the wastefulness of the old kind of housekeeping. We see already the organization of housewives' associations, of common playgrounds, which some people object to when they have a roof and are called common nurseries. There are neighborhood associations, and women's municipal leagues. There are kindergartens which take away from each mother the necessity of being an accomplished teacher of the most subtly plastic period of human life.

Now with the development of some division of labor among women, they will begin to earn salaries. To be paid for work in money is possible only when you don't do all the work. So the moment you divide the work the only way you can share the product is by paying money to each worker. A woman who does her own cooking gets no pay. A woman who does someone else's cooking gets pay. And when women introduce into the work of the home the principle of division of labor and cooperative organization, they also will receive pay, and what is called "economic independence" will be open to them.

That will, of course, be a real emancipation. If women are trained to do all the things that the existing home requires, that is, if they become amateur cooks, marketers, and Montessori mothers, and specialists in none of these things, then they have to wait till they can have a home of their own in which to display their versatility. They have to wait for a man who loves them enough to put up with their general amateurishness, or one who doesn't know any better. But the moment they specialize, so that women can do some one thing very well, they can begin to do homework before they are married. A kindergarten teacher doesn't have to bear a child before she can begin to teach a child. She has a place in the world, a livelihood, and a self-respect because she can do something which is needed. She can marry for love, because she desires children of her own, because she wants what the family can give, not because she is a detached and meaningless female until she is married.

What this will mean for everyone is almost beyond the imagination of most people today. We are just beginning to realize that the intense narrowness of women is one of the things that thwarts human effort. The number of wives who have egged their husbands on to ruthless business practices, the inventive minds that have been stunted by a fierce absorption in the little interests of the household—all the individualism of women is a constant obstacle to a larger cooperative life. If we knew the details of why men falter, why they are pulled away from common action, we should find, I believe, in unnumbered cases that there was some woman at home, a mother or a wife, who, limited in her whole vision, was clinging desperately to some immediate, personal advantage. And as for children, in their most educable period, they are surrounded by an example of isolation, made to feel that the supreme concern of human life is to look in towards the home, instead of out from it. It is no wonder that democracy is so difficult, that collective action is impeded by a thousand conflicting egotisms. Everyone of us is trained in a little watertight compartment of his own.

From the economic and spiritual subjection of his mother the child forms its ideal of the relation of men and women. We speak about the influence of the parents. It is deeper than most of us realize. The child is influenced by its parents, but not only for good, as sentimentalists seem to imagine. The boy may absorb all the admirable qualities of his father, but he is just as capable of absorbing his father's contempt for woman's mind, his father's capacity for playing the little tyrant, and his father's bad economic habits. The girl learns to obey, to wait on the lordly male, to feel unimportant in human affairs, to hold on with unremitting force to the privileges that sex gives her. And out of it all we get the people of to-day, unused to the very meaning of democracy, grasping their own with an almost hysterical tenacity.

The sense of property may be a deep instinct. But surely the nineteenth century home stimulated that instinct to the point of morbidity. For it did almost nothing to bring the child into contact with the real antidote to acquisitiveness— a sense of social property. To own things in common is, it seems to me, one of the most educating experiences in the world. Those people who can feel that they possess the parks, the libraries, the museums of their city, are likely to be far more civilized people than those who want a park which they can enclose, and who want to own a masterpiece all by themselves. It is well known that there is among sea-faring people a rare comradeship. May this not be due to the fact that the sea is there for all to use and none to own? On the high road men salute each other in passing. Farmers seem at times to have a kind of personal friendship with the weather and the turning seasons, and those things which no single man can appropriate.

A new kind of home could instill in the child a sense of social property.

Now in the complicated civilization upon which we are entering, it will be impossible for many people to enjoy the primitive sense of absolute possession. We shall need men and women who can take an interest in collective property, who can feel personally and vividly about it. One of the great promises of the conservation movement is the evidence it gave of a passionate attachment to public possessions. But that attachment is something that almost everyone to-day has had to acquire after he was grown up. We are all of us compelled to overcome the habits and ideals of a childhood where social property was almost unknown. In this respect the only child is perhaps the most deeply miseducated. He has had what he had as his in fee simple. But all children have far too little contact with other children—too few toys that are owned in common, too few group nurseries. Now boys, when they grow to be a bit older, do come in for a little social education. The gang is a fine experience, even though a few windows are smashed. The boy who can talk about "us fellers" has a better start for the modern world than the little girl of the same age who is imitating her mother's housekeeping. From the gang to the athletic team, class spirit, school spirit—with all their faults and misdirected energy—they do mean loyalty to something larger than the petty details of the moment.

THE HOME

Feminism will socialize the home. What does Lippmann mean?

One of the supreme values of feminism is that it will have to socialize the home. When women seek a career they have to specialize. When they specialize they have to cooperate. They have to abandon more and more the self-sufficient individualism of the older family. They will have to market through associations. They will do a great deal more of the housework through associations, just as they are now beginning to have bread baked outside and the washing done by laundries that are not part of the home. If they are not satisfied with the kind of work that is done for the home but outside of it, they will have to learn that difficult business of democracy which consists in expressing and enforcing their desires upon industry. And just as from the kindergarten up, education has become a collective function, so undoubtedly a great deal of the care and training of infants will become specialized.

This doesn't mean baby-farms or barracks or any of the other nightmares of the hysterical imagination. Nobody is proposing to separate the child from its parents any more than the child is now separated. It is curious how readily any woman who can afford it will trust her infant to the most ignorant nurse-girl, and then be horribly shocked at the idea of trusting her child to day nurseries in charge of trained women. The private nurse-girl often abuses the child in unmentionable ways, but she is preferred because she seems somehow to satisfy the feeling of possession. The penalty that grown-ups pay for the sins of the superstitious and unsocialized nursery is something that we are just beginning to understand from the researches of the psychiatrists.

There is one question about feminism which is sure to have risen in the mind of any reader who has followed the argument up to this point. Does the awakening of women mean an attack upon monogamy? For the moment anyone dares to criticize any arrangement of the existing home he might as well be prepared to find himself classed as a sexual anarchist. It is curious how little faith conservatives have in the institution of the family. They will tell you how deep it is in the needs of mankind, and they will turn around and act as if the home were so fragile that collapse would follow the first whiff of criticism.

THE FAMILY

Will feminism destroy the family? Monogamy?

Now I believe that the family *is* deeply grounded in the needs of mankind, or it would never survive the destructive attacks made upon it, not by radical theorists, mind you, but by social conditions. At the present moment over half the men of the working-class do not earn enough to support a family, and that's why their wives and their daughters are drawn into industry. The family survives that, men and women do still want to marry and have children. But we put every kind of obstacle in their way. We pay such wages that young men can't afford to marry. We do not teach them the elementary facts of sex. We allow them to pick up knowledge in whispered and hidden ways. We surround them with the tingle and glare of cities, stimulate them, and then fall upon them with a morality which shows no quarter. We support a large class of women in idleness, the soil in which every foolish freak can flourish. We thrust people into marriage and forbid them with fearful penalties to learn any way of controlling their own fertility. We do almost no single, sensible, and deliberate thing to make family life a success. And still the family survives.

It has survived all manner of stupidity. It will survive the application of intelligence. It will not collapse because the home is no longer the scene of drudgery and wasted labor or because children are reared to meet modern civilization. It will not collapse because women have become educated, or because they have attained a new self-respect.

But in answer to the direct question whether monogamy is to go by the board, the only possible answer is this: there is no reason for supposing that there will be any less of it than there is to-day. That is not saying very much, perhaps, but more than that no honest person can guarantee. He can believe that when the thousand irritations of married life are reduced, the irritations of an unsound economic status, of ignorance in the art of love, then the family will have a better chance than it has ever had. How many homes have been wrecked by the sheer inability of men and women to understand each other can be seen by the enormous use made of the theme in modern literature. It does not seem to me that education and a growing sensitiveness are likely to make for promiscuity.

For you have to hold yourself very cheaply to endure the appalling and unselective intimacy that promiscuity means. To treat women as things and yourself as a predatory animal is the product not of emancipation and self-respect, but of ignorance and inferiority. The uprising of women as personalities is not likely to make them value themselves less, nor is it likely that they will be satisfied with the fragments of love they now attain. Of course, every movement attracts what Roosevelt calls its "lunatic fringe," and feminism has collected about it a great rag-tag of bohemianism. But it cannot be judged by that; it must be judged by its effect on the great mass of women who, half-consciously for the most part, are seeking not a new form of studio and cafe life, but a readjustment to work and love and interest. There is among them, so far as I can see, no indication of any desire for an impressionistic sexual career.

To be sure they don't treat a woman who has had relations out of marriage as if she were a leper. They are not inclined to visit upon the offspring of illegitimacy the curse of patriarchal Judaea. But so far as their own demands go they are set in overwhelming measure upon greater sexual sincerity. They are, if anything, too stern in their morality and, perhaps, too naive. But the legislation they initiate, the books they write, look almost entirely to the establishment of a far more enduring and intelligently directed family.

THE WOMEN'S MOVEMENT AND ITS PROMISE FOR THE FUTURE

The effect of the woman's movement will accumulate with the generations. The results are bound to be so far-reaching that we can hardly guess them to-day. For we are tapping a reservoir of possibilities when women begin to use not only their generalized womanliness but their special abilities. For the child it means, as I have tried to suggest, a change in the very conditions where the property sense is aggravated and where the need for authority and individual assertiveness is built up. The greatest obstacles to a cooperative civilization are under fire from the feminists. Those obstacles today are more than anything else a childhood in which the antisocial impulses are fixed. The awakening of women points straight to the discipline of cooperation. And so it is laying the real foundations for the modern world.

For understand that the forms of cooperation are of precious little value without a people trained to use them. The old family with its dominating father, its submissive and amateurish mother produced inevitably men who had little sense of a common life, and women who were jealous of an enlarging civilization. It is this that feminism comes to correct, and that is why its promise reaches far beyond the present bewilderment.

MARGARET SANGER

"Aim," *The Woman Rebel: No Gods, No Masters,* March 1914

Sanger's short-lived journal The Woman Rebel *challenges just about every mainstream institution and belief about women and woman's nature. Perhaps the most radical is her assertion of women's sexuality at a time when U.S. urban societies were at the height of their attack on "vice" and "white slavery," the terms coined for prostitution. Social reformers established committees to study the matter, while theatrical productions and the new "movies" thrilled as they frightened mass audiences with the perils befalling women who left the home and walked freely on city streets. As you read, note how Sanger understands women's sexual desire and how she counters arguments against legal contraception.*

SOURCE: The Woman Rebel. *Vol. 1, No.1, March 1914. 1.*

*T*his paper will not be the champion of any "ism."

All rebel women are invited to contribute to its columns.

The majority of papers usually adjust themselves to the ideas of their readers but the WOMAN REBEL will obstinately refuse to be adjusted.

The aim of this paper will be to stimulate working women to think for themselves and to build up a conscious fighting character.

An early feature will be a series of articles written by the editor for girls from fourteen to eighteen years of age. In this present chaos of sex atmosphere it is difficult for the girl of this uncertain age to know just what to do or really what constitutes clean living without prudishness. All this slushy talk about white slavery, the man painted and described as a hideous vulture pouncing down upon the young, pure and innocent girl, drugging her through the medium of grape juice and lemonade and then dragging her off to his foul den for other men equally as vicious to feed and fatten on her enforced slavery—surely this picture is enough to sicken and disgust every thinking woman and man, who has lived even a few years past the adolescent age. Could any more repulsive and foul conception of sex be given to adolescent girls as a preparation for life than this picture that is being perpetuated by the stupidly ignorant in the name of "sex education"!

If it were possible to get the truth from girls who work in prostitution today, I believe most of them would tell you that the first sex experience was with a sweetheart or through the desire for a sweetheart or something impelling within themselves, the nature of which they knew not, neither could they control. Society does not forgive this act when it is based upon the natural impulses and feelings of a young girl. It prefers the other story of the grape juice procurer which makes it easy to shift the blame from its own shoulders, to cast the stone and to evade the unpleasant facts that it alone is responsible for. It sheds sympathetic tears over white slavery, holds the often mythical procurer up as a target, while in reality it is supported by the misery it engenders.

If, as reported, there are approximately 35,000 women working as prostitutes in New York City alone, is it not sane to conclude that some force, some living, powerful, social force is at play to compel these women to work at a trade which involves police persecution, social ostracism and the constant danger of exposure to venereal diseases. From my own knowledge of adolescent girls and from sincere expressions of women working as prostitutes inspired by mutual understanding and confidence I claim that the first sexual act of these so-called wayward girls is partly given, partly desired yet reluctantly so because of the fear of the consequences together with the dread of lost respect of the man. These fears interfere with mutuality of expression—the man becomes conscious of the responsibility of the set and often refuses to see her again, sometimes leaving the town and usually denouncing her as having been with "other fellows." His sole aim is to throw off responsibility. The same uncertainty in these emotions is experienced by girls in marriage in as great a proportion as in the unmarried. After the first experience the life of a girl varies. All these girls do not necessarily go into prostitution. They have had an experience which has not "ruined" them, but rather given them a larger vision of life, stronger feelings and a broader understanding of human nature. The adolescent girl does not understand herself. She is full of contradictions, whims, emotions. For her emotional nature longs for caresses, to touch, to kiss. She is often as well satisfied to hold hands or to go arm in arm with a girl as in the companionship of a boy.

It is these and kindred facts upon which the WOMAN REBEL will dwell from time to time and from which it is hoped the young girl will derive some knowledge of her nature, and conduct her life upon such knowledge.

It will also be the aim of the WOMAN REBEL to advocate the prevention of conception and to impart such knowledge in the columns of this paper.

Other subjects, including the slavery through motherhood; through things, the home, public opinion and so forth, will be dealt with.

It is also the aim of this paper to circulate among those women who work in prostitution; to voice their wrongs; to expose the police persecution which hovers over them and to give free expression to their thoughts, hopes and opinions.

And at all times the WOMAN REBEL will strenuously advocate economic emancipation.

THE PREVENTION OF CONCEPTION

Is there any reason why women should not receive clean, harmless, scientific knowledge on how to prevent conception? Everybody is aware that the old, stupid fallacy that such knowledge will cause a girl to enter into prostitution has long been shattered. Seldom does a prostitute become pregnant. Seldom does the girl practicing promiscuity become pregnant. The woman of the upper middle class have all available knowledge and implements to prevent conception. The woman of the lower middle class is struggling for this knowledge. She tries various methods of prevention, and after a few years of experience plus medical advice succeeds in discovering some method suitable to her individual self. The woman of the people is the only one left in ignorance of this information. Her neighbors, relatives and friends tell her stories of special devices and the success of them all. They tell her also of the blood-sucking men with M. D. after their names who perform operations for the price of so-and-so. But the working woman's purse is thin. It's far cheaper to have a baby, "though God knows what it will do after it gets here." Then, too, all other classes of women live in places where there is at least a semblance of privacy and sanitation. It is easier for them to care for themselves whereas the large majority of the women of the people have no bathing or sanitary conveniences. This accounts too for the fact that the higher the standard of living, the more care can be taken and fewer children result. No plagues, famine or wars could ever frighten the capitalist class so much as the universal practice of the prevention of conception. On the other hand no better method could be utilized for increasing the wages of the workers.

As is well known, a law exists forbidding the imparting of information on this subject, the penalty being several years' imprisonment. Is it not time to defy this law! And what fitter place could be found than in the pages of the WOMAN REBEL!

MARRIAGE

Marriage, which is a personal agreement between a man and a woman, should be no concern of the State or of the Church. Never have either of these institutions interested themselves in the happiness or health of the individual. Never have they concerned themselves that children be born in healthy and clean surroundings, which might insure their highest development. The Church has been and is anxious only if a child be trained Catholic, Baptist, Methodist and so forth. The State and the Church are concerned only in maintaining and perpetuating themselves even to the detriment and sacrifice of the human race. In the willingness to accept without protest or question the indignities imposed through the barbarities of the Law, together with the stupid superstitions of the Church, can be traced a great proportion of the world's misery.

That there exists in all Nature an attraction which takes place between particles of bodies and unites to form a chemical compound is not doubted. This same attraction exists in men and women and will, unconsciously perhaps, cause them to seek a mate just as other organisms do.

Priests and marriage laws have no power or control over this attraction nor can they make desirable a union where this attraction does not exist.

Marriage laws abrogate the freedom of woman by enforcing upon her a continuous sexual slavery and a compulsory motherhood.

Marriage laws have been dictated and dominated by the Church always and ever upon the unquestionable grounds of the wisdom of the Bible.

A man and woman who under a natural condition avow their love for each other should be immediately qualified by this to give expression to their love or to perpetuate the race without the necessity of a public declaration.

A reciprocal, spontaneous voluntary declaration of love and mutual feelings by a man and woman is the expression of Nature's desires. Were it not natural it would not be so and being natural it is right.

The marriage institution viewed from the light of human experience and the demands of the individual has proven a failure. Statistical reports show that one out of every twelve marriages in the United States has resulted in a divorce— which does not include the thousands of women who want divorces—but on account of the Church and conventions are restrained from obtaining them. Nor does it mention the thousands of women too poor to obtain the price to set in motion the ponderous machinery of the divorce courts. The divorce courts give us only a hint of the dissatisfaction and unhappiness underlying the institution of marriage.

Superstition; blind following; unthinking obedience on the part of working women; together with the pretense, hypocrisy and sham morality of the women of the middle class have been the greatest obstacles in the obtaining of woman's freedom.

Every change in social life is accomplished only by a struggle. Rebel women of the world must fight for the freedom to harmonize their actions with the natural desires of their being, for their deeds are but the concrete expressions of their thoughts.

THE POST OFFICE BAN

The woman rebel feels proud the post office authorities did not approve of her.

She shall blush with shame if ever she be approved of by officialism of "comstockism."[1]

REBEL WOMEN WANTED

Who deny the right of the State to deprive women of such knowledge as would enable them to take upon themselves voluntary motherhood.

Who deny the right of the State to prohibit such knowledge which would add to the freedom and happiness of the people.

Who demand that those desiring to live together in love shall be provided with such knowledge and experience as Science has developed, which would prevent conception.

Who will assist in the work of increasing the demand for this information.

Who have the courage and backbone to fight with "THE WOMAN REBEL" against this outrageous suppression, whereby a woman has no control of the function of motherhood.

Who are willing to enter this fight, and continue to the end.

---

1. Refers to Anthony Comstock. See the footnote on 209.

NEITH BOYCE

"Constancy: A Dialogue," 1916

This play was first presented in the Provincetown, Massachusetts, living room of Hutchins Hapgood and Neith Boyce. Joe O'Brien (new husband of Mary Heaton Vorse) played Rex; Neith Boyce played Moira. Boyce wrote the play about the relationship between Jack Reed and Mabel Dodge.

Boyce's characters, while modern in their demands for personal independence, also cling to the emotional patterns of an earlier age: romantic love, true womanhood, male sexual freedom. The playwright gives this one-act play the title Constancy. *What could this title mean?*

SOURCE: *Adele Heller and Lois Rudnick, eds.* 1915, the Cultural Moment: The New Politics, the New Woman, the New Psychology, the New Art, and the New Theatre in America. *New Brunswick, NJ: Rutgers University Press, 1991.*

*HARACTERS*
MOIRA
REX

A room, luxurious and gay, in delicate, bright colors. Long arched windows at the back open on a balcony flooded with moonlight, overlooking the sea. In the center of the room a long sofa piled with bright cushions. Moira, sitting at a desk under a shaded lamp, writing busily. She is dressed in a robe of brocade with straight lines, brilliant in color. A whistle sounds under the balcony. She looks up, glances at a tiny clock on the desk, which delicately chimes twelve, smiles and finishes her phrase. A second whistle, prolonged. She rises and goes out on the balcony, leans over the rail.

| *What are Rex and Moira's customary ways to meet?*

REX *(Off)*: Moira.
MOIRA: Rex. There you are. Come 'round, the door is open.
REX: The door. The door. Oh, very well . . .
(Moira comes back into room, laughing softly. She glances into mirror, touching the circlet around her temples, takes cigarette, lights it, stands leaning against end of couch, looking at Rex. . . .
Enter Rex in cape and soft hat which he drops on floor as Moira lazily takes two steps to meet him, with both hands held out.)
MOIRA: Well. Well. Here you are.
REX *(Quickly)*: Yes. I've come back.

MOIRA (*Lazily*): You have come back. How well you're looking.

REX: I'm not well. I'm confoundedly ill. I'm a wreck.

MOIRA: Oh, no. Come here, let me look at you. (*Draws him nearer lamp*) Well, you're a little thinner, but it's becoming. And you do look tired. But then you've had a long journey. Come, sit down and make yourself comfortable.

(*She drops onto couch and draws him down.*)

REX: Comfortable.

MOIRA: Yes; why not there? (*Tosses cushion behind his head.*) Will you have something to eat? A drink?

REX (*Darkly*): No, Moira.

MOIRA: Have a cigarette. I think I've some of your kind left. Look over there.

REX: Oh, never mind. (*He is gazing intently at her; mutters*) I don't care what kind.

MOIRA: You don't care. And I've kept them all this time. Well then, have one of mine.

(*She leans to take one from desk, offers it to him, he lights it absently, looking at her steadily as though perplexed.*)

REX: Thanks. Moira, I must say you look well.

MOIRA: Yes, I am—very well.

REX: And—happy?

MOIRA: Oh, very busy, and—yes, pretty happy, I should say.

REX (*Gloomily*): I'm very glad.

(*She smokes luxuriously, looking at him. He smokes nervously, looking at her.*)

MOIRA: And now tell me all about yourself, my dear. It seems ages since you went away and yet it's only four months . . . but such a lot of things have happened.

REX: Yes. A lot indeed. (*Abruptly*) I wrote you.

What has happened? Note the ways that Moira shows her apparent indifference.

MOIRA: Oh yes, but letters . . . There's a lot one doesn't say in letters.

REX: Yes, there is. (*Gets up, strides to railing, hurls cigarette out, comes back and stands back of couch.*) Moira, the last thing on earth I expected was that you should receive me like this.

MOIRA: But why, Rex. How did you expect me to receive you? With a dagger in one hand and a bottle of poison in the other?

REX: Well, I don't know. But (*bitterly*) I didn't expect this.

MOIRA: But what is this?

REX: You know well enough. You treat me as though I were an ordinary acquaintance, just dropped in for a chat.

MOIRA: Oh, no, no. A dear friend, Rex. . . . Always dear to me.

(*She leans over languidly, drops cigarette in tray, takes gray knitting from desk and knits.*)

REX: Friend. (*Walks away to window*) When we parted four months ago we weren't friends. We were lovers.

MOIRA (*Sweetly*): Yes, but you know a lot of things have happened since then.

(*She knits with attention.*)

REX: Well . . . (*Stops for a moment then turns toward her with indignation*) Well, even if things have happened. I don't see how you can have changed so completely.

MOIRA (*Counting stitches*): One, two, three . . . Well, my dear Rex, you've changed a good deal yourself.

REX (*Vehemently coming back*): I have not changed.

MOIRA (*Dropping her knitting and looking around at him*): Well . . . Really.

REX (*Hotly*): Of course I know what you mean. Perhaps it's natural enough for you to think so.

MOIRA (*Coolly*): Yes, I should think it was.

REX: And yet I did think you were intelligent enough to understand. But even if I had changed as completely as you thought, I still don't understand why—why you are like this.

MOIRA: This again. (*Puts up hand to him*) My dear Rex, I'm awfully glad to see you again. Do come, sit down and let us talk about everything.

REX (*Dolefully*): Glad to see me. (*He sits at end of sofa*) I didn't think you'd let me in the door.

MOIRA: You didn't? (*Springs up suddenly, drops knitting.*) Rex, you didn't expect to come by the ladder, did you?

REX: Well, no—

MOIRA: I believe you did. This romantic hour, your boat, your whistle—just the same—I know you looked for the ladder.

REX: No, no, I didn't. I tell you I didn't think you'd see me at all. But what have you done with it, Moira?

MOIRA: The ladder? (*Walks across to table, opens drawer, drags out rope ladder, comes back to couch.*) Here it is.

REX: So—you've kept it.

MOIRA: Yes—as a remembrance.

REX: Only that?

MOIRA: Absolutely. If you like I'll give it to you now.

REX: To me.

MOIRA: Yes. You might find use for it some time.

REX: Moira.

MOIRA (*Laughing*): Well, you know, my dear Rex, you are incurably romantic—and then, you're still young. As for me, my days of romance are over.

REX (*Leaning towards her, violently*): I don't believe it. I believe you love some one else. I've believed it ever since your telegram to me. Otherwise you couldn't have behaved so—so—

MOIRA: So well?

REX: If you call it that.

MOIRA: I do, of course. I think I behaved admirably. But you're wrong about the reason. I don't love anyone else and I don't intend to. I've done with all that.

REX (*Softened, taking her hand*): No, Moira.

MOIRA; Yes, indeed. (*Sits up, drawing her hand away, more coolly.*) As to my telegram, what else could I do? You had fallen in love with Ellen. You telegraphed me, "Let us part friends"—

| What does the ladder mean to Rex and Moira?

REX: But, Moira—

We learn the details of the separation. MOIRA (*Quickly*): Then came your letter telling me that you and Ellen loved one another; that this was the real love at last, that you felt you never had loved me—

REX: Yes, but Moira—

MOIRA: You reminded me how unhappy you and I had been together—how we had quarreled—how we had hurt one another—

REX: Yes, yes, I know, but listen—

MOIRA: And then you begged me to forgive you for leaving me—so—I did forgive you. What else could I do if I couldn't hold on to you when you loved and wanted to marry another woman.

REX: Moira, if you won't listen to a word from me, how can I explain to you?

MOIRA: Why, Rex, I'll listen to you all night if you like . . . but I don't see that you have anything to explain.

REX: Well, I have, though. You've got an entirely wrong idea of this business . . .

MOIRA: I don't see that. Your letters were quite explicit. You were tired of me—

REX: I was not.

MOIRA: You fell in love with another woman, younger, more beautiful—

REX: Moira—

Moira's view of men. MOIRA: That's all natural enough. I know what men are. They're restless, changeable. You wanted to marry this one—just as—

REX: I didn't want to marry her.

MOIRA: You didn't? You wrote me—

REX: Well, perhaps I did, or thought I did, just then. . . . But really it was she that wanted to marry me.

MOIRA: Oh, Rex, you wrote me—

REX: Oh, I admit I was in love with her. Yes, I was, for a while and I was willing to do anything she wanted, then.

MOIRA: Well, then.

REX: But, Moira, what I can't understand is your giving me up like that—like a shot, without a struggle.

MOIRA: But, my dear Rex, what else—

REX: When I think what you were last year. What scenes you made if I even looked at another woman. How you threatened to kill yourself when I had just a casual adventure.

MOIRA: Yes—that's true—I did.

REX: Well, what can I think now except that you have absolutely ceased to love me.

MOIRA: But, my dear Rex, did you want me to go on loving you when you had left me for another woman?

REX: I never left you.

MOIRA: Oh.

REX (*Hastily*): But, anyhow, it isn't a question of what I wanted. It's a question of fact. You stopped loving me. The real truth is you never never loved me.

MOIRA: Oh, yes, I did, Rex.

REX: No, else you couldn't have stopped. It's true; it's true. "Love is not love that alters when it alteration finds or bends with the remover to remove."

MOIRA: Oh, my dear Rex, you are really wonderful. How about you? You stopped loving me.

REX: I never stopped loving you.

MOIRA: Oh, heavens. You wrote me that you never had loved me.

REX: Never mind what I wrote. I was in a very excited frame of mind—and wrote a lot of things I didn't mean. And you must remember Ellen was there at my elbow, and of course her point of view influenced me a lot.

MOIRA *(Coldly)*: Naturally. And what was her point of view?

REX: Why that we were fatally in love; had fallen in love at first sight and that we were to marry and settle down together.

MOIRA: Well, that certainly seemed to be your point of view.

REX: I tell you, Ellen was right there, influencing me. . . . And there's no doubt I was in love with her at the time. She's lovely, you know. I was mad about her.

MOIRA: Why do you say was—was—was? You're still in love with her, aren't you?

REX: No, Moira, I don't believe I am. Of course I have a feeling about her— she is beautiful—But even if I were in love with her, Moira, this about marrying—

MOIRA: Well, what about it?

REX *(Springing up and pacing the floor)*: Moira, I don't want to marry. As to settling down, I simply can't.

MOIRA: But you promised her, didn't you?

REX: I did. And of course if she insists, I suppose I'll have to keep my promise. That is, I'll marry her, but I won't settle down. That I cannot do. Why, Moira, listen— *(Throws himself in corner of couch, leans forward.)* What do you think she expects? She expects me to live with her in a little suburban house, and come back every night to dinner, and have a yard with vegetables, and a sleeping porch facing the east. Oh, Moira. *(Buries his face in his hands.)*

MOIRA: Well, my dear Rex, if you love her—

REX *(Savagely)*: I couldn't love anyone like that.

MOIRA: Well, how do you love her, then?

REX *(Moodily)*: Why—I loved her as a beautiful, poetical creature, a ▐ *Rex's ideal of woman.* bit of plastic loveliness—Moira, you ought to see her; she is lovely— er—she was unhappy, too. She needed to be made love to. I made love to her; I loved her in a way, but, oh, Moira, not as I loved you.

MOIRA: What? My dear boy . . .

REX *(Surprised)*: Surely you know Moira that I have loved you ever since we met; that I never ceased loving you; that I could never love anyone else as I love you.

MOIRA: But, my dear Rex, you wrote me.

REX: Oh, I wrote you, I wrote you. . . . I've already explained to you that I wasn't in a state of mind to know what I meant then. You remember, too, that you and I parted with a quarrel.

MOIRA: What of it? You wrote me right after that quarrel that you adored me more than ever . . .

REX: Well, so I did. . . . But don't you see, the fact that we had quarreled so terribly, just at parting—well, it made me feel desperate. And so—

MOIRA *(Ironically)*: And so—you fell in love with Ellen.

REX: Well, yes, that's only natural, just at first. But now, you see, I've had time to think it over and I know—why, what did you think I meant when I wrote you that I was coming back?

MOIRA: Meant? Meant? Why I supposed you meant you were coming to pay me a friendly visit and make sure of my forgiveness.

REX: Forgiveness, yes, but real forgiveness, Moira.

MOIRA: Yes, yes, I do really forgive you. I don't bear you any malice at all.

REX: Then you do really love me, Moira, after all.

MOIRA: I'm very fond of you, my dear, and always shall be.

REX: No, no, that isn't what I mean and you know it. I love you just as I always did, only more, I think. I've come back to you, Moira.

MOIRA: But—my dear Rex—Ellen.

REX: I've written Ellen that I can't honestly promise to do what she wants. . . . I've told her that I will marry her if she still wants me to, but that I can't settle down. . . . That I must have my freedom—and that probably she wouldn't be happy with me. I have been as honest with her as I could be—Just as I was always honest with you.

MOIRA *(Smiling pensively)*: Yes, you always told me that, too.

REX: You see, I haven't deceived either of you. I may have deceived myself at times—when I thought I didn't love you, for instance. But I know now that I do and always shall. And so, Moira, do you forgive me?

MOIRA: I've told you so.

REX: And love me?

MOIRA: In a way, yes—I always shall.

REX: No, not in a way. As you did before, Moira. Surely you haven't altogether stopped loving me.

Moira explains her response to Rex.

MOIRA: No, not as I did before. That was a disease, a madness. I was mad with jealousy of you. . . . I was miserable. I tried to keep you faithful to me—and I couldn't. I don't want to go back to that.

REX: You don't want to go back?

MOIRA: *No.* To have you leave me again in a few months—or weeks—for another woman? *No.*

REX: Moira, I was always faithful to you, really. I always shall be. I should always come back.

MOIRA: That is your idea of fidelity. You would always come back.

REX: Yes, always. I couldn't help myself. I couldn't stay away for long. I couldn't forget you.

MOIRA: You forgot me easily.

REX: I never forgot you. Didn't I write you nearly every day? You were always on my mind. I saw you suffering, wounded, desperate, perhaps even doing what you threatened once—you know—

MOIRA: Kill myself?

REX: I thought everything. I was in despair about you. Even your letters, so calm and generous, didn't reassure me. I knew your pride.

MOIRA: So you thought I was wearing a mask of cheerfulness and resignation.

REX: Yes, and I thought it noble of you.

MOIRA: And at the same time you thought I must be in love with some one else. You said so.

REX: Well, I didn't know what to think. That's the truth.

MOIRA: The one thing you couldn't believe was that I had ceased to feel about you as a lover.

REX: Yes, that was it; I admit it.

MOIRA: And yet you'll admit, too, that it was the right and reasonable thing to do.

REX: Oh, right and reasonable.

MOIRA: If I had behaved like a jealous fury, showered reproaches on you, threatened you, pursued you, tried to get you away from Ellen, that from your point of view would have been the natural thing for me to do.

REX: Yes, if you loved me.

MOIRA: Well, Rex, I don't think so. I knew that you would leave me some day. You're young, and as you say yourself, you must have your freedom. So when it came I took the blow, for it was a blow. I adjusted myself to the change.

REX: Very easily.

MOIRA: Well, it is done, now.

REX: And you don't want to undo it? You don't want me back?

MOIRA: As a friend, yes; always. Love passes. Friendship endures.

REX: Love never ends—real love. But you know nothing about it. You never loved me.

MOIRA: I did, Rex. I lived only for you for a year and I wasn't happy. Don't you remember how I absorbed myself in you, gave up all my other interests, gave up my friends, could see nothing and nobody but you; was careless and indifferent to everyone but you? And I wasn't happy.

REX: That is exactly it. Did I want you to give up your interests and your friends? Did I want you to see nothing and nobody but me? Didn't I want you to be free of me and let me be free of you—sometimes.

MOIRA: In love one cannot be free. I was constant to you every moment, while I loved you.

What is Moira's idea of constancy? What is Rex's?

REX: While you loved me. That's not my idea of constancy.

MOIRA: No, your idea of constancy is to love a hundred other women and at intervals to come back—to me.

REX: Moira, you drove it too hard. You tied yourself and me down hand and foot. And now you say it is ended for you. Now because I've been what you call unfaithful you throw me off. And that is your idea of constancy.

MOIRA: I can't endure love without fidelity. It tortures me. I don't want to be the head of a harem. Yes, it is ended.

REX *(Goes to balcony, stands looking out)*: Look. How many times have I come to you; come up over this balcony? And you were happy then. You didn't want to push me away then.

MOIRA: It was a fever. What is real is what I feel for you now; a warm affection, a—

REX: I don't want that. I want you back as you were before.

MOIRA: You want to make me miserable again. No, Rex.

REX: *(Kneels on couch, leans toward her and takes her in his arms. She does not resist.)* I can't believe you mean it. Kiss me. *(She kisses him. He draws back suddenly and lets her go.)* You do mean it. You don't care any more. *(He drops down on couch. She leans over and caresses his hair.)*

MOIRA: Now, Rex, you are just a boy, crying for the moon. As long as you haven't got it you are dying for it. When you get it you go on to something else. I understand you very well and I think you are the most charming and amusing person I know, and I shall always be really fonder of you than of anyone else.

REX: *(Jumping to his feet)* The moon. You are the moon, I suppose, and you are certainly as inconstant. How can you change like this? I come back to you loving you as I always did, the same as ever, and I find you completely changed; your love for me gone as though it had never been. And you tell me it is no new love that has driven it out. I could understand that, but this . . . It is true, as Weininger said, women have no soul, no memory. They are incapable of fidelity.[1]

MOIRA: Fidelity.

REX: Yes, fidelity. Haven't I been essentially faithful to you. I may have fancies for other women but haven't I come back to you?

MOIRA *(Looking at him with admiration)*: Oh, Rex, you are perfect; you are a perfect man.

REX: Well, I can say with sincerity that you are a complete woman.

MOIRA: After that I suppose there is no more to say. We have annihilated one another.

REX *(Furiously snatching up cloak and hat)*: I shall leave you.

MOIRA: But you will come back.

REX: Come back. *(He turns to her)* You know I shall. I can't help it. And we shall see.

MOIRA: Yes, shan't we. Oh, by the way, I promised you this. *(Holds up the ladder)*

---

1. Austrian philosopher Otto Weininger (1880–1903) provides this definition of woman in his *Sex and Character* (1903).

REX: You'd better keep it.

MOIRA: No, Rex. *(Drops the ladder at his feet.)*

REX: I am going. You never loved me.

MOIRA: Oh, yes I did, Rex. Have you forgotten?

REX: I have forgotten nothing. It is you who have forgotten. It is you who have been unfaithful. I come back to you and you treat me like a stranger. You turn me out. You say you no longer love me. *(Regarding her with passionate reproach.)* And you told me you had forgiven me.

MOIRA: So I have.

REX: You mean—by ceasing to love me. Do you think anyone wants that sort of forgiveness?

MOIRA: That's the only sort anyone ever gets.

REX: No. *(with emotion)* Forgiving means forgetting.

MOIRA *(With a wide gesture)*: Well, I have forgotten—everything.

REX *(With a violent movement toward her)*: You—*(Stops and they stand looking at another)* And you have called me inconstant. *(He backs toward the door with a savage laugh)* Constancy! *(Moira stands looking at him, motionless.)*

> *The conflicts between new freedoms and old ways of thinking and feeling have an impact on this relationship. How do you understand Moira's decision to push Rex away?*

CURTAIN.

RANDOLPH BOURNE

"Trans-National America," *The Atlantic Monthly,* 1916

In this article, Bourne explores the possibilities of an American nationalism that is not only inclusive of immigrants and their many cultures, but also transformed by continual arrival of new peoples. Rejecting the notion that America must be "Anglo-Saxon," Bourne is free to imagine a "trans-national" America. How does he counter beliefs that the United States should be a "melting-pot"? What does he propose instead of the assimilation of the newcomer?

Note that the notion of the United States as a melting pot, where immigrants would transform themselves into Americans, comes from Israel Zangwill's play The Melting-Pot *(1908). There a character states: "America is God's Crucible, where all races of Europe are melting and reforming."*

SOURCE: The Atlantic Monthly. *CXVII. April, 1916. http://catalog.hathitrust.org/Record/000597656*

I.

No reverberatory effect of the great war has caused American public opinion more solicitude than the failure of the "melting-pot." The discovery of diverse nationalistic feelings among our great alien population has come to most people as an intense shock. It has brought out the unpleasant inconsistencies of our traditional beliefs. We have had to watch hard-hearted old Brahmins virtuously indignant at the spectacle of the immigrant refusing to be melted, while they jeer at patriots like Mary Antin who write about our "forefathers."[1] We have had to listen to publicists who express themselves as stunned by the evidence of vigorous traditionalistic and cultural movements in this country among Germans, Scandinavians, Bohemians and Poles, while in the same breath they insist that the alien shall be forcibly assimilated to that Anglo-Saxon tradition which they unquestionably label "American."

As the unpleasant truth has come upon us that assimilation in this country was proceeding on lines very different from those we had marked out for it, we found ourselves inclined to blame those who were thwarting our prophecies. The truth became culpable. We blamed the war, we blamed the Germans. And then we discovered with a moral shock that these movements had been making great headway even before the war even began. We found that the tendency, reprehensible and paradoxical as it might be, has been for the national clusters of immigrants, as they became more and more firmly established and more and more prosperous, to cultivate more and more assiduously the literatures and cultural traditions of their homelands. Assimilation, in other words, instead of washing out the memories of Europe, made them more and more intensely real. Just as these clusters became more and more objectively American, did they become more and more German or Scandinavian or Bohemian or Polish.

Bourne asserts that there is no melting-pot.

To face the fact that our aliens are already strong enough to take a share in the direction of their own destiny, and that the strong cultural movements represented by the foreign press, schools, and colonies are a challenge to our facile attempts, is not, however, to admit the failure of Americanization. It is not to fear the failure of democracy. It is rather to urge us to an investigation of what Americanism may rightly mean. It is to ask ourselves whether our ideal has been broad or narrow—whether perhaps the time has not come to assert a higher ideal than the "melting-pot." Surely we cannot be certain of our spiritual democracy when, claiming to melt the nations within us to a comprehension of our free and democratic institutions, we fly into panic at the first sign of their own will and tendency. We act as if we wanted Americanization to take place only on our own terms, and not by

---

1. Mary Antin (1889–1949), a Jewish immigrant, writer, and speaker, embraced the ideal of public education as a "melting-pot" for the creation of new Americans.

the consent of the governed. All our elaborate machinery of settlement and school and union, of social and political naturalization, however, will move with friction just in so far as it neglects to take into account this strong and virile insistence that America shall be what the immigrant will have a hand in making it, and not what a ruling class, descendant of those British stocks which were the first permanent immigrants, decide that America shall be made. This is the condition which confronts us, and which demands a clear and general readjustment of our attitude and our ideal. Mary Antin is right when she looks upon our foreign-born as the people who missed the Mayflower and came over on the first boat they could find. But she forgets that when they did come it was not upon other Mayflowers, but upon a "Maiblume," a "Fleur de Mai," a "Fior di Maggio," a "Majblomst." These people were not mere arrivals from the same family, to be welcomed as understood and long-loved, but strangers to the neighborhood, with whom a long process of settling down had to take place. For they brought with them their national and racial characters, and each new national quota had to wear slowly away the contempt with which its mere alienness got itself greeted. Each had to make its way slowly from the lowest strata of unskilled labor up to a level where it satisfied the accredited norms of social success.

We are all foreign-born or the descendants of foreign-born, and if distinctions are to be made between us they should rightly be on some other ground than indigenousness. The early colonists came over with motives no less colonial than the later. They did not come to be assimilated in an American melting-pot. They did not come to adopt the culture of the American Indian. They had not the smallest intention of "giving themselves without reservation" to the new country. They came to get freedom to live as they wanted. They came to escape from the stifling air and chaos of the old world; they came to make their fortune in a new land. They invented no new social framework. Rather they brought over bodily the old ways to which they had been accustomed. Tightly concentrated on a hostile frontier, they were conservative beyond belief. Their pioneer daring was reserved for the objective conquest of material resources. In their folkways, in their social and political institutions, they were, like every colonial people, slavishly imitative of the mother-country. So that, in spite of the "Revolution," our whole legal and political system remained more English than the English, petrified and unchanging, while in England law developed to meet the needs of the changing times.

> Moreover, the first English settlers did not seek to join an existing native culture.

It is just this English-American conservatism that has been our chief obstacle to social advance. We have needed the new peoples—the order of the German and Scandinavian, the turbulence of the Slav and Hun—to save us from our own stagnation. I do not mean that the illiterate Slav is now the equal of the New Englander of pure descent. He is raw material to be educated, not into a New Englander, but into a socialized American along such lines as those thirty nationalities are being educated in the amazing schools of Gary [Indiana]. I do not believe that this process is to be one of decades of evolution. The spectacle of Japan's sudden jump from mediaevalism to post-modernism should have destroyed that superstition. We are not dealing with individuals who are to "evolve." We are dealing with their children, who, with that education we are about to have, will start level with all of us. Let us cease to think of ideals like democracy as magical qualities inherent in certain peoples. Let us speak, not of inferior races, but of inferior civilizations. We are all to educate and to be educated. These peoples in America are in a common enterprise. It is not what we are now that concerns us, but what this plastic next generation may become in the light of a new cosmopolitan ideal. . . .

Bourne asserts that the Anglo-Saxon has imposed his culture on minority groups.

If freedom means the right to do pretty much as one pleases, so long as one does not interfere with others, the immigrant has found freedom, and the ruling element has been singularly liberal in its treatment of the invading hordes. But if freedom means a democratic cooperation in determining the ideals and purposes and industrial and social institutions of a country, then the immigrant has not been free, and the Anglo-Saxon element is guilty of just what every dominant race is guilty of in every European country: the imposition of its own culture upon the minority peoples. The fact that this imposition has been so mild and, indeed, semi-conscious does not alter its quality. And the war has brought out just the degree to which that purpose of "Americanizing," that is, "Anglo-Saxonizing," the immigrant has failed.

For the Anglo-Saxon now in his bitterness to turn upon the other peoples, talk about their "arrogance," scold them for not being melted in a pot which never existed, is to betray the unconscious purpose which lay at the bottom of his heart. It betrays too the possession of a racial jealousy similar to that of which he is now accusing the so-called "hyphenates." Let the Anglo-Saxon be proud enough of the heroic toil and heroic sacrifices which moulded the nation. But let him ask himself,

Bourne challenges the value of a dominant Anglo-Saxon culture.

if he had had to depend on the English descendants, where he would have been living to-day. To those of us who see in the exploitation of unskilled labor the strident red *leit-motif* of our civilization, the settling of the country presents a great social drama as the waves of immigration broke over it. Let the Anglo-Saxon ask himself where he would have been if these races had not come? Let those who feel the inferiority of the non-Anglo-Saxon immigrant contemplate that region of the States which has remained the most distinctively "American," the South. Let him ask himself whether he would really like to see the foreign hordes Americanized into such an Americanization. Let him ask himself how superior this native civilization is to the great "alien" states of Wisconsin and Minnesota, where Scandinavians, Poles, and Germans have self-consciously labored to preserve their traditional culture, while being outwardly and satisfactorily American. Let him ask himself how much more wisdom, intelligence, industry and social leadership has come out of these alien states than out of all the truly American ones. The South, in fact, while this vast Northern development has gone on, still remains an English colony, stagnant and

complacent, having progressed scarcely beyond the early Victorian era. It is culturally sterile because it has had no advantage of cross-fertilization like the Northern
states. What has happened in states such as Wisconsin and Minnesota is that strong
foreign cultures have struck root in a new and fertile soil. America has meant liberation, and German and Scandinavian political ideas and social energies have
expanded to a new potency. The process has not been at all the fancied "assimilation" of the Scandinavian or Teuton. Rather has it been a process of their assimilation of us—I speak as an Anglo-Saxon. The foreign cultures have not been melted
down or run together, made into some homogeneous Americanism, but have
remained distinct but cooperating to the greater glory and benefit, not only of
themselves but of all the native "Americanism" around them.

What we emphatically do not want is that these distinctive qualities should be washed out into a tasteless, colorless fluid of uniformity.
Already we have far too much of this insipidity, masses of people who
are cultural half-breeds, neither assimilated Anglo-Saxons nor nation-
als of another culture. Each national colony in this country seems
to retain in its foreign press, its vernacular literature, its schools, its

Bourne gives a sarcastic appraisal both of those who lose their vibrant foreign culture and the superficial American culture that they accept.

intellectual and patriotic leaders, a central cultural nucleus. From this nucleus the
colony extends out by imperceptible gradations to a fringe where national characteristics are all but lost. Our cities are filled with these half-breeds who retain
their foreign names but have lost the foreign savor. This does not mean that they
have actually been changed into New Englanders or Middle Westerners. It does
not mean that they have been really Americanized. It means that, letting slip from
them whatever native culture they had, they have substituted for it only the most
rudimentary American—the American culture of the cheap newspaper, the "movies," the popular song, the ubiquitous automobile. The unthinking who survey
this class call them assimilated, Americanized. The great American public school
has done its work. With these people our institutions are safe. We may thrill with
dread at the aggressive hyphenate, but this tame flabbiness is accepted as Americanization. The same moulders of opinion whose ideal is to melt the different
races into Anglo-Saxon gold hail this poor product as the satisfying result of their
alchemy.

Yet a truer cultural sense would have told us that it is not the self-conscious
cultural nuclei that sap at our American life, but these fringes. It is not the Jew
who sticks proudly to the faith of his fathers and boasts of that venerable culture
of his who is dangerous to America, but the Jew who has lost the Jewish fire and
become a mere elementary grasping animal. It is not the Bohemian who supports
the Bohemian schools in Chicago whose influence is sinister, but the Bohemian
who has made money and has got into ward politics.[2] Just so surely as we tend to

---

2. Bohemian here refers to Czech.

disintegrate these nuclei of nationalistic culture do we tend to create hordes of men and women without a spiritual country, cultural outlaws, without taste, without standards but those of the mob. We sentence them to live on the most rudimentary planes of American life. The influences at the centre of the nuclei are centripetal. They make for the intelligence and the social values which mean an enhancement of life. And just because the foreign-born retains this expressiveness is he likely to be a better citizen of the American community. The influences at the fringe, however, are centrifugal, anarchical. They make for detached fragments of peoples. Those who came to find liberty achieve only license. They become the flotsam and jetsam of American life, the downward undertow of our civilization with its leering cheapness and falseness of taste and spiritual outlook, the absence of mind and sincere feeling which we see in our slovenly towns, our vapid moving pictures, our popular novels, and in the vacuous faces of the crowds on the city street. This is the cultural wreckage of our time, and it is from the fringes of the Anglo-Saxon as well as the other stocks that it falls. America has as yet no impelling integrating force. It makes too easily for this detritus of cultures. In our loose, free country, no constraining national purpose, no tenacious folk-tradition and folk-style hold the people to a line.

The war has shown us that not in any magical formula will this purpose be found. No intense nationalism of the European plan can be ours. But do we not begin to see a new and more adventurous ideal? Do we not see how the national colonies in America, deriving power from the deep cultural heart of Europe and yet living here in mutual toleration, freed from the age-long tangles of races, creeds, and dynasties, may work out a federated ideal? America is transplanted Europe, but a Europe that has not been disintegrated and scattered in the transplanting as in some Dispersion. Its colonies live here inextricably mingled, yet not homogeneous. They merge but they do not fuse. America is a unique sociological fabric, and it bespeaks poverty of imagination not to be thrilled at the incalculable potentialities of so novel a union of men. To seek no other goal than the weary old nationalism, belligerent, exclusive, inbreeding, the poison of which we are witnessing now in Europe, is to make patriotism a hollow sham, and to declare that, in spite of our boastings, America must ever be a follower and not a leader of nations. . . .

III.

. . . [I]t is not uncommon for the eager Anglo-Saxon who goes to a vivid American university to-day to find his true friends not among his own race but among the acclimatized German or Austrian, the acclimatized Jew, the acclimatized Scandinavian or Italian. In them he finds the cosmopolitan note. In these youths, foreign-born or the children of foreign-born parents, he is likely to find many of his old inbred morbid problems washed away. These friends are oblivious to the repressions of that tight little society in which he so provincially grew up. He has a pleasurable sense of liberation from the stale and familiar attitudes of those whose ingrowing culture has scarcely created anything vital for his America of to-day. He breathes a larger air. In his new enthusiasms for continental literature, for unplumbed Russian depths, for French clarity of thought, for Teuton philosophies of power, he feels himself citizen of a larger world. He may be absurdly superficial, his outward-reaching wonder may ignore all the stiller and homelier virtues of his Anglo-Saxon home, but he has at least found the clue to that international mind which will be essential to all men and women of good-will if they are ever to save this Western world of ours from suicide. His new friends have gone through a similar revolution. America has burned most of the baser metal also from them. Meeting now with this common American background, all of them may yet retain that distinctiveness of their native cultures and their national spiritual slants. They are more valuable and interesting to each other for being different, yet that difference could not be creative were it not for this new cosmopolitan outlook which America has given them and which they all equally possess.

The university as a place for the development of a cosmopolitan outlook and identity.

A college where such a spirit is possible even to the smallest degree, has within itself already the seeds of this international intellectual world of the future. It suggests that the contribution of America will be an intellectual internationalism which goes far beyond the mere exchange of scientific ideas and discoveries and the cold recording of facts. It will be an intellectual sympathy which is not satisfied until it has got at the heart of the different cultural expressions, and felt as they feel. It may have immense preferences, but it will make understanding and not indignation its end. Such a sympathy will unite and not divide. Against the thinly disguised panic which calls itself "patriotism" and the thinly disguised militarism which calls itself "preparedness" the cosmopolitan ideal is set. This does not mean that those who hold it are for a policy of drift. They, too, long passionately for an integrated and disciplined America. But they do not want one which is integrated only for domestic economic exploitation of the workers or for predatory economic imperialism among the weaker peoples. They do not want one that is integrated by coercion or militarism, or for the truculent assertion of a mediæval code of honor and of doubtful rights. They believe that the most effective integration will be one which coordinates the diverse elements and turns them consciously toward working out together the place of

Bourne describes a cosmopolitan ideal of America.

America in the world-situation. They demand for integration a genuine integrity, a wholeness and soundness of enthusiasm and purpose which can only come when no national colony within our America feels that it is being discriminated against or that its cultural case is being prejudged. This strength of cooperation, this feeling that all who are here may have a hand in the destiny of America, will make for a finer spirit of integration than any narrow "Americanism" or forced chauvinism. In this effort we may have to accept some form of that dual citizenship which meets with so much articulate horror among us. Dual citizenship we may have to recognize as the rudimentary form of that international citizenship to which, if our words mean anything, we aspire. We have assumed unquestioningly that mere participation in the political life of the United States must cut the new citizen off from all sympathy with his old allegiance. Anything but a bodily transfer of devotion from one sovereignty to another has been viewed as a sort of moral treason against the Republic. We have insisted that the immigrant whom we welcomed escaping from the very exclusive nationalism of his European home shall forthwith adopt a nationalism just as exclusive, just as narrow, and even less legitimate because it is founded on no warm traditions of his own. Yet a nation like France is

Legal dual citizenship ▌ said to permit a formal and legal dual citizenship even at the present time. Though a citizen of hers may pretend to cast off his allegiance in favor of some other sovereignty, he is still subject to her laws when he returns. Once a citizen, always a citizen, no matter how many new-citizenships he may embrace. And such a dual citizenship seems to us sound and right. For it recognizes that, although the Frenchman may accept the formal institutional framework of his new country and indeed become intensely loyal to it, yet his Frenchness he will never lose. What makes up the fabric of his soul will always be of this Frenchness, so that unless he becomes utterly degenerate he will always to some degree dwell still in his native environment.

Indeed, does not the cultivated American who goes to Europe practice a dual citizenship, which, if not formal, is no less real? The American who lives abroad

The spirit of dual citizenship ▌ may be the least expatriate of men. If he falls in love with French ways and French thinking and French democracy and seeks to saturate himself with the new spirit, he is guilty of at least a dual spiritual citizenship. He may be still American, yet he feels himself through sympathy also a Frenchman. And he finds that this expansion involves no shameful conflict within him, no surrender of his native attitude. He has rather for the first time caught a glimpse of the cosmopolitan spirit. And after wandering about through many races and civilizations he may return to America to find them all here living vividly and crudely, seeking the same adjustment that he made. He sees the new peoples here with a new vision. They are no longer masses of aliens, waiting to be "assimilated," waiting to be melted down into the indistinguishable dough of Anglo-Saxonism. They are rather threads of living and potent cultures, blindly striving to weave themselves into a novel international nation, the first the world has seen. In an Austria-Hungary or a Prussia the stronger of these cultures would be moving almost instinctively to subjugate the weaker. But in America those wills-to-power are turned in a different direction into learning how to live together.

Along with dual citizenship we shall have to accept, I think, that

The importance of a migratory habit among immigrants. ▌ free and mobile passage of the immigrant between America and his native land again which now arouses so much prejudice among us. We shall have to accept the immigrant's return for the same reason that we consider justified our own flitting about the earth. To stigmatize the alien who works in America for a few years and returns to his own land, only perhaps to seek American fortune again, is to think in narrow nationalistic terms. It is to ignore the cosmopolitan significance of this migration. It is to ignore the fact that the returning immigrant is often a missionary to an inferior civilization.

This migratory habit has been especially common with the unskilled laborers who have been pouring into the United States in the last dozen years from every country in southeastern Europe. Many of them return to spend their earnings in their own country or to serve their country in war. But they return with an entirely new critical outlook, and a sense of the superiority of American organization to the primitive living around them. This continued passage to and fro has already raised the material standard of living in many regions of these backward countries. For these regions are thus endowed with exactly what they need, the capital for the exploitation of their natural resources, and the spirit of enterprise. America is thus educating these laggard peoples from the very bottom of society up, awakening vast masses to a new-born hope for the future. In the migratory Greek, therefore, we have not the parasitic alien, the doubtful American asset, but a symbol of that cosmopolitan interchange which is coming, in spite of all war and national exclusiveness.

Only America, by reason of the unique liberty of opportunity and traditional isolation for which she seems to stand, can lead in this cosmopolitan enterprise. Only the American—and in this category I include the migratory alien who has lived with us and caught the pioneer spirit and a sense of new social vistas—has the chance to become that citizen of the world. America is coming to be, not a nationality but a transnationality, a weaving back and forth, with the other lands, of many threads of all sizes and colors. Any movement which attempts to thwart this weaving, or to dye the fabric any one color, or disentangle the threads of the strands, is false to this cosmopolitan vision. I do not mean that we shall necessarily glut ourselves with the raw product of humanity. It would be folly to absorb the nations faster than we could weave them. We have no duty either to admit or reject. It is purely a question of expediency. What concerns us is the fact that the strands are here. We must have a policy and an ideal for an actual situation. Our question is, What shall we do with our America? How are we likely to get the more creative America by confining our imaginations to the ideal of the melting-pot, or broadening them to some such cosmopolitan conception as I have been vaguely sketching? . . . We cannot Americanize America worthily by sentimentalizing and moralizing history. When the best schools are expressly renouncing the questionable duty of teaching patriotism by means of history, it is not the time to force shibboleth upon the immigrant. This form of Americanization has been heard because it appealed to the vestiges of our old sentimentalized and moralized patriotism. This has so far held the field as the expression of the new American's new devotion. The inflections of other voices

Bourne presents his vision of a transnational America. What does he mean?

have been drowned. They must be heard. We must see if the lesson of the war has not been for hundreds of these later Americans a vivid realization of their transnationality, a new consciousness of what America meant to them as a citizenship in the world. It is the vague historic idealisms which have provided the fuel for the European flame. Our American ideal can make no progress until we do away with this romantic gilding of the past.

All our idealisms must be those of future social goals in which all can participate, the good life of personality lived in the environment of the Beloved Community. No mere doubtful triumphs of the past, which redound to the glory of only one of our transnationalities, can satisfy us. It must be a future America, on which all can unite, which pulls us irresistibly toward it, as we understand each other more warmly.

To make real this striving amid dangers and apathies is work for a younger *intelligentsia* of America. Here is an enterprise of integration into which we can all pour ourselves, of a spiritual welding which should make us, if the final menace ever came, not weaker, but infinitely strong.

ENDNOTES

1. Ross Wetzsteon, "Republic of Dreams," in *Greenwich Village: The American Bohemia, 1910–1960* (New York: Simon & Schuster, 2002), 4–14; Rick Beard and Leslie Cohen Berlowitz, eds., *Greenwich Village: Culture and Counterculture* (New Brunswick: Rutgers University Press, 1993), ix.

2. Barbara Welter, "The Cult of True Womanhood: 1820–1860," *American Quarterly* 18, no. 2 (Summer 1966): 151–174.

3. Nell Irvin Painter, "Voices of Suffrage: Sojourner Truth, Frances Watkins Harper, and the Struggle for Woman Suffrage," in *Votes for Women: The Struggle for Suffrage Revisited*, ed. Jean H. Baker (New York: Oxford University Press, 2002), 42–55.

4. Margaret Finnegan, *Selling Suffrage: Consumer Culture and Votes for Women* (New York: Columbia University Press, 1999).

5. Eleanor Flexner and Ellen Fitzpatrick, *Century of Struggle: The Woman's Rights Movement in the United States*, enlarged ed. (Cambridge: Harvard University Press, 1996), 223.

6. Alice Kessler-Harris, *Gendering Labor History* (Urbana: University of Illinois Press, 2007), 97–128.

7. Industrial Workers of the World, "The Internationale," in *We Shall Be All: A History of the Industrial Workers of the World*, Melvyn Dubofsky (New York: Quadrangle, 1969), 154.

8. David Glassberg, *American Historical Pageantry: The Uses of Tradition in the Early Twentieth Century* (Chapel Hill: University of North Carolina Press, 1990).

9. Mary Chapman, *Making Noise, Making News: Suffrage Print Culture and U.S. Modernism* (New York: Oxford University Press, 2014), 60–71.

10. Karen J. Blair, *The Torchbearers: Women & Their Amateur Arts Associations in America, 1890–1930* (Bloomington: Indiana University Press, 1994), 137.

11. Glassberg, *American Historical Pageantry*, 128.

12. Leslie Fishbein, "The Paterson Pageant: The Birth of Docudrama as a Weapon in the Class Struggle," *New York History: Quarterly Journal of the New York State Historical Association* 72, no. 2 (1991): 197–233.

13. Sandra Adickes, *To Be Young Was Very Heaven: Women in New York Before the First World War* (New York: St. Martin's Press, 1997), 35.

14. Christine Stansell, *American Moderns: Bohemian New York and the Creation of a New Century* (New York: Henry Holt, 2000), 225.

15. Ibid., 227.

16. Adickes, *To Be Young*, 90.

17. June Sochen, *Movers and Shakers* (New York: Quadrangle, 1973), 38.

18. Rheta Childe Dorr, *A Woman of Fifty* (New York: Funk & Wagnalls, 1924), 268.

19. Leslie Fishbein, *Rebels in Bohemia: The Radicals of the Masses, 1911–1917* (Chapel Hill: University of North Carolina, 1982), 157.

20. Ibid., 138.

21. Joanne E. Passet, *Sex Radicals and the Quest for Women's Equality* (Urbana: University of Illinois Press, 2003).

22. Nancy F. Cott, *The Grounding of Modern Feminism* (New Haven: Yale University Press, 1987), 39.

23. Stansell, *American Moderns*, 227, 248.

24. Jean V. Matthews, *The Rise of the New Woman: The Women's Movement in America, 1875–1930* (Chicago: Ivan R. Dee, 2003), 102–3.

25. Carroll Smith-Rosenberg, *Disorderly Conduct: Visions of Gender in Victorian America* (New York: Oxford University Press, 1985).

26. Max Eastman, *Enjoyment of Living* (New York: Harper and Brothers, 1948), 310.

27. Ibid., 313.

ACKNOWLEDGMENTS

I would like to thank Mark Carnes, Dana Johnson, and the first Reacting to the Past Advisory Board for their support with this project. The faculty and students who tested *Greenwich Village, 1913* in its pilot forms have provided invaluable comments and suggestions. I particularly appreciated the exchanges in the formative years with Professors Kathleen Clark, Mark David Higbee, Ben Maegi, Suzanne Marilley, Bill Offutt, Nicolas Proctor, Rebecca Stanton, Lara Vapnek, and Ross Wheeler. Professor Proctor has become my go-to colleague for all things concerning the development of this game. The current RTTP Consortium and RTTP colleagues continue to astound me with their creativity and ideas on how to develop *Greenwich Village, 1913* for all manner of courses and groups. I thank them all for their deep thinking and rich exchanges.

Brittany Backhaus and Alexandria Eveleth (Simmons College '09) have been an extraordinary help with their close readings of this text and their players' insights into how to make this game really work. Jennifer Ferguson, Simmons College librarian par excellence, has tracked down the most hidden of primary sources and made possible access to several of the core texts.

And a special thanks to Justin Cahill, editor and creative force behind the Norton RTTP project.

CREDITS

TEXT:

p. 239 Neith Boyce: *Constancy: A Dialogue*. Premiered July 15, 1915, Provincetown, MA. Reprinted by permission of Fred Hapgood.

PHOTOS:

p. 104 Godey's Lady's Book. Vol. 42. January, 1851. Courtesy Project Gutenberg. http://www.gutenberg.org/files/15080/15080-h/15080-h.htm.

p. 128 "United We Stand: Anti-Suffrage Meeting," by Cornelia Barns, *The Masses*, November 1914.

p. 172 Women's Trade Union League Seal by Julia Bracken Wendt, *Proceedings of the Second Biennial Convention of the National Women's Trade Union League of America*, September 27–October 1, 1909.

p. 188 "Uncle Sam Ruled Out," by Art Young, *Solidarity*, June 7, 1913. Original image courtesy of the Industrial Workers of the World (www.iww.org).